LOST in

the

Suburbs

LOST in the Suburbs

A Political Travelogue

Stephen Dale

Published in 1999 by Stoddart Publishing Co. Limited
34 Lesmill Road, Toronto, Canada M3B 2T6
180 Varick Street, 9th Floor, New York, New York 10014

Distributed in Canada by:
General Distribution Services Ltd.
325 Humber College Boulevard, Toronto, Canada M9W 7C3
Tel. (416) 213-1919   Fax (416) 213-1917
Email customer.service@ccmailgw.genpub.com

Distributed in the United States by:
General Distribution Services Inc.
85 River Rock Drive, Suite 202, Buffalo, New York 14207
Toll-free Tel.1-800-805-1083   Toll-free Fax 1-800-481-6207
Email gdsinc@genpub.com

03 02 01 00 99 1 2 3 4 5

Canadian Cataloguing in Publication Data

Dale, Stephen, 1958–
Lost in the suburbs: a political travelogue

Includes bibliographical references and index.
ISBN 0-7737-3204-7

1. Ontario – Politics and government – 1995-   .*
2. California – Politics and government – 1951–   .   3. Reagan, Ronald.
4. Harris, Mike, 1945–   .   I. Title.

FC3077.2.D34 1999   971'.3'04   C99-931537-4
F1058.D34 1999

Jacket Design: Angel Guerra
Text Design: Tannice Goddard

THE CANADA COUNCIL | LE CONSEIL DES ARTS
FOR THE ARTS | DU CANADA
SINCE 1957 | DEPUIS 1957

*We acknowledge for their financial support of our publishing
program the Canada Council, the Ontario Arts Council, and
the Government of Canada through the Book Publishing
Industry Development Program (BPIDP).*

Printed and bound in Canada

To my parents,
Freda Dale and the late Bob Dale,
who gave me a suburban childhood
filled with love and hope

Contents

	Acknowledgements	ix
part 1	**High Angst Somewhere in Ontario**	
1	A New Kind of Place, A New Kind of Politics?	3
2	The Nature of the Beast	27
3	The Populist Challenge	73
part 2	**California Dreams and Nightmares**	
4	The Lie of the Land, the Lot of the People	125
5	Orange County and the Origins of the Middle-Class Revolt	144
6	Ballot-Box Gunslingers and the Fight for the New West	162
7	Keeping the Sacred Flame Burning	185
8	A Liberal Renaissance?	217
9	It Comes Down to Neighbourhoods	259
part 3	**Where Does It Go from Here?**	
10	Encore: Back in the 905	283
	Notes	323
	Bibliography	337
	Index	341

Acknowledgements

I'm grateful to a number of people whose enthusiasm and talent made this book a reality. I thank the folks at Stoddart, in particular Don Bastian, who kept things on track and had many kind and encouraging words, and Angel Guerra, whose enthusiasm for this project got things rolling in the first place.

I'm fortunate to have worked with David Kilgour, a superb and intuitive editor who knew exactly what this book was about and how it should end. Copy editor Maryan Gibson has a keen eye and an even keener mind. Both David and Maryan rescued me from a number of literary and logical gaffes.

A hearty thanks to my agent David Johnston of Livingston-Cooke for his faith in this project and for his persistence.

I tip my cap as well to ex-Californian Matthew Behrens, who read much of the manuscript, and Andrew van Velzen, who supplied some critical research material.

I gratefully acknowledge the generous financial support of the Canada Council for the Arts and the Ontario Arts Council, without which this book could not have been written.

As always, I have a million reasons to thank Laura Macdonald, who made many contributions to this project, both tangible and intangible, and whose presence made the task seem lighter. I'd also like to thank Ben and Matthew Macdonald-Dale, who are a joy to be around, whatever city or suburb we happen to be in.

Stephen Dale
Ottawa
July 1999

part 1 | High Angst Somewhere in Ontario

1 | A New Kind of Place,
A New Kind of Politics?

It is late May 1997, and most of the talk on radio newscasts and open-line spleenfests centres on the upcoming federal election, set to take place in about ten days. This is being hyped as an historic contest, one that could determine the direction of Canadian politics for perhaps decades to come by providing answers to some crucial questions: Will the Bloc Québécois, which has served as the official Opposition for the past four years, keep the separatist issue front and centre in the federal arena by replaying its earlier triumph, or will its vote collapse? Will Preston Manning's Reform Party achieve the breakthrough it is looking for in rural and suburban Ontario, thereby creating a truly national presence for his right-wing, Western populist party? Will the Progressive Conservatives — the party of Confederation and of two solid majority governments in the 1980s — continue their slide into oblivion, or will it rebuild from its pathetic two-seat showing of the last Parliament? And what impact will the relative showings of Reform and the PCs have on the crusade to bring Canada's two right-wing parties under a single banner?[1]

The question of particular interest to me is the one about the rural and suburban Ontario vote — well, actually, just the suburban Ontario vote. In 1995, when Mike Harris's reconstituted far-right Conservative party swept into power provincially, the newspapers all started carrying stories about the "905 belt," 905 being the telephone area code of much of Toronto's sprawling suburban fringe. Evidently the region was hugely receptive to the Ontario Tories' US-style platform promoting privatization, tax cuts, workfare, and deregulation, and mesmerized by its American-inspired advertising campaign attacking welfare recipients, racial- and gender-based hiring targets, and pay equity.[2]

— — —

Fascinated by this shock to the normally placid and polite Canadian political scene, I make it my mission to journey into the heart of these suburban badlands as the political gladiators engaged in battle once again, this time jousting for position in the federal arena. And so, after throwing briefcase and garment bag into the back seat of a rented Nissan Sentra with automatic transmission, push-button radio, the lingering scent of new upholstery, and the faint trace of stale cigarette smoke — I pull out of the driveway of my modest Ottawa row house and head for the exotic destination of Aurora, Ontario, on the eastern tip of the federal riding of Vaughan-King-Aurora and somewhere towards the centre of the elongated blob that is 905. The Liberal party's book of constituency profiles lists Vaughan-King-Aurora as the wealthiest riding in Canada, with an average household income of $80,439. Apart from this tidbit, I know little of life in the area. Having lived in downtown Toronto for most of the 1980s before moving to the nation's capital, I was one of those smug urbanites for whom it is a point of pride to remain completely ignorant of everything that happens north of Eglinton Avenue.

By the mid-1990s, however, these outer suburbs have become increasingly difficult to ignore. Rapid population growth created by the suburban construction boom of the previous fifteen years has given the 905ers a pivotal influence over provincial politics, which they exercised in 1995 with their almost unanimous support of the Tories' so-called "Common Sense Revolution." This came as a big shock to most newspaper columnists and political pundits, who had been following the Ontario scene over the long term. They watched in disbelief as a sector of society that nobody had previously identified as a cohesive or ideologically distinct entity led the charge against a century-old Ontario tradition of enlightened government intervention in economic development — for example, huge investments in Ontario Hydro and the school system — and social harmony. Commentators marvelled at how this "revolution" could happen here, in Ontario, where people had long prided themselves on being so much more caring than Americans. One had only to compare the urban landscapes, so the traditional thinking went, to see how much more sense our approach made. While cities on the US side of the border had decaying urban cores and rotting, dismal housing projects, Toronto won international praise for its vibrant, garbage-free streets and co-op housing ventures that actually worked. While visitors to the downtowns of many nearby American cities risked death at the hands of gun-toting, knife-wielding thugs, Ontario residents could credit the comprehensive Canadian social safety net for decreasing social tensions and keeping the streets of our cities comparatively safe.

By the mid-1990s, things had changed. The extravagant dreams of the 1980s (fuelled by the real-estate boom) were punctured by recession. There had been migration of traditional industries to low-wage zones and increased unemployment. Meanwhile the provincial debt soared under the watch of a nominally socialist NDP government. So many Ontarians, particularly those in the suburbs, seemed willing to abandon the caring Ontario society. Instead they threw their lot behind a party advocating a US-style of politics, centred on personal initiative, a diminished role for government, and a stern approach to social welfare. The speed with which voters' preferences shifted from a compassionate liberalism to a granite-hard conservatism — budget cuts for social agencies and "boot camps" for young offenders were the new lightning rods for the electorate's hostile mood — invited a number of unflattering historical comparisons.

In the pages of the *Ottawa Citizen*, for instance, civic columnist Randall Denley fiercely attacked a writer of a local computer "chat room" who had suggested that the demonization of welfare recipients in Harris's Ontario, supported by "propagandists" like Denley himself, bore similarities to the way Adolf Hitler had harnessed middle-class resentments against Jews. What prompted the writer to make this comparison was the Harris government's swift and gleeful execution of one of its key election promises — an immediate twenty percent reduction in welfare rates. Critics have since charged that the government's restrictive welfare policies have been responsible for a dramatic rise in homelessness in the province.[3]

Despite the odd surface similarity, the Hitler analogy seemed overblown to me, although I'm sure it would seem less so to people who have been kicked off welfare and face freezing to death on the streets. And so, winding my way through the brilliant green pastures of rural eastern Ontario in the shiny new Sentra, with the radio and the air-conditioning cranked up, I certainly do not expect to find that York Region is some neo-fascist enclave. Instead, I expect it to be a little piece of the United States, somehow transplanted deep into the heart of Ontario.

I was primed for this by a number of newspaper articles that pegged this new urban-suburban political split as a long-established US phenomenon. South of the border, voting patterns are often polarized between the support by city-dwellers for the old politics of benevolent government meddling, and the endorsement by suburbanites of slash-and-burn neo-conservatism. And many American political fixers have made a lucrative niche out of translating suburban angst and resentment into explosive TV ads.

Clearly the Ontario Tories were inspired by the American example. *Toronto Star* reporter William Walker, for instance, visited New Jersey and found that Republican governor Christine Todd Whitman's surprise upset of Democratic incumbent James Florio in 1993 bore striking similarities to Harris's 1995 electoral triumph in Ontario. Both candidates had been trailing badly coming into their respective elections: Whitman's popularity was twenty-two percent lower than her rival's, and polls put Harris's Tories in third place as the Ontario contest began. What rocketed both candidates to convincing victories were virtually identical platforms promising 30 percent tax cuts, privatization of government services, welfare cuts, and those juvenile boot camps. Walker also observed similarities in rhetorical tone — while Harris touted his Common Sense Revolution, Whitman also spoke of "common sense," using the phrase more than half a dozen times in her 1996 budget address — which suggests that the "suburban backlash" campaign strategy might be something you can buy off the rack and have altered to fit your particular regional circumstances. Indeed, Walker maintained that the 1995 Ontario Tory campaign was consciously modelled on Whitman's, with Harris's executive assistant Bill King having studied her tax-cut strategy beginning in 1993, and with Harris himself meeting with the New Jersey governor a year later to pick up pointers on how to run his campaign.[4]

One other key similarity between the Ontario and New Jersey campaigns, of course, was that they were both played out on landscapes that had become largely suburbanized. While the Harris revolution found its strongest core of supporters amongst the 905ers, New Jersey is also a highly suburban state, sharply divided between crumbling, poverty-stricken cities such as Camden, Trenton, Newark, and Jersey City, and the more populous and affluent suburban tracts that have swallowed up much of the countryside. The same is true of Michigan, where an advanced network of highways and simmering racial tensions have encouraged the "white flight" to the suburbs since the 1950s, reducing to rubble parts of the once-majestic city of Detroit. The state's tax-cutting, service-slashing, tough-on-crime Republican governor John Engler is also said to have served as a model for Harris and his revolutionary zealots.

The original template for suburban revolt, however, is clearly found in the first phase of the Reagan revolution, fought out at the state level in California in the mid-1960s. In one jolting moment, Reagan's suburban-driven, anti-government campaign, the legacy of which I will examine in detail in the second part of this book, managed to overturn decades of interventionist government policies aimed at stoking the state's economy and levelling social inequalities. At the same time, it provided the initial spark that ignited the worldwide political brushfire later to be identified as neo-conservatism, a movement that, with its insistence that prosperity and the natural order demand lower taxes, less government, and a more "pragmatic" view of what society can do to comfort the afflicted, has since over-turned many of the certainties of the post–World War II era.

The American writer William Schneider, in his article "The Suburban Century Begins," published in *Atlantic Monthly* magazine, says it's entirely logical that the neo-conservative movement's capture of the political mainstream would be powered by its support amongst suburbanites, since "suburbanization means the privatization of American life and culture. To move to the suburbs is to express a preference for the private over the public."

Schneider acknowledges that this kind of geographic determinism, in which a whole society's political outlook is seen as a product of the way communities are structured, presents for many people a rather apocalyptic vision. It's due, he says, to the social shortcomings of the suburban form, which has dominated planners' vision for the latter half of the twentieth century. He quotes from architects Andres Duany and Elizabeth Plater-Zyberk, founders of the "New Urbanism" architectural movement, who characterize the suburb as "less a community than an agglomeration of houses, shops, and offices connected to one another by cars, not by the fabric of human life" and as "the last word in privatization, perhaps even its lethal consummation, [which] spells the end of authentic civic life."[5]

But people who live in suburbia do not view it so negatively. Says Schneider:

> There is a reason why people want to be confined to their houses and cars. They want a secure and controlled environment. Suburban commuters show a determined preference for private over public transportation. Automobiles may not be efficient, but they give people a sense of security and control. With a car you can go anywhere you want, anytime you want, in the comfort of your own private space.

The attributes exemplified by the private automobile can also be found in the new types of entertainment technologies, which similarly reinforce the essential character of suburbia. Continues Schneider:

> Entertainment has also been privatized. Suburbanites watch cable television and rent videos. They can watch anything they want, anytime they want, in the comfort of their own private space. People have control over what they see — remote control. And they don't have to put up with the insecurity and disorder of public spaces. Historically, enjoying public spaces was one of the reasons people lived in cities.

In Schneider's estimation, it doesn't take much of a leap to divine suburbanites' political preferences from those rituals of everyday life. Suburban consumers who are used to buying or renting their own transportation or entertainment, rather than partaking in the more communal experiences of riding a bus or going to the movies, quite naturally expect "to be able to buy their own government," says Schneider. "These people resent it when politicians take their money and use it to solve other people's problems, especially when they don't believe that government can actually solve those problems." Thus, the suburbanite will quite happily pay user fees to cover the costs of a service he or she uses, but will chafe at writing a cheque for taxes to be applied to some greater but more distant public good. The attitude that citizens should have to pay taxes only to support services they directly use is also encouraged by the compartmentalized nature of suburban life; it's difficult to see any greater social good arising from government spending when you pass most of your day in the work-place, at home, and in your car, spending little time in public places and having few opportunities to glimpse into the lives of people who are less well-off and more likely to be in need of some kind of government assistance.

To Schneider, the fact that most people in the United States now live in suburbia goes a long way towards explaining the strength of the American right. The 1990 census showed that about half of the American people lived in suburbs, up from a third in 1960, when the population was split almost evenly between rural, urban, and suburban dwellers. Working through the arcane mathematics that determines victory in a US presidential election campaign, Schneider concluded that if Democrats (whose pro-social welfare policies had traditionally appealed to urban dwellers) continued to ignore the fact that six of the ten most populous states (California, Pennsylvania, Ohio, Michigan, Florida, and New Jersey) had majority suburban populations, they would be fated to continual failure. Since Schneider penned his article in 1992, the Democrats have apparently heeded his advice, promoting a fiscal program that promises to "spend broadly and tax narrowly" — an edict that favours user fees over broad-based taxes and assigns federal funds more to universal programs such as social security and road-building rather than to targeted initiatives suburbanites perceive as benefitting a remote group — for example, the urban poor — at their expense.[6]

Meanwhile, the author Joel Garreau attributes the shift in the polit-ical centre of gravity in the US not just to the growth in the size and population of America's suburbs, but also to the increasingly self-contained nature of those places. In his trail-blazing book *Edge*

City: Life on the New Frontier, Garreau traces the post-war spread of the typically "suburban" style of decentralized, low-rise, and auto-mobile-centred communities through three distinct phases: first was the "suburbanization" phase when housing tracts went up on the outskirts of traditional city centres; second was the "malling of America," when suburbanites were freed from the trip to the city to do their shopping; and third was the migration of (mostly white-collar and technological) jobs out to the burbs, where the housing and the malls had gone. Garreau makes a convincing case for the stance that when your suburb reaches stage three, it isn't a suburb anymore; it is now an Edge City, a new kind of beast no longer defined by its proximity to a traditional city, a separate geographic entity that boasts the same complex mix of residential, retail, and business functions as a typical city, but looks and feels a lot more like a suburb.

How do you know when the soil you're standing on is part of an Edge City? Garreau sets out some strict criteria for membership in this club. The place must have at least five million square feet of leasable office space and 600,000 square feet of leasable retail space. It must also have more jobs than bedrooms and be a mixed-use community (that is, it should serve as a destination as well as a starting point). Finally it must be new, having sprung from cow pasture or scrubland since the early 1960s and bearing little physical resemblance to a traditional city. Though not part of Garreau's formal definition, Edge Cities are also likely to have indistinct borders (since they are often the product of a suburban sprawl that has bled across political bound-aries and swallowed once-separate communities) and to have such a low-definition sense of self that they are quite likely to be known by such names as "287 and 78" (the closest intersecting highways) or "West Houston Energy Corridor."

As uninspiring as these monikers may be, Garreau agrees with Schneider that the communities they describe have become a defining force within American society — partly because they are so numerous and so big. The author identifies dozens of Edge Cities that have larger populations than mid-range cities like Portland, Oregon, and

Tucson, Arizona. Many of them have accumulated considerable economic clout too. By the early 1990s, when Garreau's book was published, two-thirds of American offices were located in Edge Cities. The Edge Cities close to New York, for instance, contained far more office space than downtown Manhattan did.

Garreau's portrayal of the rise of these suburban cities also tends to support Schneider's idea that suburbanites have become the kingmakers of US politics — an influential breed with a distinctive mentality and the will to see their own agenda carried out. They can act as an autonomous force partly because they are much less dependent on the older cities than in the past. Consider, for instance, that census data from the early 1990s show the typical suburb-to-downtown commute to be much less common than the commute between points within the suburban frontier. (Garreau also maintains that commuters' travelling time and fuel consumption have been reduced since jobs began flooding into suburbia, because workplaces and homes are now more likely to be located close together.)

And does Garreau agree with Schneider that these Edge City folk can be counted on to exercise their new political muscle in support of an anti-government, survival-of-the-fittest conservatism? To answer that, Garreau defers to the American cultural historian Leo Marx and to the landscape itself. The spread-out and generally low-rise design of these new outer cities, Garreau believes, reveals a desire to maintain aspects of country life within the context of a mechanized and complex economy and society. Which leads Marx to observe that these communities are a reaction against what is perceived as "too much restraint, oppression, and hierarchy" within American society, a return to the Jeffersonian ideal of "a land that is midway between too much and too little civilization." So, yes, the very look of these places implies that its inhabitants have rejected the intrusiveness of government, the most obvious manifestation of too much civilization, opting instead for a return to a fabled time when Americans' survival was dependent on their relationship with the land, rather than on government programs.[7]

- - -

Maybe it's because I'm a Canadian that I can't see these places as expressions of the deep yearnings of a people. Garreau looks at the new suburban behemoths that have sprung up since the 1960s and sees an architectural attempt to heal a conflicted national psyche, to forge a reconciliation "between our reverence for 'unspoiled' nature and our enduring devotion to 'progress,'" as he puts it. Call me prosaic, a philistine, a Canuck, but I look at these places and see only endless, uniform subdivisions spoiling what was once a pastoral view from the highway. I see great, boxy temples to the gods of consumerism, places with brazenly unimaginative names like Home Depot, Sports Warehouse, Kitchen Superstore; I see places that are totally blind to any aspect of the human experience that can't be bought or driven to in a private automobile.

But then again, in the spring of 1997 I'm not sure I have ever been to an Edge City. That's why, as my rented Japanese car comes to the end of the rolling countryside of southern Ontario and enters the undifferentiated North American-ness that is suburbia, I'm ready to learn. I want to know what the federal riding of Vaughan-King-Aurora and the Region of York in which it is cradled are all about. Does this place represent a capitulation to the thoroughly American ideals represented by Garreau's Edge City? Is this area's firm support of Mike Harris's privatizing, welfare-slashing, public-servant-bashing Tories a confirmation of Duany and Plater-Zyberk's idea that the suburb "spells the end of authentic civic life?" And, if the answers to the above questions are yes, could this place somehow be redeemed?

The first thing I observe about Aurora is how different it is from the suburb in which I grew up during the '60s and '70s. Most things in the working-class suburban fringe surrounding Hamilton, the industrial city where I was born, had a utilitarian feel about them; for me, the images that linger from my childhood are of large grocery stores, Canadian Tire outlets, a multitude of gas stations, and, of course, the shopping malls. The suburban project of the immediate post-war period was essentially aimed at moving factory workers and their families out of the dingy downtown row houses where they had lived, away from the satanic mills where they toiled, and relocating them in these bucolic blue-collar paradises where the air was comparatively fresh and kids had backyards and unpaved school playgrounds to romp in. Just moving out from under the shadows of those hulking steel mills was reward enough; it wasn't as if the new suburbs of the '50s and '60s needed to be constructed with any great sense of art to make the move worth it. As the real estate agents say, what matters is "location, location, and location," and the suburb where I grew up certainly had that: perched atop a piece of the Niagara Escarpment known as "the Mountain," its primary attraction was a deep ridge of rock that served as a comforting barrier between the new residential neighbourhoods and the old, dirty industrial city below. With that much location, who needs design? It was only natural, then, that when a hockey arena was built close to my neighbourhood, its exterior projected all the grace and charm that can possibly emanate from a building whose painted concrete surface has been trimmed with versatile and culturally significant (for a steel town) strips of corrugated sheet metal.

Of course, this utilitarian aesthetic remains a part of newer suburbs, like the ones that have sprouted in York Region, where "big box" retail outlets such as Wal-Mart dominate the landscape like late-twentieth-century versions of Stonehenge. Yet that's not all there is in these places. Driving into Aurora — until fairly recently a distinctive rural burg, since fused into the greater sprawl of York Region — what's immediately apparent is the effort that's been made to retain some of the character of the original town. In fact, as I motor from the east towards my final destination of the Aurora Howard Johnson's, what's common to a number of distinct pockets of suburbia that I pass through is that, in each case, new subdivisions have been built outward from an old town crossroads, with that intersection being retained as a community focal point and a touchstone to the past.

Aurora's main crossroads, at Wellington and Yonge, serves as a fitting emblem for the newer suburbs of the '80s and '90s, a snapshot of the disparate influences and aspirations that have shaped these places. For a start, the corner is architecturally the same as it might have been a hundred years ago, with Victorian commercial buildings — storefronts on the ground floor, apartments or offices above — on each of the four corners, facing what might be considered the central square. That this crossroads has retained its prominence and continues to generate some street life seems to support Joel Garreau's observation that the denizens of Edge Cities want to revive their links to a simpler past, to at least create the illusion for themselves of living outside an era when human settlements have come to resemble beehives, when the complexity of our lives has necessitated ceding power to large bureaucracies and the other "oppressive forces" Garreau speaks of.

But while the transplanted urbanites who live here may have one eye on the past, their other eye is on the future. There are no haberdasheries or hardware stores at the centre of town in Aurora. Instead, one corner storefront is occupied by a New Age bookstore, which seems to do a brisk trade, while directly across from it are the offices of an advertising agency where multiple television screens cast continuous, overlapping loops of rock-and-roll imagery out onto the street. This is only fitting perhaps, since Aurora's rebirth as a part of suburbia came about in an era when culture (broadly defined) had become arguably a bigger industry in Canada than steel- or car-making, and when the staid Protestantism of earlier decades had largely been replaced by more esoteric turns of mind.

As I venture farther south down Yonge Street, the buildings are newer and more classically suburban — but there are signs of attempts to erase, or at least modify, the convention of blandness that has dominated in suburbia for most of the past half-century. I see a Speedy Muffler King and immediately recognize it as an artifact of post-war suburban utilitarianism that would have been right at home on the Mountain in Hamilton: it's a boxy building with automotive bays and corporate logos in front, no more distinctive than a typical gas station. But wait — what's this? One corner of the building has been set aside for use as a coffee shop, and stepping into it for a cappuccino is like crossing the threshold into Oz. The decor speaks of some other, more urbane world: the wallpaper is elegant, the furniture luxurious and stylish and more evocative of some fashionable coffee bar in Milan than a hole-in-the-wall café adjoining a suburban muffler shop. The floor has also been set at different levels, so the serving staff glide up and down on their way between tables. And, the pièce de résistance is the cappuccino machine. Set at centre stage like a prized work of sculpture, it's a glistening technological marvel that's as awe-inspiring as the engine of a Maserati or the control panel of a spaceship.

I have a similar experience a couple of evenings later a bit farther south in the suburb of Richmond Hill. I sit down for dinner in an Italian restaurant that advertises "fine cuisine" on one of those illuminated portable signs on wheels with a trailer hitch up front. The sign didn't lie; the food is great, served by waiters in black tie, in an elegantly appointed room. The view, of course, is pathetic: glance outside through the plate-glass window and what you see is parked cars and truck traffic, exactly what you'd expect to observe from a small-scale suburban strip mall at nine in the evening.

This dissonance between the interior and exterior images makes sense. Both the muffler-shop-cappuccino joint and the "fine cuisine" strip-mall restaurant are evidence that people who moved out to the burbs in the 1980s — unlike earlier waves of urban émigrés whose first concern was securing the essentials of life — are products of an era when the middle class, or at least its upper end, had already accumulated substantial material wealth. Now they were turning their gaze towards the cultural trappings, the intangibles that bespeak a certain spirit of urbanity that's able to rise above the shortcomings of the suburban form. In many cases, those cultural trappings involved some statement of ethnic identity. This part of York Region, which is a good chunk of the riding of Vaughan-King-Aurora, has an Italian flair, reflective of its many émigrés being from the Little Italy neighbourhood of downtown Toronto. In nearby Markham the accent is Asian; venture south and east to that upscale community and you'll see it's as easy to find dim sum as it is to order a burger.

Does this newly conquered terrain on the northern fringe of Toronto fit Joel Garreau's description of an Edge City? It is certainly evolving in that direction. Much like its American cousins, the area forms a spread-out and multi-purpose landscape with a variety of commercial and industrial focal points rather than one central urban core, and a mix of residential and job-centred functions that make it both a starting point and a destination for travellers. There are shopping malls, high-tech industries, warehouses, high-rise towers, and low-rise subdivisions, and they are mostly linked, in typical Edge City fashion, by a menacing grid of highways and arterial roads.

Still, in one key respect this area is closer to a typical suburb than an Edge City. By all the anecdotal accounts I collected, this area is populated more heavily by commuters who work in downtown Toronto than by full-fledged Edge citizens who work and live in the same hinterland. Dick Illingworth, a former high-ranking official with the Ontario Ministry of Municipal Affairs who was also twice elected mayor of Aurora, told me that while a short time ago the towns up here were almost exclusively "bedroom communities" serving downtown Toronto, today there is a three-way split: a third of the region's residents commute to Toronto, another third work locally, and the final third are employed in some other place that would also be considered suburban.

Because downtown Toronto continues to provide many people here with a livelihood, the fate of Aurora is kept tied more closely to the old downtown core than its autonomous American counterparts. This is explained partly by the newness of the place: businesses simply haven't had time to relocate their offices closer to where many of their workers live.

But the situation also shows that urban-suburban relations in most

Canadian cities have followed a very different pattern than those in the United States, where racial animosity and "white flight" from the city to the suburbs have, for well over a generation, helped to erect strong barriers between largely black (and typically impoverished) urban areas, and whiter and more affluent suburbs. American suburbs have had decades of practice trying to disconnect themselves from the cities that spawned them. In fact, celebrated urban-watcher Jane Jacobs, in her introduction to former Toronto mayor John Sewell's book *The Shape of the City*, suggests that white Canadians' unwillingness to create distinct racial ghettos was one reason downtown Toronto remained intact and healthy during a period when many city cores in the US crumbled. (The other main reasons, says Jacobs, are that Canadian banks did not "redline" inner-city neighbourhoods as ineligible for loans, as their US counterparts did; that in Canada federal funds were not available to finance new, neighbourhood-destroying expressways, as they were in the US; and that misguided urban renewal schemes were introduced later in Canada than in the US, by which time many of their negative effects had been documented.) Racial ghettoization, Jacobs points out, is actually very difficult to accomplish, requiring the creation of complex "blockbusting" schemes and property-value panics to "empty whites out of ghettos-to-be."[8]

Current events indicate that these elaborate efforts to exclude blacks and other minorities from white America's post-war suburban dream seem to have been at least partly successful. While sociologist J. John Palen points out that in the US "residential suburbs have become . . . racially diverse to a degree unthought of even two decades ago," with, for example, the once-rigidly segregated suburbs around Washington, D.C., and Atlanta, Georgia, having become home to "more than a million, overwhelmingly middle-class black suburbanites,"[9] in other cases residents of mostly black urban neighbourhoods are still virtually quarantined by deliberately restrictive routings of freeways and bus lines.

Americans were shown a tragic illustration of the way "bus route discrimination" works when seventeen-year-old Cynthia Wiggins, a black woman from an inner-city neighbourhood of Buffalo, was killed after attempting to cross a busy freeway late in 1995. She was trying to get to her job as a cashier at an Arthur Treacher's Fish and Chips in suburban Cheektowaga's upscale Walden Galleria mall, a popular destination, incidentally, for Canadians on cross-border shopping trips. Since the mall owners did not allow the bus from Wiggins's neighbourhood to stop on their property, her normal routine was to disembark on the highway and sprint across seven lanes of fast-moving traffic. One morning in December, with snow piled high by the roadside, she was hit by a car while performing this risky manoeuvre.

According to Buffalo community worker Warren Galloway, quoted in *Time* magazine, Wiggins's death shows how old strategies of block-busting and outright discrimination have been replaced by "a kind of racism that is often played out in battles between cities and suburbs. It doesn't say no blacks allowed, but the effect is the same." *Time* also reported that this form of segregation-through-transit-route-rigging is thought to be common throughout the United States, as white suburban politicians seek to bar blacks from their neighbourhoods in ways that don't violate federal anti-discrimination laws. US Secretary of Housing and Urban Development (HUD) Henry Cisneros saw in the Wiggins tragedy a hardening of attitudes not just in racial matters but in the arena of inter-class conflict. "Success and prestige today means not having to look at people who are poor," he told *Time*. "That's what the [lack of a] bus stop at the mall said: 'Don't remind us; don't force us to see it.'"[10]

Journey 150 miles or so north of Buffalo and you'll find that York Region has no history of institutionalized racial discrimination and no mechanisms in place to keep out ethnic minorities. If you live in Toronto's Regent Park or the Jane-Finch corridor, you can travel here by GO bus or commuter train, and face only the same amount of inconvenience as would anyone else who chooses to take public transit into this car-dependent realm.

Regardless, there are barriers to acceptance in this part of the world based on more subtle measures of class. These are kept in place not by devious manipulation of the bus routes or urban planning that walls poor minorities into ghettos, but rather by the simple realities of the real estate market, which in recent years have gone unchallenged by any level of government.

That York Region has developed overwhelmingly as an economically homogeneous community may be an accident of timing. Most of its growth occurred during the 1980s, an era that saw private moxy exhalted and government do-goodism disdained. Middle-class, white-collar folks were exhorted to take risks, to aim high, which meant developing a muscular stock portfolio or riding the runaway real estate market. This is the thinking that shaped today's York region; much of the housing was built for the carriage trade, with practically no land set aside for lower-income or subsidized accommodation, as would have been mandated in growing jurisdictions during previous booms. But even though York Region attained its exclusive aura more by inertia than by conspiracy — nobody seemed to want to challenge the prevailing pro-market ethos of the day — the result is much the same as what Henry Cisneros observed in the outskirts of Buffalo: a social landscape where the privileged can choose not to look at poverty or deprivation, where attitudes towards those of a lower station can be cultivated in a comfortable vacuum, without having to be tested against real life.

To be fair, it must be stated that the local politicians who resolved, in the optimistic '80s, to exclude social housing from their development plans may have been motivated partly by a desire not to repeat the mistakes of the past, many of which had been immortalized in steel-reinforced concrete a few short miles away. Venture across York Region's southern perimeter, as the Sentra and I did one evening after touring the monied splendour of the Caledon Hills (in the western half of the region), and you'll discover that there's only a thin threshold of green separating this quasi-paradise from an area notorious across North America as a prime example of how bad planning can sabotage good intentions.

I speak, of course, of the Jane-Finch corridor. Finch Avenue is, for the most part, a grim boulevard of dingy malls and industrial parks, populated by both light manufacturing concerns and strip clubs, pushed out here by the local bylaws that bar them from residential areas. On Finch Avenue immigrants to Canada learn that their adopted homeland is a place of constant truck traffic, commercial fortresses fashioned from plain concrete blocks, and the garish neon signs of those strip clubs. Surrounding some sections of this thoroughfare are low-rise subdivisions, but never far from view are the daunting apartment towers for which the area is famous, commanding the eye like some kind of Emerald City gone awry.

As John Sewell recounts in his book *The Shape of the City*, the Jane-Finch corridor was at one time — that is, when it was still on the artists' drawing board — a place of hope. The idea behind it was that combining high-rise accommodation with low-density housing would create the opportunity even for low-income tenants in subsidized accommodation to experience the restorative effects of open space and countrylike vistas. Building skyward would, of course, increase density on those sites, but if density in the overall area was capped, big chunks of land would be left as rolling green meadows where children could play and families could picnic; it would also provide a pastoral view to soothe the nerves of weary residents gazing down from above. This design theory was first made into reality with the construction of the Flemingdon Park project (closer to downtown Toronto) in the 1950s, and imported to Jane-Finch in the 1960s. But after a while its shortcomings became apparent in both locations; planners had not taken into account the obvious fact, for instance, that while parents felt comfortable leaving their children to play in a small backyard attached to a house, they were highly reluctant to allow them to play in a vast park separated from their living space by a twenty-storey elevator ride.

As Sewell concludes, the lofty theory behind Jane-Finch (suburban-scale densities + highrise living + lots of open space = Utopia) didn't meet the tests of everyday life. The more "suburban" aspects of the design, which were supposed to make life more pleasant, in reality just exacerbated old problems.

> The vast amount of common space both inside and outside the buildings seems ideal for drug dealing and anonymous crime; the distance of buildings from public streets makes using public transit a most unpleasant experience, although the low income of many Jane/Finch residents leaves them no option but to travel by transit; generally low suburban densities mean that transit service is not exemplary, certainly not up to the standards of denser parts of the city; and the high-rise and other multiple-unit buildings are inappropriate for the many children living in the area. Other complaints — such as the lack of social services in the area — relate more to the inability of the Jane/Finch community to influence the political system, but that too might be a result of urban form, in that those who can choose to live some place more pleasant have made that choice. In the 1980s, a Jane-Finch address was considered perhaps the least desirable in Metro Toronto.[11]

In a perverse kind of way, the enduring and fearsome monument of Jane-Finch, sitting across York Region's southern fringe, was a major influence on the style of development that would take place to the north. Dick Illingworth confirms that those imposing towers were emblematic of everything people arriving here wanted to avoid. "When people moved out of the city," he says, "they wanted to get away from the high-rise, they wanted to get away from higher densities. They wanted single-family homes." Many were also not crazy about having subsidized housing nearby, even though social housing advocates had learned a lot since the 1960s, with such newer forms of subsidized housing as mixed-income co-operatives having received good reviews. The St. Lawrence housing co-op in downtown Toronto, for instance, is far more aesthetically pleasing than any of those fortresslike monster homes that began to sprout on the streets of older suburbs during the boom years of the 1980s.

Meanwhile, if the builders who set to work in York Region during the '80s saw the landscape to the south as a cautionary tale, looking off in other directions they found more positive inspiration. To the east, the west, and the north are the icons of an aristocratic heritage — the equestrian clubs and golf courses, the pricy craft shops in well-groomed rural hamlets, the impressive mansions that peer haughtily over the Caledon Hills — of which many newcomers hoped to become part.

Of course, the problem with moving to a new suburb to purchase something resembling a dignified life in the country is that a lot of other people have the same idea at the same time, so country living becomes something other than country living. Though large pockets of York Region have stayed green and rural, what I remember most about my stay there are the traffic jams — often due to road construction — and the wall-to-wall shopping malls and big-box retailers on a strip of Yonge Street between Aurora and Newmarket.

These newer suburbs have assumed such critical mass that they are starting to define life in the metropolis. When people talk today about living in Toronto, often they don't mean Toronto, or even the Toronto megacity that has swallowed up the post-war suburbs of Scarborough, North York, and Etobicoke. They may well mean they live in the far-flung outposts of Markham or Aurora to the north, or Whitby or Ajax to the east, or Mississauga or Milton along the western curve of Lake Ontario.

This is in keeping with the idea, current among many urban theorists, that we no longer live in suburbs or in cities, but in "metropolitan regions." In Ontario the practical implications of this notion have taken political form in the continual wrangling — by a vast collection of municipal mayors as well as provincial officials — over the issues said to be of common concern to the region known as the Greater Toronto Area, or GTA. The GTA — an informal amalgam of regions and municipalities previously thought of as independent and self-contained — encompasses a huge chunk of southern Ontario. The former Metro Toronto has only 10 percent of the land surface and 50 percent of the 4.5 million population of the GTA, which embraces the urban 416 area code plus most of suburban 905. The primary issue that has gripped this region is the question of whether wealthier suburbs should shoulder some of the higher social service costs of downtown Toronto. Mayors of suburban cities have reacted mostly with expected defensiveness, telling downtowners they should pay for their own problems. But the mere fact that the issue has been raised is somehow a recognition of the interconnectedness of this sprawling economic region, and a general acceptance of the proposition that if one part of the GTA starts to rot, the disease may well spread throughout the organism.

If this massive territory has indeed become one entity — the GTA, or Toronto, for short — perhaps it's time to alter the associations that come to mind with the phrase "living in Toronto." The emblematic images of life in T.O. — streetcars rolling across the urban landscape, people strolling through funky neighbourhoods where outdoor vegetable stands line the streets — have been propagated widely by the city's booming film and TV industry, but today they are a reality for only a small minority within the metropolis. This is true even for people who spend their working days in downtown Toronto and live way out in the boonies. If they toil in the office towers of the financial district — a massive, self-contained chunk of suburban logic grafted onto the city core and given life support by an arterial network of subways, walkways, highways, and commuter rail lines that lead to the burbs — they can enter and exit the land of commerce without setting foot in the real city, without, essentially, leaving the warm embrace of Shopping Mall Land.

Toronto's civic mythology, which hasn't changed much in thirty years, gives short shrift to the fact that most people who think of themselves as living in Toronto live a suburban rather than an urban life. In his book *Accidental City*, Robert Fulford writes that Toronto was for most of its life an intensely inward-looking city that finally acquired a sense of public life when Nathan Phillips Square, the long-awaited plaza adjoining the new city hall, was opened in 1965. Since that event, says Fulford, "in Toronto, city building has become an art of public revelation rather than private expression. Toronto is a private city that finally became public, and gradually acquired a desire to be seen and understood."[12] This sudden blossoming caused the world to take notice — and caused Torontonians to take notice of the world taking notice. Architecture critic Leon Whiteson opened his homage to Toronto, *The Liveable City*, with a reference to *Fortune* magazine's 1975 description of Toronto as "the world's newest great city." What entranced outsiders and made the city "liveable" for residents, Whiteson believed, was the strength of its neighbourhoods — distinct little "urban villages" that functioned as an antidote to the anomie of big city life, providing human-scale focus, a shelter for the individual, and a familiar street on which to walk.[13] This appealing mélange continues to win praise from down south; over two decades after *Fortune* delivered its "newest great city" kudos, the *Utne Reader* declared that Toronto remained "North America's most liveable big city" by virtue of its "low crime rates, excellent public transportation, charming residential neighbourhoods, cosmopolitan energy, and sophisticated cultural scene."[14] (On a micro-level, a handful of issues later, the same periodical chose Toronto's College-and-Clinton neighbourhood as "one of the hippest places to live in North America.")[15]

But the moment you notice something in your rear-view mirror, to adapt an observation of Marshall McLuhan's, you know that it's past, receded into history. As the media were busy gushing over how different Toronto was from US cities, how its safe and friendly public spaces contrasted with the insular civic lives of a nation that had abandoned its great urban areas in favour of suburbia, many Torontonians were jumping ship and moving out to northern versions of the Edge City that could just as easily have been located in New Jersey or Ohio. This is "living in Toronto" for a big chunk of the populace on the cusp of the millennium: You spend your nights in the quiet suburbs in front of the tube or computer screen, and divide your day between a car and an office cubicle. And so Fulford's story of Toronto transforming itself from a private to a public city has come full circle: for the majority (those in the remote suburbs, at least), living in Toronto is once more a private experience, not as in a secluded Victorian drawing room, but as in twenty-first-century Edge City, revolving around private automobiles and video machines. Today, shopping malls, parking lots, and Wal-Marts take up a lot of space, both on the land and in people's lives. So perhaps, in the course of trying to take the pulse of the ever-enlarging metropolis known as the GTA, referred to in shorthand as Toronto, it is more representative to forgo a colourful trip down to Queen and Spadina, and head out instead to Yonge and Wellington, in charming downtown Aurora.

2 | The Nature of the Beast

Dick Illingworth remembers his family's move to Aurora as if it were yesterday. The year was 1954, and the community of Willowdale, to which the Illingworths were about to bid farewell, was just beginning to establish itself as one of Toronto's most popular post-war commuter suburbs. Although Willowdale remained, at that point, positively rustic compared with what it would become, it was developed enough by the mid-1950s that its promise of a tranquil, crime-free life had become tarnished, and populous enough that fear and suspicion began to spread.

"We have a daughter who was two and a half at the time," recalls Illingworth, explaining the rationale for leaving, "and there had been one of those unfortunate incidents where a child had been molested — well, not close, but in the area. So my wife and I decided we should move up here. Since I was travelling all the time [as a salesman] it didn't make any difference to me where I lived."

This is a story that's probably been played out many millions of times across North America: A young couple with a child moves to the suburbs so their offspring will have a clean and safe place to grow up. When that suburb starts to feel more like the urban area it's been built around, they move again, and in this way the suburban frontier gets pushed farther outward with each pulse of development pressure. In the 1950s, a couple of decades before *Sesame Street* rehabilitated the idea of the city neighbourhood as a hospitable place for kids, and when agricultural land on the urban periphery appeared boundless — this must have seemed the most practical course for many families.

Illingworth says he has never regretted the decision to move northward; that fate brought his family to its own Shangri-la. "We came up and lived two miles out of town, right by the Hunt Club," he recalls. "It was beautiful. Our daughter grew up watching the horses and the hunting dogs. Every Sunday morning you would see the hunters in their red jackets going off into the fields."

What Illingworth himself got out of the move was a social niche and a life's work. First elected as a school trustee in 1963, he moved up to the office of town councillor two years later and in 1969 was elected mayor. While occupying the mayor's chair, he also held down a day job as a bureaucrat with the province's Ministry of Trade and Development, but had to give up public office when a transfer to the Ministry of Municipal Affairs in 1973 presented the potential for conflict of interest. After his retirement in 1982, however, Illingworth put his name back on the ballot and was once again elected mayor. Altogether he has served more than twenty years as an elected politician and civic affairs bureaucrat. The kicker to the story is that since 1985 Dick Illingworth has kept up with local politics by freelancing for local newspapers and radio stations, a task that — judging by the appearance of his byline on the front pages of several regional news organs this particular week in 1997 — the eighty-one-year-old writer attacks with more vigour than most cub reporters.

It would be an absurd understatement to say that Aurora has changed a lot in the near half-century since Dick Illingworth moved here. As in suburban outposts everywhere, what were not long ago fields and pasture are now parking lots, subdivisions, and Wal-Marts and their ilk. What's remained constant throughout the years, however, is the political conflict over the question of how much development should be allowed. Recent arrivals invariably want the floodgates closed the minute they're safely inside; the realization that the nice open field beside the house they've just bought will soon afford a view of other people's backyards is sure to stir outrage and high-decibel protest.

Back in the 1950s the anti-development impulse was directed not so much against the plunder of the landscape as against the threat it posed to a comfortable and long-established social order. "Some of these old towns, they're very cliquish, and it takes awhile to break that down," Illingworth recalls. "Even when I got on council, I was still treated like the new boy."

This coolness towards newcomers was so pronounced that for years a kind of caste system existed that separated old-stock villagers and the first new waves of suburbanites. Aurora contained some 5,000 inhabitants when the Illingworths first arrived, but the town's population bulged in the late 1950s with the construction of two new subdivisions — one in the south end of town had about seven hundred homes, another in the north had between five and six hundred. "Now we had three towns," Illingworth says, "and it was rather strange — some of the retailers on the street would ask you where you lived. If you were from the old town you could run a charge account. But if you were from the north town or the south town, it was strictly COD."

This divide persisted until 1969, the first year Illingworth was mayor. "We had the Little NHL hockey tournament here. There were over a thousand boys from across Ontario coming to play, and they had to billet them. Well, for the first time, that event brought the town together, and from then on it was one town." This event also marked the birth of what Illingworth refers to — repeatedly, and with the imploring earnestness of someone who believes it's a former mayor's lifelong duty to boost the hometown — as "the Aurora spirit."

"When people move here, usually a good 95 percent catch it," he explains. "Now it takes four or five years on average. Because they move up from Toronto, their connections are still down there — maybe they are still working there, and they don't become involved in the community because Toronto is still their community. But as their kids start to go into school and they start meeting their neighbours, and they start having a street party or something, they get the Aurora spirit."

As we talk, I am sitting in a lushly upholstered armchair at the Aurora Golf and County Club across from Illingworth, a tall man with a neatly trimmed moustache and a cowboy-style string tie. We're both knocking back morning coffee and occasionally glancing through the Plexiglas panel that separates this cosy mezzanine from the swimming pool below. I feel some scepticism about the existence of this "Aurora spirit." It springs partly from the things I have read about how the shape of suburbia has torn asunder the sense of community and social connectedness that may once have existed in places like this. I've only been here a day, but I've seen the enormous, anonymous shopping mall farther north on Yonge Street where Aurora bleeds into Newmarket, toured some of those sprawling subdivisions, and seen the traffic jams at rush hour. To me, this all speaks of a place populated by workaholic commuters who are inseparable from their cell phones and who see home mostly as a post-workplace netherworld where they can slip into the narcotic release of cable TV or a video from Blockbuster.

I'm not saying that Illingworth's view of Aurora life is bogus. It's just that I wonder if looking at things from the vantage point of the Aurora Golf and Country Club might skew the view a bit. Most people here this morning appear to be (a) retired, and (b) well off — a combination of circumstances that might provide a greater opportunity to commune with one's neighbours and participate in civic life than the average, overworked, insecure white-collar toiler of the late 1990s would have.

Well, not everyone in this room is retired. Not Doug Clark, for instance, who saunters over to our table and begins to quiz Illingworth about whether he has any new information on the quasi-scandal that links the source of local federal Liberal MP Maurizio Bevilacqua's campaign funds to an alleged (and now deceased) Russian mobster named Josef Sigalov. (There is nothing to suggest that Bevilacqua knew that the source of the money was linked to the Russian mob.) Clark is a local Reform Party organizer who is currently the official agent for Reform candidate Maralyn Hazelgrove. Clark, Illingworth tells me later, was also a major mover behind the surprise victory of Frank Klees, Mike Harris's man in these parts during the last provincial election, who buried favoured Liberal Charles Beer partly on the strength of Reform's formidable grassroots machine, which was put at the service of the provincial Tories.[1]

This morning Clark is thinking about strategy for tonight's all-candidates meeting at the Aurora Town Hall, and he's stuck on the Sigalov story. One of the arrows in his team's quiver is a recent story by Elaine Dewar in *Toronto Life* magazine, which names Bevilacqua as one of four Liberal candidates to receive campaign contributions from the alleged mobster in the previous federal contest. The Dewar article claims that Sigalov, who had been linked to the Russian mafia by the FBI, had gained his introduction to Liberal circles through a former member of Vaughan city council. Having failed to check the Russian émigré's credentials, Liberal officials then faced the embarrassing dilemma of not knowing to whom to return the contributions to after Sigalov's death from brain cancer.[2] Clark is clearly frustrated that the story has not ballooned into a major scandal, and Illingworth echoes his surprise that the national media have not given it extensive play (in fact, the *Globe and Mail* did run one front-page story on Sigalov's contributions to Liberal candidates). With these words of commiseration, but no more ammunition for tonight's debate, Clark is off.

This little encounter may seem like a modern-day equivalent of the casual chat at the small-town barbershop or the hardware store, but I still contend that what goes on under this roof is probably not typical of the town as a whole. The Aurora Golf and Country Club may bear some similarities to the place that used to be — that old, rural Ontario burg, run by an exclusive clique, where political insight was traded casually and everyone knew everyone else's business. My sense, however, is that the modern suburb that's supplanted old Aurora is now just another island in the metropolitan mainstream, a place where most people are probably too busy to know their neighbours' names, let alone their business. That, at least, is the preconception I bring to this terrain, and it fits in well with the recent political history of the area. Based on what Schneider and Garreau have written about the interaction between politics and architectural form, I'm assuming that the reason people here voted en masse for Mike Harris in the last election is that, since they see very little of the effects of public projects but do see a lot of shopping malls, they've come to believe that the rightful purpose of their money is to buy them more consumer goods, rather than to advance some nebulous notion of the public good. And if other people further down the social ladder suffer as a result of this, well, tough; living in a quiet, secluded suburb such as this, you never have to see them.

When I put a gentler version of this hypothesis to Dick Illingworth, asking if he agrees that the migration of the last wave of go-getting professionals from the city has eroded the typical Canadian sense of civic duty, he sticks with his earlier story about "the Aurora spirit."

"That 'get out of my face' attitude might be there when they first arrive," Illingworth concedes, "but as they become involved in the community and they start volunteering — it might be with a service club or with the Cancer Society or something — I don't see it any-more. I think they get the Aurora spirit. I've no other explanation, except that they become a part of the community and they see the needs and they see that we are our brothers' keepers and that we have to help. I may be a dreamer, but that's what I believe."

In Illingworth's estimation, Mike Harris's sweep across the 905 belt was due less to suburbanites adopting American values and more to the peculiar dynamics of that particular election. This, of course, may be partly wishful thinking, since Illingworth's disdain for the Harris crew is clearly evident in his other remarks about the need for a backbench revolt at Queen's Park or a replay of the Upper Canada Rebellion. Although this octogenarian reporter dutifully served as a bureaucrat under successive Tory premiers in the '70s and '80s, those were a different breed of Tory. Now it especially galls Illingworth that the task he was personally responsible for during his years at Municipal Affairs — trying to build co-operative relationships between the province and the municipalities — apparently has no value for a government intent on downloading a multitude of funding responsibilities to the municipalities without consultation and often without explanation. Wishful thinking or not, Illingworth's view of the last provincial election is that people voted Tory simply because the party appeared more organized and coherent than the NDP, which was perceived to have botched its time in power, and the Liberals, whose leader, Lynn McLeod, had an image problem. So the question, in Illingworth's mind, is more who people voted against, rather than who they endorsed.

At the all-candidates meeting that takes place later in the day, it strikes me that Dick Illingworth may be right. The people who have gathered at the Aurora Town Hall — a glistening new building surrounded, like many in the municipality, by huge mounds of earth and idle construction vehicles — will ask questions reflecting a wide range of political views, often presenting them in understated ways. They may be an unrepresentative sampling, of course — about 50 percent of the close-to-capacity crowd appears to be either retired or too young to vote — but as a group they display little of the right-wing, revolutionary zeal that made the headlines after the last provincial election.

The candidates, on the other hand, clearly reflect how far the Canadian political mainstream has drifted to the right. The incumbent, Liberal Maurizio Bevilacqua, who won by an enormous margin last time around and is set to repeat that feat in the upcoming contest, identifies himself almost completely with the side of the Liberal party that concerns itself with no-nonsense issues like balancing the books. He talks incessantly of fiscal responsibility and never broaches the question of social programs. He mentions Paul Martin a couple of times but never Jean Chrétien. He crows that the biggest accomplishment of the previous Liberal Parliament was to enact those painful cuts that brought the conquest of the deficit within sight. "Times have changed," he tells the crowd. "The *Wall Street Journal* is not laughing at Canada anymore. The IMF is not closing down our finance department. Things are better in this country."

This deficit-cutting bandwagon seems to have become awfully crowded of late. The federal Progressive Conservative party is also running on a right-wing economic platform, largely lifted from Mike Harris's program in Ontario; local candidate Lara Coombs, whose campaign literature bears her image electronically fused into a tête-à-tête with party leader Jean Charest, repeatedly talks about income and payroll tax cuts, each time waving a copy of the Tory policy book as proof of her intentions. Cutting taxes and slashing government is old hat for the Reform Party, so candidate Maralyn Hazelgrove makes only a perfunctory mention of these economic policies, preferring to concentrate on the more touchy-feely aspects of Reform's platform, like its commitment to hunt down child pornographers and other members of the criminal element.

It is Hazelgrove, in fact, who sparks the biggest fireworks of the meeting, though none of those explosions will have anything to do with economic issues. Perhaps as a desperate ploy to distract attention from a losing campaign — or maybe, conversely, as part of a brilliant strategy to uncover some hidden panic, some deep existential angst beneath these calm suburban surfaces — Hazelgrove hammers away at the personal integrity issues, so as to suggest that the good people here have entrusted their government to an elite cabal of chisellers. Hazelgrove is perfect for the role. She sits stone-faced for much of the meeting, often adopting a look of disgust when she starts to speak, her manner suggesting that she has no interest in playing the typical polite Canadian. She begins with an attack on the incumbent that would be standard issue for many populist politicos in the United States, stating that she really doesn't enjoy running for political office but that "somebody's got to do it, or else the job will be left to the professional politicians like Maurizio Bevilacqua." She also picks a fight with Lara Coombs by implying that the PCs are an untrustworthy lot who reneged on an understanding with Reform. "We agreed to help get the Conservatives elected in the last provincial election and they agreed to help us get elected in this election," Hazelgrove says, prompting Coombs to shoot back with, "We would never help to get a party elected that would divide this country." Hazelgrove later takes a run at the NDP, characterizing it as a gang of irresponsible pot-smokers, a reference to NDP Leader Alexa McDonough's confession that she has smoked marijuana "and I did inhale." This jab causes NDP candidate Robert Navarretta to grin broadly and shake his head.

But things move from the comic to the combative when Hazelgrove plays the Sigalov card. Early in the meeting, she hammers Bevilacqua for failing to investigate who it was that sent him a $10,000 cheque, insisting that the name should have rung alarm bells, since Sigalov's criminal connections had been reported in the *Toronto Star* more than a year earlier. Bevilacqua can only produce an uncharacteristically lame answer about how, in a democracy, people will either write a $10 cheque or a $100,000 cheque "according to their ability," and these cheques should all be treated equally. Bevilacqua is obviously unprepared for this line of questioning; Hazelgrove sees an opportunity to return to this ground and ratchet up the pressure towards the end of the meeting, when a member of the audience asks what each candidate has done for the riding. "I can only take credit for one good deed," Hazelgrove begins, "and that is that I brought to the attention of all our constituents the fact that Mr. Bevilacqua accepted campaign contributions —" Before she can finish, a Bevilacqua supporter attempts to shout down the Reform candidate by yelling, "Stop the mudslinging! Stick to the issues!" The moderator then fires back at the heckler, "Hey, hey, shut up, you," and Hazelgrove finishes her sentence: "— accepted campaign funds from the Russian mob." In the awkward hush that follows there is isolated applause, a few titters of laughter, and an undercurrent of *ohs* from the crowd. Bevilacqua is red-faced and fuming.

Compared with this display, taxes — the foremost "hot button" issue of the previous provincial contest — register considerably lower on this audience's political Geiger counters. When someone raises the question of how tax policy relates to job creation, a civilized discussion ensues that provokes some unexpected responses from the crowd. Bevilacqua, who was head of the Commons finance committee, delivers a scholarly answer on the nuances of various types of taxes as economic stimuli or depressants. Both Coombs and Hazelgrove recite their parties' policies on delivering income tax cuts as a way to rev up consumer spending and create new jobs, but they receive only lukewarm applause. At this point the two voices in the wilderness off to the left of the conservative consensus seem to score a hit with the assembled observers. When Robert Navarretta, a veteran union organizer who's flying the NDP's colours in this area, contests the idea that tax cuts will automatically lead to job growth, the applause-o-meter goes off the scale. Meanwhile, independent candidate Andrew James, a former Tory who's now flogging a form of green economics, deepens the tone of the debate by suggesting that politicians have to move beyond "band-aid" policies by addressing the "deep structural concerns" that arise from wrenching changes like the globalization of trade or the impact of computerization on employment levels.

There is even — right here in the heart of 905 — a call for *new* taxes. An elderly man steps up to the microphone and proposes that the candidates consider the merits of the Tobin tax, a proposed levy favoured by several agencies of the United Nations, which would skim a tiny percentage off international financial transactions and apply the proceeds to global social programs.

But is this range of opinion representative of the broader electorate in Vaughan-King-Aurora? Well, if you trust what the experts say about suburban alienation, this gathering by its very nature must be an aberration. Typical suburbanites would not come to such a meeting, since typical suburbanites prefer to stay at home, insulated against the intrusions of the outside world, learning all they need to know about politics from those catchy ads the parties run during the commercial breaks in *NYPD Blue*. The debate in the Aurora Town Hall may be indicative of nothing other the mindset of a handful of political junkies and local cranks. And so it's time for a reality check, time to venture off into the places where people live and work to drop my journalistic dipstick into the well of daily affairs.

There is no better person to provide a measure of the political mood in these parts than Craig Proctor, local boy and real estate salesman extraordinaire. Proctor was the top-selling Re/Max agent in Canada for three years running, and in 1996 was the sales leader of the 45,000 Re/Max associates worldwide. "What blows people away," Proctor tells me, "is that I'm from Newmarket. They figure, 'What, do you live in New York, Los Angeles, San Francisco, London, England? Where is Newmarket on the globe?'"

Across York Region, an image of Proctor's restrained smile and youthful blond curls can be seen on the backs of the multitude of park benches. In person, he can sometimes be found at the Newmarket Re/Max office — a striking building of metal and glass, all atriums and plant-lined walkways inside — that seems slightly out of place amidst the bland and predictable right angles of the commercial park where it stands.

On the day I am to meet Craig Proctor at his office, I have seriously miscalculated the time it would take to drive from Woodbridge, in the southwest part of the region, to Newmarket, in the northeast. After crawling through stop-and-stall traffic in the middle of the day, I arrive forty minutes late, but am spared embarrassment because Proctor, who is driving up from Toronto, is twenty minutes later than I am. After his arrival, it doesn't take long for the conversation to turn to traffic — one of the minuses of living in these distant burbs.

"I meet a lot of people who just can't handle it," says Proctor. "They move up to Newmarket or Aurora for a couple of years and then say, 'You know what? I can't take it anymore. I'll have to move to a condo, or rent a house in Toronto. I know it's a lot more expensive and I won't be able to afford the type of home I have here, but I can't do it anymore, I've reached the limit.' The travelling, the commuting, takes its toll. You take someone who works maybe a nine-hour day, and you add an hour commute on either side, there's eleven hours of your day. So it doesn't leave a lot of time to do anything else."

It's unnerving at first to hear such candid talk from somebody who wants to sell houses in these parts. In fact, what's most startling about the next hour or so of conversation is how many bad things Proctor has to say about life in York Region. He claims, however, that this is one of the secrets of his success. He tries to let people know about the pros and cons of suburban living; even though it may cost him a commission, he will walk them through a twenty-four-hour day in the life of a commuter and try to dissuade clients from buying if he thinks they are overextending themselves. The pay off, says Proctor, especially during a market downturn when lots of quick-buck artists have gotten out of the business, is the trust he instils in his clients and a constant stream of new referrals. Proctor's approach also elevates the real estate agent to the status of psychoanalyst/confessor/priest, a mystic personage who can guide lost souls through the dark vicissitudes of the real estate market, a trusted figure who is allowed a rare view of the lives and psyches of his clients. Proctor has peered plenty into those suburban psyches, and what he invariably sees are people stressed beyond imagination.

"I meet a lot of people who are frustrated," he relates. "They work hard for their money. Their houses went down in value, they're killing themselves, the husband works, the wife works. There's a lot of pressure on people today . . . I sit down with my customers and I say, 'What do you want? What do you want to achieve here?' 'Gee, my family's important . . . You know, I've got two kids, I never get to see them.' 'Well, what's your life like?' 'Our marriage isn't that great, we don't do anything anymore, we're under stress with work.' 'What would make you happy?' 'Well, our mortgage is killing us, I'd like to have more time with my family — I don't want to have to work over-time every day to make ends meet.'"

This is a far cry from the life that Proctor remembers in the relaxed Newmarket of his youth. "I'm the fifth-generation Proctor born here, and I was actually born on the Proctor farm right on Yonge Street," he recounts. "To live here thirty-five years and see all the changes, it's almost like it's a different place." The biggest single step in the transformation of this area happened in 1987-88, when real estate prices soared and "the market went nuts." A pent-up demand for housing exploded into an extravagant building boom that changed the face of the region. Craig Proctor played no small role in this process, and he harbours some mixed feelings about it.

"I'm in real estate, so a part of me says, 'Yeah, this is fantastic, lots of development, more houses; means I get to sell more.' But on the other side of the coin, the roads are busier, it's less personal, and the community isn't so much a community anymore . . . Especially being raised on a farm, and remembering Newmarket, how it used to be. You know, as a kid you remember fields you used to play in and just how nice the scenery was."

But changes to the scenery are probably the least of the transfor-mation. It's the way of life, the psychology of the place, that's now completely different. With the new buildings have come a frantic pace, more pressure, a sense of alienation.

In the old town "everybody sort of knew each other," continues Proctor, sinking deep into nostalgia, "and it was more of a commu-nity back then. We had a hockey team, the Newmarket Redmen, and everyone was behind it. But now a lot of people don't work in the area — don't really feel they are part of the community. They are really Toronto people. They come up here to sleep, but everything they do socially — their friends, their relatives, their social life — is all back in Toronto. They may know their [immediate] neighbour but that's about the extent of their community involvement."

Suddenly the pieces of this psychological profile start to fit together. It makes sense that this area would throw its weight behind the slash-and-burn politics of Mike Harris — to which the label "mean-spirited" has frequently been applied — since the conditions of many people's lives here, so it appears, could be expected to promote irritability and, yes, meanness. They endure too little personal time, too many responsibilities, and probably they get far too little sleep. Is it logical to expect people to sympathize with homeless people on the streets of downtown Toronto when they live in this kind of isolation? When they work and commute for so many hours that they may get to see their own kids for only an hour or so a day? When their impression of human society is formed largely in the mad dash of chrome and pistons up the highway towards home at night — when their fellow man is the guy up ahead who, with one unsignalled lane change, could bring their lives to a crashing halt?

If these factors create the psychological conditions necessary for supporting the politics of cruelty, Proctor says they are undergirded by a set of circumstances that go a long way towards explaining why many people around here voted for the man who promised to cut welfare payments to finance a tax cut for the upper middle class. Some of these people live in debtors' prison. They bought their homes when the market was high, are now unable to sell, and spend huge amounts of money paying off the paper value of a house that's completely out of line with current market value. This explains, in some cases, why people who make good salaries — people who are among the upper-income earners in society — consider themselves poor and oppressed, and jump at every dime the government promises them in tax cuts.

It's a woeful story of the exuberant expectations of the 1980s being crushed by the grim tide of retreat that rolled in during the 1990s. Proctor has seen many of the monuments to those grand dreams turn into prisons for their owners. "We have one development,

Stonehaven," he offers by way of example. "All big estate homes — 3,000 square feet up to 6,000 square feet — and the prices probably went down $100,000 to $200,000 just because of the market. Your most expensive house there would have started around $600,000, and now you'd be lucky to get $400,000 for it."

The buyers, of course, were not innocent victims in all this. It's not as if they are poor sharecroppers working their fingers to the bone for the Man, or simple Midwestern bumpkins about to be evicted from the family farm by an evil bank manager. Although Proctor is too diplomatic to say it, in many cases people find themselves facing hard times because of their own greed.

"A lot of people were speculating," Proctor confirms. "They said, 'I own a house now, and it went up, and therefore let's buy a really big house because if it's big it's got to be better and it's going to go up more.' And, of course, the opposite happened. The market crashed and the economy went soft. A lot of people lost their jobs and ended up having to sell their house — they just couldn't afford it."

Those who lost their homes, however, may have been the lucky ones — for them it was a quick death. Others — Proctor believes this probably applies to 15 percent of people living in the area — found themselves unable to sell homes that they couldn't afford, and are now on a fast-moving treadmill just trying to keep up with their mortgage payments.

"You see, these people never bought the house — in a lot of cases — to live in," the realtor explains. "They bought the house on speculation. 'If I pay six, like this house used to be five last year, therefore a year from now it will be worth seven. I could flip it around for an easy hundred and I'm off to the races.' They didn't count on having to own it and live in it and carry it.

"You see, that's when you know there's a problem. When the average Joe starts to get in there and buy and flip and speculate, you know the market is ripe for the downward crash. And what happened was, you know, the average guy's at work, Joe's at work, and his buddy John says, 'You know what? I made fifty grand last year by flipping one house.' And Joe says, 'Hell, that's more than we make all year long. And I had to *work* for that — you didn't have to do anything.' So Joe goes out and he buys a house.

"Problem is, John's timing was much better than Joe's timing. Neither one of them had any specialized knowledge, it's just that John . . . he lucked out — bought in and got out — and Joe, he buys the same house, probably pays a little more because his timing was a little off, and sells it for a lot less when the market crashes. And they are average guys working at average jobs; they can't afford to carry a $400,000 to $600,000 house."

The result is that the dream of a grand life, a shot at real prosperity through the magic of the free market, suddenly turns into a nightmare. And the problem is not just the mortgage; it's the whole package, the whole lifestyle that comes with the bricks and mortar. "There's a small percentage of people here that are trapped. They've bought a house, they've got in over their heads. They hate their jobs, but of course they need the job to pay all their obligations, whether it be a big car, a big house, or whatever. They made a decision when they purchased — based on how the real estate market was, how the economy was, how driving down the 404 was, and everything all of a sudden became worse. More people move in, more traffic, chances are there's cutbacks at work so you're making less money, the housing market crashes and you can't get out from under because you can't sell the house to cover your mortgage."

— — —

I hear a similar story of misery from Brian Kirlik, acting editor at the *Era-Banner*, the local newspaper for Aurora, Newmarket, and a few smaller communities. Kirlik moved to Aurora in 1985 when the town's population was just 13,500. Twelve years later, the number of inhabitants had almost tripled to 35,000; with the town now physically big enough that to get from one end to the other, "you're talking a fifteen- to twenty-minute drive, which is straight driving, not heavy traffic. It's not a small town anymore." Growth across the whole region of York, after having levelled off with the crash of the early 1990s, has since resumed its upward trajectory, hitting 614,000 by 1997 and expected to reach 1.1 million around the year 2021.[3]

Kirlik says the population growth has forced the *Era-Banner* to transform itself from a typical community newspaper focused on social notes and "lots of pictures of kids playing in the parks," to a news organ that deals mostly with the political and social challenges arising from development. And though he's kept a keen professional eye on these changes, he still chooses to live outside the region, in Scarborough, the post-World War II Toronto suburb that served as the inspiration for Mike Myers's "Wayne's World" films. Scarborough was built during a time when people had different priorities. Kirlik says he wouldn't think of trading up for the bigger square footage and design frills that are available in houses closer to his workplace.

"I tell people, 'You're nuts to buy a house in York Region,'" says Kirlik, a personable guy in his mid-thirties who sports a neatly trimmed moustache and a reporter's paunch. "My publisher might not like me to say that, but I tell people, 'Think about it before you go. There's a serious hospital situation, there's a serious police situation, there's a serious tax situation, there's no public transit — think about those things.'

"The house might be beautiful," he adds, "but you're not buying the house, you're buying the community . . . Think about it before you move up here; ask yourself the question, where do you want your kid to go to school? Next door? It's not going to happen. They're going to be bused [from Newmarket] to Aurora, or maybe to the other side of Newmarket."

Even new homeowners who are assured that new schools are being built are often disappointed if they don't read the fine print carefully, the editor says. "This situation here, when they were selling houses for development just across the street, they referred to a brand-new school in all the literature — well, that school is full. The kids are being bused to a holding school that's a hundred years old in downtown Newmarket. Did anybody bother to ask [about] that? They've got signs up in developments now that say, 'This is the site of a public school.' It may not be built until two or three years from now. The homes are being built there now, but the school board doesn't have approval to build the school, it doesn't have the funds.

"Well, what are these parents going to do with their kids? You know, it's a beautiful home, but there are all these social issues. Call me a cynic, but I know that in Scarborough my kids are going to go to the same school that's right over here, it's a short little walk, all residential streets. Here that's not the case."

Name any aspect of life you choose, says Kirlik, and you will find a drastic shortage of social amenities. It's not just the school boards that need to build more schools at $20 million a pop but don't have the money. It's also the hospitals — designed to serve a sparsely populated area and overwhelmed by the region's explosive growth — that are so inadequate they are close to posing a threat to public safety. Then there are the jammed commuter highways leading to Toronto, which provide a daily illustration of the need for more people to use public transit. With one GO train leaving for Toronto in the morning and only one returning at night, however, rail travel remains impractical for commuters who can't count on an absolutely fixed work schedule — and to hope for better rail service would be wildly naive in the current climate of spending restraint, which has seen the provincial government reduce, rather than expand, its support for transit. The police force, meanwhile, can't grow fast enough to patrol the streets. And looming just over the horizon is a water-and-sewage crisis, with the need to construct a huge water-intake pipe, ranging over several regions and slicing through cities, to draw water from Lake Ontario. As Dick Illingworth explained to me, the problem is simply that the underground sources that have provided the region's water are now running dry because of increased demand. Kirlik's summation is that "they are looking at billions of dollars on the region's infrastructure bill to accommodate the growth," and nobody knows where it will come from.

But who's to blame? If the social calamity that sprang from the Jane-Finch project in the '70s and '80s was a product of public-sector bungling — a crisis born of too much faith in government and its planning gurus — then the social and fiscal squeeze new northern suburbs face in the '90s and beyond is its mirror image: a malaise that can be laid at the doorstep of private developers and a citizenry willing to foresake valuable public oversight in favour of an unfettered free market. It's not that there was any shortage of resources to plan in advance for the infrastructural needs of new communities. The 1980s, Kirlik recalls, were "a period of unprecedented boom" when "money was never an object for anyone who was living here. People were spending it, borrowing it, and building houses, and York Region rolled along." Huge fortunes were made, palatial homes constructed, and bank profits and speculators' incomes buoyed by the frenzy of buying and selling.

Things might have been different if there had been greater control over how this river of money was spent. If surcharges on new development, for instance, had risen to reflect the greater burden that larger and more spread-out suburban homes placed on the environment and the infrastructure, or if there had been an effective speculation tax, then per-house profits might have been slimmer and the new homes less grandiose. But at the same time, a more meaningful chunk of that '80s bonanza might have been invested in providing the services so desperately needed now. (Journalist Linda McQuaig recalls that during the southern Ontario housing boom of the '80s, a tax on speculation was touted as having multiple benefits: not only would some of this money have been used for needed public projects, but the tax would also have served as an alternative to the hiking of interest rates. Those rate hikes were enacted by the Bank of Canada to dampen a round of inflation spurred by the massive growth of Toronto-area real estate prices, but their overall effects were to dampen economic growth across Canada.) Still, such measures would have defied the mood of the time. The '80s were an era when government was perceived as the problem; the solution was to deregulate, to reduce taxes on corporations, to allow private business to get on with the tasks of creating wealth and jobs and dreams and to unleash the creativity of the individual.

What was the consequence of this approach? In York Region, perhaps, it was that people wound up buying an overstuffed status symbol, rather than a stake in a future community. Few people had been thinking about unresolved longer-term issues such as the need for schools, roads, and sewers created by runaway growth, and how to pay for them.

One consolation is that it could have been worse. In Canada houses were actually built, even if there were too few hospitals, schools, or transit services. But in the United States — where the deregulation of mortgage-providing savings-and-loan institutions was one manifestation of the Reagan administration's manic attempt to get government out of business's hair — often high-rolling real estate projects existed only on paper, while other times so little attention was paid to construction standards that completed buildings were uninhabitable.

Financial writer J.L. Davis recounts this sordid tale in his bitterly humorous account of the S&L disaster that appeared in *Harper's* magazine in 1990. According to Davis, deregulating the S&Ls, or "thrifts," provided unscrupulous financiers and real estate developers with an embossed invitation to loot those institutions, with any losses — at the end of the '80s, they were conservatively estimated at $500 billion — being underwritten by the federal government's deposit-insurance program. Envisioned by Franklin D. Roosevelt in the 1930s as a vehicle to allow modest-income people to buy their own homes, the S&Ls were once strictly regulated institutions; the deal was that deposit insurance would be made available in exchange for close government scrutiny. Under Reagan, however, some key regulations were dispensed with. They were that S&Ls must be owned by small depositors within a radius of 150 square miles, that assets worth a small percentage of outstanding loans must be held at the S&L, and that loans be used solely to finance mortgages. Without these regulations, the S&Ls, some of them opened or bought by shady dealers, suddenly began to accept millions in "hot money" from Wall Street. Instead of being used to finance the family homes of ordinary working people, the money was parcelled up in lots of $100,000, the maximum amount insurable by the government, and pumped into high-yield, high-risk, sometimes hare-brained or fraudulent schemes. The government insurance ensured that investors couldn't lose; they'd get their money back no matter how faulty the investment.

As Davis details, speculation became the sole object of the game in the new, deregulated world of S&Ls, occasionally to the extent that the land-development schemes S&L transactions were said to be financing existed only on the terrain of the imagination. Davis cites the case of a real estate promoter in Texas who would gather his associates to "sit around a table doing a 'land flip' — i.e., trading a piece of property at ever-increasing prices. (No real estate ever changed hands during a flip.) Every time a piece of property was sold, the thrift made a new loan to cover the purchase price. Each time a loan was made, the thrift owner or owners pocketed fees — loan fees for negotiating the deal, origination fees for preparing the documents — all of which provided him or them with a handsome and ever-increasing income." In other cases, half-hearted attempts at construction were made to justify the loans; at one uninhabitable condominium project, also in Texas, the developer parked junked cars in front of the building to make it look as if people were living there.[4]

But a national border does make a difference, even in the age of globalization, and there has been no suggestion that the type of widespread criminal activity encouraged by S&L deregulation in the US was practised in Canada. Still, a similar social climate existed north of the border and, in fact, across most of the western world, with conservative governments holding office in virtually every developed country. In the face of the ascendent worldwide agenda for deregulation, privatization, and the banishment of government from the business of business, it was unlikely, in our tiny corner of the globe, that government would have had an easy time imposing new terms, conditions, and costs on the developers, who were at that point revelling in the massive demand for new homes and rolling in dough. This is too bad because, as John Sewell notes in *The Shape of the City*, as early as 1970, Ontario's government (then old-style, red Tory) had foreseen that uncontrolled suburban development would lead to massive infrastructure costs and such related problems as congestion, inadequate services, escalating land prices, and gridlock on the highways, and it had a pretty good idea how to avoid them.

The Toronto-Centred Region Plan — one of a series of studies dating back to the early 1960s and designed to help Ontario grapple with the expected population explosion around Metro Toronto — proposed to corral development in such a way that growth would not outstrip the ability to provide services. One key proviso was that development in the Yonge Street corridor — that is, York Region and environs, where massive growth did indeed take place in subsequent years — was to be discouraged because, as Sewell explains, "water and sewage services were much easier to provide to municipalities with direct access to Lake Ontario than to those blocked from the Lake by Metro Toronto." Instead of pushing north, then, there would be "a strong east-west linear configuration" that directed new development into the lengthy corridor running alongside Lake Ontario between Oshawa and Hamilton. There would also be a greenbelt running east-west at the northern edge of Metro Toronto, with development above it remaining sporadic; most of this northern region would stay rural.

The other crucial component of the plan was to "encourage a compact form to ensure efficiency in public spending on matters such as servicing and transit." After the plan had been officially released in 1971, Municipal Affairs Minister Darcy McKeough emphasized the logic that compact building — building houses taller rather than wider on smaller lots and beside narrower roadways, which produces higher densities and a reduced appetite for land — would lower servicing costs. "The provision of trunk services, whether sewers, water, transit or communication, is expensive and must be rationalized," he said. "We will assist and encourage growth in a compact form, properly staged by the economies of servicing."

In fact, the Toronto-Centred Region Plan did not have to wait for the deregulation mania of the greedy '80s to meet its demise. Sewell recounts that the plan withered during the '70s, in the face of opposition from developers who had assembled large land packages for development, and from local politicians who believed that the future of their communities and their own careers depended on growth, not restraint. Within ten years the plan "had been battered into little more than a thin, grey servicing corridor," Sewell writes, while growth restrictions in the Yonge Street corridor had been lifted, allowing the town of Markham, for instance — originally predicted to have 20,000 inhabitants by 1990 — to hit the 100,000 mark by 1985.[5]

A drive through almost any part of the new York Region also reveals that little of the development that took place in the 1980s was of the "compact" variety promoted by McKeough, although homes constructed during the downturn of the '90s were, of necessity, more likely to be smaller and cheaper and to occupy less land. But while large numbers of grand boom-town houses sit contentedly on their large lots — a monument to the buoyant spirit of the '80s and a kind of thumbed nose at the politicians who wanted to rein in the developers' vision — it is not correct to assume that McKeough's plan for a more compact and rational style of suburban development has been lost to the dark recesses of history. On the contrary, the ongoing and intertwined fiscal and social squeezes that have gripped the new suburbs have brought those ideas back into the public debate and given them a new sense of urgency.

In a report titled *The Economics of Urban Form*, for instance, prepared for the Greater Toronto Area (GTA) Task Force in the mid-1990s, economist Dr. Pamela Blais warns that a failure to finally accept the need for compact development in the suburbs will create future fiscal and service crises against which today's problems will pale. The bottom line, according to her study, is that it's just too expensive for governments to provide services and infrastructure for the type of subdivisions that developers are accustomed to building.

"If the low-density greenfields development pattern that character-izes urban development in the GTA today is maintained, future growth is estimated to require some $90 billion in supporting capital investment over the next 25 years," Blais's report states. This isn't counting the massive costs of maintaining and replacing existing infra-structure, and the possible $1 billion in annual "external costs" for such services as additional road policing, automobile-emissions reduc-tion, and the health costs associated with intensified automobile use.

But it needn't be this way. The good news, Blais reports, is that "an urban form that relies to a greater degree on reurbanization, more compact development, and mixed land use would decrease the capital investment required . . . by an estimated $10 billion to $16 billion and decrease operating and maintenance costs by $2.5 to $4 billion." Where Blais's report differs from the Toronto-Centred Region Plan of 1970, however, is in not calling for government regulation to promote compact development; instead, it advocates a "market-oriented" user-pay system based on the principles of true-cost accounting, whereby the development charges or user fees applied to "low-density green-fields" developments, would be scaled upwards to reflect the real costs of service provision and also to account for the "external costs," which are not immediately apparent. (This additional burden would presumably discourage construction of low-density subdivisions located ten or twenty kilometres out from existing pockets of popula-tion, while ensuring that those who still choose to live in the "greenfields" style would pick up the full tab for servicing.)

According to Blais's report, all the mechanisms that Ontario has used to pay for new suburban infrastructure — property tax, devel-opment charges, user fees, provincial income tax — are skewed so that residents of higher-density areas provide a subsidy to those who live in the sprawling suburban style.[6] The economist's conclusion is consistent with Sewell's observation in his 1994 volume *Houses and*

Homes that, despite municipalities' application of lot levies that sometimes reached $20,000 per new home by the late 1980s — levies that
were attacked as "capricious" by developers and then replaced by the
province with fees regularized through the Development Charges Act,
which in turn were challenged by developers as unconstitutional —
there was still a shortfall in funding new services, which compelled
municipalities to dip into property taxes and the province to contribute from income taxes.[7] It's those contributions from income and
property taxes that constitute the biggest subsidies for suburban
sprawl.

So the potential remedy to a wide range of problems becomes clear:
remove public subsidies for sprawl and more land will be preserved,
servicing and related costs will decline, communities will be built that
will be easier to serve by public transit, and housing may even be
cheaper. The main barrier to this solution, though, is politics. Blais's
formulation — that suburbanites who drive long distances to work
and live in large houses on large lots are getting a free ride on the
backs of more frugal urbanites — turns the dominant political logic
of the 905 belt on its head. Mike Harris's triumph here was based on
the very opposite notion: that hard-working suburbanites now live in
misery because they are being overtaxed in order to pay for downtown welfare cases. The crisis in services currently being experienced
in the new suburbs tends to support this view; why are we paying all
these taxes, suburbanites wonder, when there's no school in our neighbourhood and the hospital is too crowded? Part of the answer is that
public money is flowing into projects people rarely think about —
amenities like roads and sewers. Another is that you can get more
for your tax money in areas of urban compactness, so funds spent
in the spread-out burbs may not produce a very big bang. While
Toronto's TTC receives provincial subsidies equal to 60 cents a ride,
for instance, the province's outlay for a ride on the bus increases to
$3.34 in spread-out, car-dependent Richmond Hill.[8]

Still, don't expect this logic to produce any sea changes in development policy anytime soon. The notion of 905 as a victim of the

avaricious urban vortex has become a matter of ideological commitment. Removing subsidies to suburban development, as Blais has
proposed, might entail overturning that increasingly entrenched
mindset. In the meantime, Brian Kirlik says, there is a policy void, and
planning continues through inertia: local governments still approve
the same old style of development, without having any real idea of
how they will pay for the service requirements these new developments generate.

"What we're saying to the politicians over and over again, through
editorials and through features," he insists, "is that every time you
guys approve a subdivision with seven hundred to eight hundred
homes, you're not thinking about the infrastructure." For example? I
ask. The editor gives a backwards nod over his shoulder, directing my
gaze towards the giant earth-moving machines kicking up clouds of
dust and snarling traffic fifty metres or so from his window. "You
drive out this street here, Mulock Drive, and it's disgraceful," he
laments. "You know, this is the second time they've rebuilt it in the ten
years that I've been working in this office. The first time they paved
it, and now they're rebuilding it to four lanes, and it's still not going
to be enough to accommodate the intensification they're putting along
this strip of land. You drive straight out Mulock to Yonge Street and
there's a huge new development called Summerhill that by itself is
going to take Newmarket's population up 30 percent. An extra lane
of traffic isn't going to cut it, but that's all they could afford to build."

For Kirlik, this and the dozens of other stories of stress and strain
in York Region underscore the reality that "we can't afford to keep
building on these vast tracts of open land. There's the environmental
concern, and there's also the cost factor. It costs a lot of money to run
a sewage pipe to a subdivision twenty miles outside of town."

But if the political will does not exist to deal with these environmental and economic problems by having suburban development pay
for itself, what other options remain? Well, for the Harris government
there have been attempts to take tax money from established areas
and reassign them to housing-rich but services-poor new suburban

cities. There have also been efforts to deregulate development, in the hope that a stimulated market will increase the cash flow across the 905 frontier and keep everyone happy a little while longer.

But although the Harris Tories have kept a close eye on the interests of their stalwart supporters in the suburban belt, its attempts to reward its constituents have been marked by controversy and clumsy retreats. Suburban issues are a minefield of conflicting interests and confused priorities, and it is impossible to act decisively without incurring the wrath of at least one of the entrenched and powerful interests — developers, municipal taxpayers, local governments — that cling to opposing sides of the issues.

On the question of development levies, for instance, the government failed to consider that the interests of land developers (who are keen on building as much as possible) and suburban residents and taxpayers (who generally favour caps on growth and certainly don't want to subsidize infrastructure for their neighbours-to-be) are not one and the same.

As Dick Illlingworth recalls it, in the late 1980s the David Peterson Liberals did move closer to the principle that new development should pay for itself. They instituted the Development Charges Act, which allowed municipalities to slap somewhere between $6,000 and $20,000 worth of levies on each new home. Yet faced with intense opposition from the Urban Development Institute, the developers' lobby, the post-1995 Tory government of Mike Harris — which was, in any case, committed to deregulation and to lowering taxes as a means of stimulating economic development — announced that it would remove this burden from the shoulders of builders.

This prompted a counterattack from the GTA mayors, who promised that if servicing costs related to new development were now to be covered by municipal property taxes, not a single new building permit would be issued. So the province backed down, opting for a compromise plan in which some service costs would be applied to municipal tax bills and others would be billed to the developers.

Brian Kirlik describes the development charges issue as "one that could definitely backfire on the Harris government," since most established residents in York Region believe that new infrastructure and service costs should be borne by developers and new residents rather than by people already living in the community. On this matter the government was caught, it seems, by conflicting loyalties to its friends in the development industry and the suburban taxpayers who voted them into office.

The Harris government's downloading initiative, an attempt to reshuffle funding responsibilities between provincial and local levels of government, is another case where the province's desire to reward its suburban base was thwarted by the complexity of the issues and the potential for disaster. Again the Tories would be forced to abruptly change their agenda — partly because of the anxieties of the suburbanites and business people who had powered the Conservative revolution into office.

As interpreted by reporter John Ibbitson in his book *Promised Land*, which chronicles the Harris Tories' first two years in power, Harris's drive to "disentangle" overlapping provincial and municipal funding responsibilities was motivated mostly by a desire to have the province assume control of education. A group of five influential cabinet ministers, Ibbitson writes, believed that the local school boards administering the public school system were responsible for creating a patchwork that was both ineffectual and overly costly.

At the same time, successive provincial governments had been grappling with how to rationalize the delivery of services, which had been complicated by the overlapping responsibilities of the cities and the province. So the government contracted former Toronto mayor and federal cabinet minister David Crombie to report on how tasks could be reassigned between the two levels, in a way that would give the province responsibility for education. But Crombie's recommendation — that Queen's Park should take control of both education and the welfare system — was unacceptable to the Harris regime, because it would have greatly increased the burden on provincial coffers and made it impossible for Harris to deliver his promised 30 percent income tax cut. So the province moved ahead with its own plan: It would take over education but download to the municipalities responsibility for funding transit, commuter rail, secondary highways, and subsidized housing, while raising to 50 percent the municipalities' responsibility for funding subsidized daycare (up from 20 percent), general welfare assistance (also up from 20 percent), and family benefits (up from zero). The municipalities would also assume total responsibility for the administration of welfare, which used to be shared. Meanwhile, the province declared it would kick in a one-time $1 billion to smooth the edges during the transition.

The downloading plans unleashed a fury of criticism. The president of Metro Toronto's Board of Trade warned that Toronto's property taxes would rise dramatically with the shift in responsibility for welfare payments, and that the city's economic viability would be threatened. David Crombie also condemned the welfare download as "wrong in principle and devastating in practice."

Ultimately, the government did yield to sustained criticism of the welfare plan, agreeing to a compromise formula put forth by the Association of Municipalities of Ontario (AMO) that would see 50 percent of education costs stay on the property tax, municipal contributions to welfare and daycare drop to 20 percent, and the province contribute $200 million to upgrade social housing stock.[9]

How you view the governments' intentions in this protracted and acrimonious battle depends on your vantage point. John Ibbitson, who crafts his account largely from information provided by insiders in the premier's office and elsewhere, accepts at face value the version that "disentanglement" began with the quest to reform education, and that what followed was a kind of spontaneous horse-trading that sought to shift duties between two levels of government in a way that was "revenue-neutral" to both parties. Opposition politicians, meanwhile, hammered the government during question period for what it saw as a brazen attempt to pay for its promised income tax cut by shifting much of its own former spending burden onto cities. In turn, cities would be faced with the choice of raising property and commercial taxes or cutting services, making them the fall guys for the province's policies.

A third way of looking at this is that Harris's redrawing of the funding map was intended from the beginning as a way of rewarding loyal 905ers, but removing mostly urban costs from the shoulders of suburbanites and allowing Queen's Park to throw more money at the pressing needs in the new burbs. For, under the Tories' plan, not all civic governments were being whacked with equal force; in fact, while urban Toronto would suffer, some suburban regions stood to benefit.

The government's seizure of education, for example, may have been motivated by more than just a desire to overhaul the curriculum. Education is of tremendous concern in the newer suburbs, where there are lots of children and a paralyzing shortage of schools. The provincial capture of the education system clearly benefits these new suburbs, not only by taking the weight of school support off suburbanites' property taxes, but also by giving the province the power to take funds from elsewhere to construct new schools in the outer burbs. This is especially true under the AMO-brokered compromise deal, which gives the province the power to scoop education-related funds raised through property taxes in Toronto and Ottawa — cities that hadn't been receiving provincial education subsidies — and reallocate them to other jurisdictions.

In other areas as well, downloading looks like a mechanism for bailing out the burbs and punishing the big downtown cores, since the items transferred to the municipal blotter are those that tend to be bigger expenses in the established cities than in the suburbs. Turning welfare over to the municipalities, for example, would be detrimental to Metro Toronto, where there are greater numbers of people receiving social assistance, but would lower those costs in places such as York Region, a more solidly upper-middle-class and upper-class area where fewer people collect welfare. Ditto for social housing: The places that have more pay more; where there's less, people pay less. Same story with public transit, which is obviously more important, extensive, and costly in the big and crowded urban areas than in the suburbs, where most residents have cars.

Add to this recipe the fact that upper-income earners (of which there are many in the northern 905 burbs) would benefit more from the government's promised personal income tax cut,[10] and there emerges a portrait of classical constituency politics: "Vote for us, and your riding will get all kinds of goodies." It appears that if many 905 suburbanites had acted like prodigal sons during the 1980s, tying up too much of their above-average incomes in lavish homes that cost too much to service, then Premier Mike Harris was prepared to act as the forgiving father and lighten their load by taking from other members of the family.

But if the great downloading extravaganza was meant to solidify the bond between governing Common Sense Revolutionaries and its suburban cheering section, it is not clear how well it worked. Many suburbanites reacted cautiously, partly because the changes would make the municipalities more vulnerable in times of economic downturn, and partly because the immediate economic benefits don't seem big enough to justify the risks.

"The region did a calculation and predicted it would be ahead by about $700,000, which is negligible," says Brian Kirlik. "For all they know, they could be up $7 million or down $12 million at the blink of an eye, the way the province was shuffling numbers and responsibilities." Dick Illingworth cites a different study indicating that York Region would benefit from downloading by $4.6 million, but he agrees that the numbers are unreliable since provincial/municipal funding splits would change with each heated exchange between the mayors and provincial officials. But the real problem, both commentators agree, is that welfare funding remains an unpredictable and potentially ruinous wild card. People in York Region saw how far you can fall when the real estate bubble of the '80s burst; they remain fearful that if the economy softened and welfare rolls ballooned in the burbs, there would be a calamitous rise in property taxes.

Many people in York Region are apparently also concerned that hitting the City of Toronto with unmanageable social service costs could send some nasty reverberations back into their own neighbourhoods. Unlike their US counterparts, many Toronto-area suburbanites are recent émigrés from the city who still make the trip downtown to work on weekdays and who like the idea of being able to take the kids to a ball game at the SkyDome on weekends without being murdered.

The way Kirlik sees it, a lot of his paper's readers are also fairminded people who accept the argument that they "benefit from Metro Toronto. They are riding Metro's transit system, they are riding the GO train into the city, they are using the provincial highways and Metro highways to get to work, yet at the end of the day they take all of their money, go back to the suburbs where the grass is green and the trees are pretty, leaving this mess in the downtown core . . . There are a lot of people here who understand that when kids from York Region run away from home, they don't run away to Richmond Hill, they run away to Toronto, and you know whose social service network they wind up on. People rely on Metro Toronto for everything from social welfare for runaways to cancer treatment at Sunnybrook."

That "mess in the downtown core" is not a reality yet; urban Toronto is still a lot healthier than most US downtowns. But some experts predict that if Toronto were forced to place a huge social services tab on its property tax, it wouldn't be long before the city was on the fast track to urban oblivion. Urban planner Ken Greenberg, who has been engaged in recent years in a project to help revive downtown Detroit, believes that if Torontonians are hit with property taxes out of proportion with those in outlying areas, taxes that in any case would likely not halt the decline in the quality of services, they will act out of rational self-interest and abandon the city en masse. In Detroit, says Greenberg, this practice of dumping social service costs onto city taxpayers was a major factor leading to the decline in population from 2.2 million to less than a million. In a situation like that, the only people left living in a city are the ones who have no other choice.

Despite Toronto's current reputation as one of the world's most "livable" cities, Greenberg sees no reason such high property taxes would not produce the same effect north of the border.[11]

The Ontario government apparently heard that message and took it to heart. Witness another about-face to match the AMO-brokered funding formula compromise. In August 1997 Municipal Affairs Minister Al Leach announced a plan for pooling social service costs so that Metro Toronto's increased burden for larger welfare rolls, a bigger stock of social housing, and larger concentrations of seniors and special-needs populations would be offset by contributions from municipalities across the GTA. There was unaccustomed applause for Leach. The *Toronto Star* editorialized that "after spending the better part of two years battering Metro Toronto with destructive policy announcements, the Tories have got this one stunningly right . . . Pooling all such costs will create a level playing field and provide an incentive to attract business to the urbanized Metro Toronto where services already have been installed, rather than allowing unchecked new growth to eat up farmland and green fields."[12] The *Globe and Mail* also hailed the move as "a great improvement over the anti-city first draft of six months ago," although it noted that the best course would have been to move the whole tab for social services, which is likely to rise dramatically during times of economic downturn, to the broader-based and more substantial reservoir of provincial income taxes, as Crombie had urged.[13] An Ekos Research poll conducted for the *Star* also indicated that the majority of GTA residents shared the editorial writers' approval of the pooling idea. Although support was greatest in Metro Toronto — 57 percent approving, 14 percent opposed, the rest saying neither or not responding — supporters con-stituted the largest group of voters in the 905 suburbs, where 43 percent approved of pooling, 29 percent opposed it, and the rest chose neither, or ventured no opinion.[14]

Suburban politicians, however, were not as warm in their reaction to the pooling idea. Brampton Mayor Peter Robertson called the introduction of pooling a "betrayal" of the suburbs, while Mississauga

Mayor Hazel McCallion said (apparently with a straight face) that it indicated "this province is moving towards socialism."[15] From Mississauga councillor Nado Iannicca came the warning of "a 905 tea party" that will signal defeat for the Tories at the next election.[16] In the end Harris's government likely made the correct judgment that Ontario's suburbanites were not prepared to cast Toronto into the same pit of decay and despair that had swallowed many American cities in order to advance their own, strictly parochial interests. But, as was the case with the development-levies issue, the tax-pooling caper showed that the politics of urban/suburban rivalry is a perilous business, one where there's always a chance of alienating a big chunk of voters. In this instance, the Tories singed the backsides of a large number of their natural 905 constituency because they weren't prepared to follow through on their rhetoric by dropping a political neutron bomb on Metro Toronto. At the same time, backing away from a plan that would have turned Toronto into Detroit is hardly enough to win the Tories new supporters in the city. To wit, four months after the province accepted the pooling idea, the new mayor of the new Toronto megacity, Mel Lastman, held a press conference to announce that he would "hit hard" against a provincial government that he accused of continuing to saddle Toronto with a $163-million shortfall in transfer payments as a result of offloading. Despite the pooling for social service costs, Toronto was still looking at a potential 6.3 percent property tax increase to cover the loss from provincial contributions, with other costs, like the new responsibility for funding the Toronto Transit Commission, still waiting to be factored in.[17]

— — —

If it's difficult to negotiate this minefield of municipal fiscal issues so as to produce a dividend for suburbanites without beggaring the urban areas into complete decay (as has happened in the US), then what's left for pro-suburban political crusaders? Well, plenty. Suburbia is more than just a geographic place — it's a state of mind — and right now that state of mind is coloured by angst and a certain amount of anger. If the portrait drawn by real estate supremo Craig Proctor is correct, most suburbanites around here are working far too hard and relaxing too little, trying to dig their way out from underneath a mountain of debt.

This is fertile ground for politicians, especially right-wing, populist politicians. People are looking for someone to blame for their troubles. They are looking for an explanation of why the good life doesn't feel so good, some way of transforming a vaporous, pervasive malaise into something solid and distinct so that it can be observed, explained, attacked, and ultimately eliminated. This desire is as tangible as the quest for a tax cut, and in the United States it has become a primary focus of politics. The "contract with America" Republicans who flooded into Congress in the mid-1990s knew that their economic program was by now bankrupt, that they would be unable to make fiscal promises that could realistically raise the standard of living of the average American. So they concentrated on the "cultural issues," proposing to voters that the discontent spreading across the land was due to some weakening of moral fibre, a diminution of the collective strength of character that once made America a place where the streets were safe to walk, families stayed together, and kids had respect for their elders.

I saw hints of this approach at the all-candidates meeting in the Aurora Town Hall. Reform candidate Maralyn Hazelgrove's second-biggest issue (next to the campaign-funding foofaraw) was rampant crime in the streets, criminals going unpunished. Maurizio Bevilacqua tried to neutralize her attack by citing statistics that show Vaughan-King-Aurora to have the lowest crime rate in the country, but Hazelgrove kept on hammering regardless, holding up the crime issue as symbolic of a failed system, the tyranny of egg-headed experts with a liberal bias, of the oppression of the law-abiding middle classes.

When I ask Brian Kirlik about the right-wing parties' fixation on the crime issue — the Ontario Tories' boot-camp hype in the last provincial election, the Reformers' tougher-punishment platform in the federal contest — he characterizes their use of the crime issue as smart marketing. "The message is very clever," he says. "It is a light-ning bolt and it strikes right into the kitchen tables of the people who live here." Youth crime in particular causes people to sweat. "You'd be hard-pressed to find anyone in this community who doesn't believe that young offenders should be treated with an iron fist."

Kirlik believes there are a lot of kids up here who rebel against their parents' expectations and run afoul of the law. But he's not sure whether this should spark the politicians' outrage or create a sense of sorrow, for often it's the kids themselves who are the biggest victims.

"When I came up here," the editor recalls, "I was struck by the number of memorial events, whether a basketball game or a fundraiser, for dead teenagers. When I was a teenager growing up in Scarborough, we didn't have teenagers dying in Mom and Dad's car on a Friday night. Up here it happens all the time. You've got those situations where kids will get in the car for something to do, they'll wind up on a country road, and three of them will die. I've gotten to know people in the community over the years, and everybody seems to know some-body — a kid, a teenager — who has died in a situation like this."

Although his impression is that this situation is improving as the area becomes more developed, Kirlik still feels "the potential for trouble is a lot greater up here" because there's much less for kids to do. If that trouble doesn't involve automobiles, it might involve vandalism or fights. On Halloween, some youths have made a practice of setting furniture alight in parks, while others have engaged in the singularly spiteful act of cutting down trees planted as memorials to dead children. This is what crime usually means in Aurora and Newmarket, and although it is not murder, armed rob-bery, or home invasion, people react to it as though it were of similar magnitude. Kirlik remembers a flood of incensed letters arriving at the *Era-Banner* after a recent case in which "a gentleman's $70,000 Audi was coloured with an indelible marker by a kid. The community was absolutely outraged."

At some point in this conversation, I offer the suggestion to Kirlik that adults' intensifying concerns about youth crime may have risen in direct proportion to the decline in their ability to play a role in their children's lives. Is it possible that parents' realization that they are too busy paying for the big house, the minivans, and the SUVs has triggered some kind of panic? Do parents want the government to play a bigger and more threatening role in keeping their kids on the straight-and-narrow — for example, in boot camps — because they themselves are now unable to oversee their kids' activities?

Kirlik indicates that this is a plausible hypothesis. Crime and vandalism stories are given significant play in his paper because "odds are the person who did this is a child who lives in the same house as one of our readers." As for the idea that children and parents in this social milieu live their lives in rarely intersecting orbits, Kirlik says you have only to look at the streams of commuters who have not yet reached home by seven o'clock on weeknights to see that this is probably true. Some parents rarely see their kids because many white-collar workers clock a fifty-hour work week with a two-way daily commute on top of that. This is why Newmarket's professional hockey team, the Newmarket Saints — a Toronto Maple Leafs farm club — had to leave town. "Nobody was going to the games on Tuesday nights," Kirlik recalls. "They did okay on weekends, but during the week they drew flies because no one was home and finished dinner and ready to go out again by seven o'clock."

It's a matter of debate whether these conditions — the removal of working parents from domestic life, the lack of time to interact with children — have indeed fed widespread enthusiasm for the idea that government agencies should play a bigger role in disciplining kids. Still, in the lead-up to the 1999 Ontario election, Tory politicians seemed convinced that the issue of crime — juvenile crime in particular — would continue to play well with its suburban supporters. In early February 1999 Education Minister Dave Johnson proposed a province-wide code of conduct for students, musing as well that uniforms for public school students might instil greater respect for authority and lead to better behaviour.[18] (Bringing in those school uniforms later became an official part of the Tories' 1999 election platform.) Premier Mike Harris extemporized on this theme during open-line radio show appearances, when he proposed that the problem of students wearing profane T-shirts represented some deep social sickness. When Liberal Leader Dalton McGuinty criticized these proposals, Harris characterized him as being "soft on crime." McGuinty shot back that "hot-button Mike" was trying to distract the electorate from the state of Ontario's health-care system.

Still, the polls seem to indicate that Harris's proposal to regulate students' dress and behaviour may find a receptive audience. John Wright of the Angus Reid polling firm reportedly said that "concern over youth conduct" has become a particularly big issue "outside of the urban centres."[19] The poll was taken months before a couple of trench-coated students armed with guns and bombs entered a high school in Littleton, Colorado, and blew away more than a dozen of their peers. That event must surely have made people feel uncomfortable in York Region, similarly populated by upper-income, workaholic adults and bored kids. Whether a tighter dress code would solve the problem of disaffected youth, however, is another question.

— — —

Some politicians obviously don't hold youth in the highest esteem. But what do kids think about the politicians, and adults in general? As it happens, a group of them got a chance to turn the tables — to pass judgment on their elders — when the Vaughan-King-Aurora federal campaign road show made a stop at King Secondary School in King City.

For a reporter, the good thing about attending a political debate in a high school is that you can have access to instant analysis. Seated right behind me are a group of five or six teenage political commentators; their presence makes this like watching Newsworld and having Peter Mansbridge or Don Newman provide simultaneous interpretation of an event. The commentary begins in earnest when incumbent Liberal Maurizio Bevilacqua enters the room. About two hundred students, all of them the eligible voting age of eighteen, have taken their places in a large classroom in this half-rural/half-suburban school; the teacher at the front of the room has beseeched several male students to take off their baseball caps; bells have rung; and the challenger candidates have all taken their places. When Bevilacqua strides through the door, he apologizes for his tardiness and sits down. But the analysts behind me are having none of it. "Slacker!" says one. "I'm not voting for him — he's late," pledges a colleague.

Having passed judgment on the candidates' ability to negotiate the morning rush hour traffic, the students next get a chance to consider their policies. Bevilacqua goes first. He focuses on the Liberal government's economic record, changing the frame of reference slightly from the other night's candidates' debate to put youth employment front and centre. Moving away from behind the candidates' table and out into the audience — a bit of choreography that gives his speech more of a MuchMusic kind of feel — he talks about how deficit reduction is enhancing Canada's ability to "compete in the new global market-place." He talks up the government's youth employment schemes intended to break the cycle of young people without job experience being unable to find the employment that would give them that experience. He also delivers an old-fashioned "stay in school" speech: "For those of you who are thinking of not going to university," he warns, with a tone of parental concern, "think again."

Tory candidate Lara Coombs also sticks close to economic themes, slagging the government for maintaining high taxes. "Every time you buy a Coke," she says, illustrating the crushing daily burden we all bear, "you pay a tax." The candidate also culls a few youth-directed promises from that ubiquitous blue Tory policy book, promises such as Jean Charest's plan to provide students with laptop computers (as if kids in this upper-income community don't already have access to laptops). There's another blast of right-wing economic logic when Reformer Maralyn Hazelgrove declares the national debt "the biggest challenge which faces your generation." But don't young people contribute to excessive government spending by partaking of subsidized post-secondary education? Well, Reform will do things differently.

It will give a $3,000 voucher directly to each student and allow universities to compete for their patronage. The theory, a variation on Harris's contrarian idea that if you remove rent controls, rents will actually *decrease*, is that if universities are allowed to compete openly for patronage, tuition fees will fall.

There's a change of pace when independent Andrew James takes the floor. He doesn't attempt to talk down to his audience or appeal to age-specific interests. Instead he launches into a riff about how you have to see employment questions in the larger light of NAFTA, globalization, and the downsizing that results from a constant frenzy of corporate mergers and acquisitions. He also wins applause from the young voters when he chides the political parties for letting environmental issues slide off the political agenda. NDPer Robert Navarretta receives a similarly warm reception for his rebellious speech about how Canada's tax system stiffs ordinary people while letting corporations and wealthy bankers shirk their share of the tithing. This favourable response seems a bit odd to me, given that King City is a horsey, aristocratic community and that many of those assembled here are likely the sons and daughters of corporate managers and bankers.

When it's time for the Q&A, it becomes apparent that these students have a quite different set of preoccupations than the political parties. While government finances are the dominant issue for most candidates, their young inquisitors are much more concerned about the intangibles, the big philosophical questions — culture, environment, aboriginal rights. It's also clear that they don't fit the label of disrespectful, crime-prone kids that "Hot Button" Mike will later try to pin on them; instead what strikes me most is their intelligence and concern.

Some of the students with questions also display a keen determination not to be placated with stock answers that don't stand up to close scrutiny. A question about gun control, for example, elicits the standard response from Reform's Hazelgrove that "guns are not the problem; criminals are." She goes on to predict that the Liberal government's proposed gun registry could be tampered with by ingenious criminals with access to computers. The discussion shifts to another issue with the next question, but the student who first raised the matter brings the gun question back into the spotlight, suggesting that it's ludicrous to fear that the average criminal would be able to hack into a government registry and change the data within it. Ultimately, though, the biggest winner on the gun-control issue is Bevilacqua, who prompts a spontaneous burst of applause after defending gun control by invoking the memory of the fourteen women massacred by a gunman at Montreal's Ecole Polytechnique.

Another sleeper issue that has captivated the attention of this young crowd is Canadian culture. When a student expresses concern about Reform's proposal to privatize the CBC, Hazelgrove responds that the model for Canadian broadcasters should be the private television network CTV, where "they make up their own rules and regulations because they know what they are doing." The student returns with the fact that CTV is a private corporation, and with companies all over downsizing their workforces, doesn't this put Canadian culture in jeopardy? Hazelgrove says that CTV, which has often been criticized for relying on US imports in prime time and for producing Canadian shows that aren't noticeably Canadian, would not downsize under Reform policies because conditions would allow them to make more money while paying less in taxes. At this point, the NDP's Navarretta steps in to play the hero. When he suggests that the CBC is "the voice of Canada" and should be retained despite its cost, there is another outbreak of applause.

After several more, generally sophisticated questions — about carbon dioxide emissions and land-use regulations, about the fate of the Canada Pension Plan and the position of aboriginal peoples in Quebec if the province separated from Canada — it is time for closing summations. Most of the candidates stick to their scripts from a few nights ago at the Aurora Town Hall, but the audience response is sometimes different. When Reform's Hazelgrove launches into her litany of ills that afflict the other parties, at one point arriving at her characterization of the NDP as a party that would promote pot-smoking, I hear an exuberant "Yeah!" behind me, and an out-break of appreciative whoops and whistles from across the room. This moment of levity aside, the continued murmuring throughout Hazelgrove's summation seems to reflect some serious misgivings here about Reform's negative tone. One of the commentators behind me is clearly offended: "That's the cheesiest speech I ever heard," he announces to his buddies. "You don't conclude your speech by putting everybody else down."

When it's all over, a few students stay behind to chat with the candidates. Most of those candidates will be on the road in a few minutes, but the independent, Andrew James — the former Tory and now born-again Green — burrows deeper into discussion with a group of a half-dozen novice voters. When he wanders off to field an inquiry elsewhere, several of the students he's been sharing his ruminations with tell me they appreciate that James was the only can-didate to raise environmental concerns. "I think a lot of the political parties are focused on money," says Kirsten Robbins. "Money is very important to the economy, but really it's just paper. If the environment is gone, a piece of paper is not worth anything."

Indeed, the students around here have seen both an influx of huge amounts of money and the disappearance of huge chunks of the natural environment, which indicates that they are talking on this matter out of experience rather than just youthful idealism. When I suggest to this congregation that environmental destruction is a necessary adjunct of development, that some of the landscape must be sacrificed so that shopping malls and department stores can be built to sell teenagers all those CDs and clothes and electronics, and so local people can have jobs — they don't buy it.

"Do we need a new Wal-Mart?" ponders a female student whose name I don't catch. "Do we need new shopping malls and stuff like that? We have enough of those. We don't need that extra crap, excuse my language. We should try to conserve our resources and decrease the amount of plastics and waste that we do have . . . to take, like, environmental approaches to our shopping habits."

The biggest gap between these novice voters and their parents seems to be the value they place on the almighty dollar. All their lives, these high-school students have been indulged with a constant flow of "stuff," and now they are bored with it. Their sights have drifted to bigger questions — What courses of action are fair and just? What gives life enduring meaning? — while their elders' gaze remains fixed on the bottom line. The business about a tax cut, the promise that catapulted Harris into the top job at Queen's Park in the last election, exemplifies the gap between the three or four students who have remained part of this discussion and the apparent consensus in the adult mainstream.

"I know where my mom comes from," offers Suzanne. "My mom works for the Ministry of Health and her big thing is, 'They are cutting me too much already. I've worked so hard for my money. I want all my money. I don't want to give it out for anything.'"

When I ask if money is, for many older people, a kind of compensation for working too hard, for not having the time to be able to appreciate other aspects of life, Suzanne seems to agree.

"I know that's what my mom feels," she says. "My mom feels kinda like, 'Well my only enjoyment in life is, like, retiring. So then I can go places and have my money. And if they are taking away all my money, how can I enjoy myself?'"

Amongst our informal group, the preoccupation with crime is similarly seen as a product of middle-aged angst. There have recently been a couple of gangland-style slayings in one section of the region, but this highly unusual occurrence is contained in a distinct subculture; it doesn't affect the average person. Overall, crime here is generally limited to stupid weekend hijinks, or else it's the stuff of myth, something people hear about but don't expect to encounter.

"I was surprised to find when I was going door-to-door in Aurora that somebody said there was a crack house nearby," offers candidate Andrew James, who has returned for the conversation in this part of the room.

Nobody seems to have heard this rumour, but Merike contributes another fragment of the local mythology that seems related.

"Well, there's a biker gang that lives in Woodbridge," she says.

"The Loners," Suzanne clarifies. "[Their clubhouse] burned down awhile ago."

"The place was so fortified the fire department couldn't get in," Merike resumes. "We drove by it after it happened."

As for the run-of-the-mill stuff — for instance, vandalism — everyone here seems to agree with Brian Kirlik that it's mostly a product of bored kids trying to get a few kicks.

"There is a bit of crime, you see it around," Linda says. "But I think it's produced because of boredom. We don't have very much entertainment around here. So people are sort of stuck in their small communities and they have nothing much to do. So they decide to hang out one night and maybe vandalize a building, or set off a smoke bomb here or there."

Suzanne thinks crime here is nothing like that in the big city, because the social conditions are so different.

"You look at the living standards that people have here," she says. "I mean, come on, the living standards are a lot. They are doing this because they are bored. There's no reason to steal, there's no reason to vandalize. You have graffiti in Toronto, but a lot of it makes a political point, a political statement. Here there's no reason for that, because people are apathetic here, nobody cares. They have their $300,000 home, they have their job — what are they worried about? They have their connections with their families so they can get a job in the summer. And their parents pay their tuition costs. They have a future."

The assertion that kids here are apathetic sparks a new debate. The three friends ponder what it would take to make people in this area passionate about public issues.

"The only time I've ever seen anyone get political in this area," Merike states, "is over the dump debate. That's purely because they don't want them to dump Toronto's garbage here."

"And also because it would make the value of their houses go down," Suzanne adds.

Clearly, this all-female collection of first-time voters are critical of the dominant values of the community they live in. The irony in this is that while people often say they moved out to a new suburb for the sake of their kids, the discussion here shows that at least some of the kids will reject this environment. And so the mentality of the suburbs becomes more difficult to characterize; you can call those places mundane, conservative, obsessively materialistic, but in the middle of this are the seeds of exactly the opposite traits. Still, this is an old story. David Bowie, to stretch for an example, said the reason the English suburbs around London gave birth to 1970s glitter rock, with its extravagant theatricality and wild face-painted excesses, was that suburban kids yearned for a dramatic kind of escape from the grey conformity of the places where they grew up. Same case today, no doubt. How many contented suburban kids today listen to rap and hip hop, the music of the urban underclass? Why does that music appeal to them? Maybe because it's so different. Because it's not "here."

Perhaps an enduring truth about the suburbs, discovered anew by succeeding generations, is that while they may be good places to grow up in, they are better places to leave. Of the three students who have stuck it out till the end of our discussion, two said they wanted to move to someplace more interesting after high school; the third said she liked the cultural diversity of a city but disliked the crowds, so was looking to divide her time between city and country. Suzanne was the most adamant about the need to get out: "I know myself I don't want to live in this environment at all," she said. "I would kind of rather go down to Africa or go up to an Inuit village somewhere, because I've had it really good for my entire life and I'd like to learn about something else that's not totally jaded. I'm just sick of it."

Linda's plans are somewhat more modest, but the sentiment is similar. "I wouldn't want to live here," she agrees. "I feel that the community I live in is too isolated. I would prefer to live somewhere where I can get more involved in things and there is more to do. I would prefer to live at the university that I am going to, and then eventually move out to BC or somewhere so I can get more involved in the environment and stuff like that."

No matter how far they roam, however, it's likely that these young suburbanites won't be able to leave the shopping malls and the Friday nights at the fast-food joints behind them. If you grew up in the burbs — trust me — it's something you always carry around inside you.

³ | The Populist Challenge

The victor has returned to the corridors of power. Or more precisely, to an office just off the corridors of power, with lush carpeting and a spacious anteroom and comfortable chairs. Maurizio Bevilacqua is re-ensconced in these patrician surroundings in Centre Block, Parliament Hill, as a consequence of his second consecutive steamrolling of all comers in the battle to represent his corner of York Region. In the 1997 federal election, Bevilacqua's capture of 32,653 votes in the contest for Vaughan-King-Aurora places him miles beyond striking distance of any of the challengers. (The second-place finisher, Tory Lara Coombs, pulls up almost 25,000 votes behind, with a tally of 8,135, followed by Reformer Maralyn Hazelgrove with 6,999 votes, the NDP's Robert Navarretta with 2,127, and independent Andrew James with 528.) Numerically Bevilacqua's performance in 1997 lacks the symbolic impact of his 1993 vote tally of 71,233 in the old riding of York North — a figure that broke a thirty-year-old Canadian record for most votes cast for one candidate — but as a percentage of total votes, his plurality in the new, reduced riding of Vaughan-King-Aurora is only slightly less formidable.

So who is this politician who has so smitten the voting public of Vaughan-King-Aurora? In conversation at his Parliament Hill office, Bevilacqua describes himself as "a centrist Liberal. I tend to be fiscally conservative," he explains, "but I'm also very much a person who wants to invest in areas like youth programming, child care, things like training, research and development. You need a balance. In order to sustain our social programs you need to generate wealth. And in order to generate wealth, you need to invest in people."

This is the kind of talk you might expect from an old-time Liberal stalwart: calm and conciliatory words bespeaking a political organization whose adeptness at walking down two sides of the street at the same time, of being all things to most people, has made it Canada's governing party for most of the post-war era and a primary instrument of the Canadian social consensus. But centrist Liberalism is somewhat out of sync with that newer image of middle-class Canada — exemplified, perhaps, by Bevilacqua's own suburban riding in York Region — as a place of restlessness, anxiety, and rebellion, more receptive to bellicose and belligerent movements like the Common Sense Revolution than to a party that still promotes, in words at least, the principles of social compassion and a role for government in addressing society's ills.

In Bevilacqua's estimation, however, that new image of suburbia is probably wrong. The characterization of the 905 belt as solidly reactionary terrain, he believes, arose from a moment of panic and confusion that moved many voters to question traditional Canadian values and to line up behind some new political movements that seemed to present a credible alternative to the status quo. The MP supports this analysis with a reference to Peter C. Newman's *The Canadian Revolution*. The central thesis of the book is that a number of overlapping and mutually reinforcing crises of public confidence —

from the abuse scandals that rocked the church to the failure of the
political elite to sell the public on the Meech Lake and Charlottetown
constitutional reform packages to the legacy of ill will that followed
the debates over free trade and the Goods and Services Tax — damaged the credibility of Canada's institutional elite and diminished
Canadians' traditional sense of deference. A new scepticism and an
appetite for (almost) revolutionary change took its place.

"A lot of Canadian institutions have faced these challenges, and
some of them have crumbled," Bevilacqua recounts. "So this creates
a mood that's against the status quo. Then along comes Mike Harris,
quote-unquote tax-fighter, and his Common Sense Revolution, and
people think he's one of us, right?"

Bevilacqua concedes that Harris's pitch was especially effective in
upper-middle-class suburban areas such as his, even among groups
that had given no indications in the past of conservative political
leanings. Take, for instance, the Italian-Canadian community, which
makes up a large segment of the population in the western sector of
York Region and accounts for a huge chunk of Bevilacqua's own
support. As city-dwellers and residents of the older suburbs, Italian-
Canadians could always be expected to tilt leftward by electing a mix
of Liberal and NDP parliamentarians, city councillors, and school
trustees. But with the move northward came a sudden lurch to the
political right. Soon Italian-Canadian voters in the new, high-end
suburbs were throwing their considerable clout behind candidates
such as Common Sense Revolutionary and former car-dealer Al
Palladini. As provincial transportation minister, Palladini became
famous for his remark that cutbacks to emergency highway patrols
did not represent a threat to public safety since all motorists these
days have cellphones in their cars.

Bevilacqua believes that there are a number of concrete, socio-
geographic reasons for this sudden rightward swing. One of them is
the all-encompassing influence of the automobile. "Everyone in the
suburbs owns at least one or two cars," the MP states, "and that in
itself has a huge impact on your financial decisions and your political

priorities." This leads Bevilacqua to his rather philosophical conclusion that "geography, the space you occupy, time and distance" play major roles in the formation of one's political outlook. Then there is the reality that many of the Italian-Canadians who moved into York Region from longer-established neighbourhoods are high-income earners, the wealthiest segment of their community. Being surrounded by other high-income people, they may see little benefit in traditional liberal values like compassion for the disadvantaged; they would quite likely agree with Palladini's remark about less need for government highway services.

But Bevilacqua doesn't see this hardening of attitudes as a threat to his own power base; rather, it's a tendency he feels he has to accommodate within a broader political synthesis. Besides, he's convinced that the sharp rightward shift of recent times is only a temporary phenomenon; the middle-class militancy that now burns in his area will be moderated by processes unfolding both on the ground in suburbia and within the national psyche. At the local level, he believes, the case for higher levels of spending on both social services and public infrastructure will seem more logical to his constituents as York Region becomes more developed and urbanized. "As urban sprawl continues and as amalgamation continues — let's say that the megacity were to extend itself to cities like Vaughan, Mississauga, Halton-Peel, and Richmond Hill — the suburban areas will adopt lots of the attitudes and concerns of the inner city."[1]

Meanwhile, on the more general theme of the weakening of the Canadian establishment and the rise of revolutionary challengers competing for Canadians' affections — the Newman hypothesis — Bevilacqua takes it more as a matter of faith that Canadians will return to traditional ground, that appeals to those old Canadian virtues of collective responsibility and social concern will once again strike a responsive chord. "Canadians are not extremists," he asserts.

True enough. "Extremist" is not a label that fits with our national self-image. Canadians are moderates and realists, and we are practical rather than ideological, or so we tell ourselves. We can see both sides of a story and will often bet on more than one horse. In this way we can be seen as conflicted, complex, or perhaps blessed with a more expansive vision than, say, Americans.

And if that is true of Canadians in general, says Toronto writer John Montesano, it is especially true of Italian-Canadians. Their experience in this country has led them to wander on both sides of the political fence, reinforcing their own particular brand of social and economic conservatism while at the same time making many of them loyal champions of the kind of interventionist, social welfare-oriented style of government that reached its pinnacle of influence in Canada in the '60s and '70s.

It was then, during the reign of Pierre Trudeau, as Montesano recounts in *This Magazine*, that

> the Liberals' bolstering of the social safety net . . . ingratiated [the party] to Italians, and why not? They were among the first to benefit from it. Unemployment insurance programs assisted seasonal construction workers stranded at home during the cold winter months. Their children would be sent to affordable universities in hopes that they might "get ahead in life." And universal health care was suddenly readily available to people who, back in Italy, would have had to go to a neighbouring town to receive effective medical care.

But while Italian families benefitted from Canadian social programs, their rapid rise up the social ladder was seen mostly as an outgrowth of their own enterprise, hard work, and self-sacrifice. Upward mobility required that new arrivals would work multiple jobs, save their money, and endure hostility from the mainstream. And so, says Montesano, "it was this struggle to cope with newfound hardships — both financial and cultural — that planted, in many ways, the seeds of conservatism." Moving quickly from poverty to affluence, many members of the community questioned why others in Canadian society could not make the same sacrifices in the service of improving their lot.

This undercurrent of conservatism rose to the surface during the 1995 Ontario election campaign, continues Montesano, after Conservative Senator Consiglio Di Nino wrote a column in the daily *Corriere Canadese* urging Italian-Canadians to see Harris's philosophy of "less government, free enterprise, personal and family values, reward for hard work, fiscal responsibility" as a reflection of their own mindset. By that time, apparently, most Italian-Canadians had forgotten their historical enmity towards the Tories, which had begun with the Diefenbaker government's introduction of more restrictive immigration legislation over thirty years earlier. (Designed to stem the flow of unskilled labourers from southern Italy and to encourage, instead, the migration of stonemasons and carpenters from the north, the measure was perceived as a hostile act towards all Italians and a black mark against the Tories.)[2]

But despite their recent conversion to the cause of lower taxes and less government — policies that now appeal to Italian-Canadians, Montesano says, because many are affluent citizens "with something to lose" — it's doubtful that people who once provided a steady pillar of support for Pierre Trudeau's "just society" feel entirely comfortable supporting parties such as the Ontario Tories or the federal Reform whose main mission is to fund tax cuts by unravelling the social safety net. And it's not just a question of nostalgia for lost idealism. Many voters in the upscale enclaves of York Region, regardless of their ethnicity, continue to view themselves as upwardly mobile. They are people trying to make it in the so-called knowledge economy, causing them to be more responsive to appeals for adequate funding for education, for instance, than to continued calls for tax cuts at all costs. It's also a fairly good bet that many suburban voters are sophisticated enough to see that the kind of wrenching cuts to social programs that produce widespread despair and upheaval are, in the long run, bad for business and for the health of their communities.

So it's not difficult to see how the platform of a self-described centrist Liberal, a man with one eye on the deficit, the other on the need for social "investments," would appeal to this constituency. Indeed, the MP himself credits those time-honoured Liberal traits of being able to embrace both sides of an issue, being able to broker understandings between competing segments of society, as chiefly responsible for his and his party's stunningly wide margin of victory in Vaughan-King-Aurora.

"We occupy a large portion of the political spectrum," he says. "Our fiscal conservatism means we get the votes of people who might consider supporting Reform or the Conservatives. But our progressive social approach wins us the votes of people who have voted for the NDP. So we got support from everyone, basically, except for the extreme left and the extreme right."

Some might argue, of course, that when the rhetoric is cast aside, a federal Liberal victory is in reality a neo-conservative victory. It's very much in keeping with the image of suburbia as a place of meanness and penny-pinching, given that the new-version Liberals under Jean Chrétien precipitated many of the provincial cuts to social programs by slashing transfer payments to the provinces. Predictably, Bevilacqua, who is chair of the Commons finance committee, disagrees. The issue of a tax cut, for instance, highlights how the Liberals are different from other, self-avowedly conservative parties. The Liberal plan, he says, is to return to its progressive roots once the government has established an annual budget surplus (which it now has) by targeting tax cuts to lower- and modest-income Canadians. This approach is obviously less appealing to the rich than competing parties' across-the-board tax-cut plans, which deliver increasingly steep returns as incomes rise.

When I ask Bevilacqua if he has trouble selling this version of tax relief to his mainly upper-income constituents, he points to two other government fiscal policies first championed by the finance committee that were obviously intended to buy the support of the upper middle class. One is the increase in the ceiling for tax-free contributions to

RRSPs; the other is a new program that offers a government top-off of private contributions to registered education savings plans (RESPs). Both these measures effectively provide subsidies to the private retirement and education savings plans of people who are wealthy enough already to be able to save or invest a chunk of their income (hardly a universal expectation these days, especially if you're paying off a big mortgage).

And thus emerges the portrait of a brand of politics whose primary strength is the ability to broker compromises and quid pro quos, and to balance competing promises made to different social groups. It demands of its practitioners little ideological zeal but a high quotient of the sort of engineering skills needed to keep this machine of social consensus in good working order. Politicians who play well within this system are unlikely to be flamboyant. Bevilacqua, for example, uses the word "balance" so much that he would probably cause most journalists — who are constantly in search of that incendiary sound bite, that spark of conflict — to fall into an uneasy slumber. His dryly even-handed style of speech, in fact, likely explains why he is a con-spicuously non-quoted politician, despite his influential role with the finance committee. But the voters of Vaughan-King-Aurora don't seem to mind his style at all. They obviously didn't want to be represented by a grandstander, by some white knight who would challenge the status quo and take aim at its shortcomings. They voted for a technocrat, a details guy, someone whose best quality seems to be competence. They wanted someone who would make the status quo work better, provided that a few incentives for them were written into the deal.

Maurizio Bevilacqua is not the only candidate to make this kind of pitch to the voters of Vaughan-King-Aurora in the spring of 1997. Second-place Tory candidate Lara Coombs, it seems to me, is cut from the same political cloth. During the campaign, I catch up with Coombs and her campaign manager Lloyd Harper at the Aurora GO station, where they were glad-handing commuters waiting for the 7:00 a.m. train into the city. Both Coombs and Harper are very much products of the establishment. Coombs tells me she's from a political family in Saskatchewan; both her great-grandfather and grandfather were MLAs and mayors, and her great-grandfather also served as a senator. Harper relates that his first political experience was to help John Turner get his start as a student politician at McGill University.

Coombs also speaks the same political vernacular as Bevilacqua — accentuating the positive, studiously avoiding any commentary that may appear negative or pessimistic. It gets a bit unnerving, really. Even an innocent little question about whether it's a tough grind having to campaign at 7:00 a.m. after an all-candidates face-off the night before is met with a fiercely upbeat "I love it. Goes with the territory. I'm a very high-energy person so . . ." And to the standard inquiry as to how the commuters have responded this morning, there is another return volley of superlatives. "Amazing. Extremely positive. Extremely," although to me it seems that most people have just smiled politely and accepted her literature.

Moving to a matter of greater substance, Coombs makes it clear that she is not running on the same "revolutionary" platform as did the Tories' provincial cousins in the 1995 Ontario election, that this is a different crew with a different approach. "We're running a positive campaign, not a negative campaign," she says. "We're not putting fear into Canadians; we haven't lost the country, it's still here. It's just time for effective leadership and a party with a broader vision than any other party."

The low-voltage style of campaign — easy on the histrionics, fed by the rhetoric of hope rather than of discontent — seems to have been a good match for the mood in suburbia during the 1997 federal election. It seems logical to suggest that this is an approach to politics that works best in good times, when the economy is relatively buoyant, when there is some optimism that things will improve in the future. That seemed to be the dominant mood in the spring of 1997.

But by now well-entrenched in this landscape is another political movement that runs on a different type of fuel. The populist politics of the federal Reform Party and of Ontario's new Tories (that is, the Common Sense Revolution Tories — Conservative in name, but largely Reform in action) has at its centre a different conception of its target constituency. This is a movement that embraces negative commentary rather than shying away from it; nothing rallies its core support more effectively than a no-holds-barred negative ad campaign, hammering away at the shortcomings of the status quo, railing against some injustice and calling for fundamental and sweeping change. It seeks this connection with its constituents based on the assumption that they are angry and alienated; that they do not believe they have been factored into social pacts so adeptly constructed by parties like the Liberals; that they are an unrepresented silent majority, as Spiro Agnew might have said.

Although the 1997 federal election results seemed to indicate that the right-wing populist movement had entered a period of dormancy, with the Liberals winning 101 of Ontario's 103 seats (one went Tory, one independent) and Reform coming up empty-handed on terrain where they had expected to win perhaps a dozen seats, the Liberal dominance was not nearly as complete in many of the suburbs surrounding Metro Toronto as it was in Vaughan-King-Aurora. Move slightly north to Newmarket (within the riding that inherited the name York North), where the houses get smaller, the average income figure drops by almost $20,000, and the threat of economic downturn and the bite of taxation hit closer to home, and the tally shows Reform ran a respectable second place. Although one has to view with scepticism the oft-heard Reform Party refrain that a right-wing party would have won perhaps thirty seats if the vote counts of Reform and federal PCs were combined — many old-line Tories would surely rather vote Liberal than support those cantankerous and vitriolic Reformers — there were ridings in Ontario where only a portion of the PC vote would have catapulted a Reform candidate into office.

Newer suburbs have characteristics that make them especially vulnerable in a downturn: the onerous mortgages of many residents and the impact of a high demand for services on the property tax being just two. When things start to fall apart, the residents of these communities will naturally get nervous, fearing that their dream is in jeopardy, and the populist cries of protest will strike a more resonant chord. In 1995 Mike Harris's American-style negative ads had the impact of neutron bombs at a time when conditions were only marginally worse than in 1997; people were spooked by the size of the provincial debt perhaps, and interest rates were a few points higher. But what if a real crisis were to descend on suburbia? Who knows what kind of success the populists would have if the mood in the suburbs suddenly turned really sour.

— —

Before the rise of Reform throughout the 1980s and 1990s, the populist movement that had the greatest impact in Canada was the quasi-socialist New Democratic Party. Now contained within a few pockets of electoral strength in the urban cores, in prairie towns, and more recently in Atlantic Canada, the party still valiantly maintains campaign offices across the breadth of the country, one of which was located, during the election of 1997, in a small storefront office in Market Square, in the town of Woodbridge, Region of York.

The first thing that strikes you about Market Square is that it shouldn't be here. It's a four-sided congregation of outdoor cafés and cobblestone walkways, a piece of Europe transposed onto the blank suburban landscape like some replica assembled on a Hollywood backlot. A few minutes' drive away are the four-lane arterial roads and red-brick subdivisions more typical of this region — except that you can't drive directly from there to here. This pre-suburban enclave is so car-unfriendly that you've got to park on one of the streets nearby and walk to your final destination. The effect is somehow disorienting. Finding this vision of European-style urban intimacy here in the heart of Shopping Mall Land is about as unlikely as, say, finding a crusading trade union activist running for public office in an upper-middle-class bedroom community.

But he's here too, in that storefront plastered with green-and-orange election signs. Robert Navarretta may not expect to win this contest, but he is campaigning hard in order to be heard. In any other affluent suburb, his candidacy might be dismissed as a joke. But Navarretta has a certain credibility here, a moral authority perhaps, because he knows the Toronto Italian community well and can speak to that portion of its history and aspirations that have been bound up with progressive politics, trade unions, and the fight for the underdog. A staff representative with the Industrial, Wood and Allied Workers of Canada, he has spent twenty-four years in the trenches dealing with the nitty-gritty issues of workers' compensation, layoffs, pay rates, health and safety. His focus during the campaign has been an obvious reflection of this experience: he speaks passionately about the tragedy of disappearing jobs, the need to halt public-sector cutbacks, the moral and practical rationales for raising the rate of corporate taxation.

You'd think this message would be lost on the voters of Vaughan-King-Aurora. This is, after all, an area of obvious wealth; job cuts have not been a pressing concern for the upper middle class, and management types would see no direct payoff in raising the taxes on corporations that reward their higher-tier employees quite handsomely. But Navarretta maintains that things out here are not quite what they seem. In the Italian-Canadian portion of his riding, at least, he believes that only about half of the people on whose doors he has been knocking are high-income professionals or successful entrepreneurs. The others are ordinary people working ordinary jobs who scrimped and saved during the '50s, '60s, and '70s to pay off the mortgages on modest downtown houses, and then discovered that they were sitting on gold mines when the boom of the 1980s doubled or tripled the value of inner-city real estate. That's when they decided to move north, to big houses with new wiring and new plumbing, where the air was clean and there was grass all around.

"There is a misconception," Navarretta explains, "that the person who buys a house up here that costs $300,000 or more has to be a rich person. Well, sometimes it's a husband and wife who are working in two different factories and they are probably getting a combined income of, say, $50,000 to $60,000. Because they had a house paid for, they said, 'Let's buy another one — it's our dream.'"

And the dream of much of their community, in fact. In the culture of Italian immigrants, Navarretta continues, a big house with some land around it is the most potent symbol of arrival, of success, and a strong measure of personal security. Accordingly, most new immigrants tend to pour the bulk of their money and energy into their homes, the foundation for their lives in a new country. The bigger the house, the more ambitious the trade-up, and the more successful they have been.

But in the aftermath of the '80s boom, the extension of a once-surefire, conservative economic strategy has, for many, turned high-risk. For the family with all its accumulated equity tied up in a new, expensive home, the sudden loss of one of the incomes needed to pay the new mortgage may raise the disconcerting question, says Navarretta, "of whether they can keep what they worked all their lives for. In other words, they have much more at stake; they can lose much more than someone who is just entering the workforce."

So appearances here are deceiving. Beneath the outward glow of optimism and expansion is a chilling undercurrent of fear and trepidation.

"A lot of people don't understand this," Navarretta says. "Like, I work down in the city and people say, 'Where do you live?' I say, 'I live in Woodbridge,' and then it's 'Oh yeah, people in Woodbridge, they are doing okay.' No, I beg your pardon, we are doing worse than other people because where for most people the loss of a job is the loss of a job, for some people the loss of a job means the end of everything they have worked towards for all their lives."

In addition to this looming threat of economic cataclysm in the form of foreclosure, Navarretta believes that many recent arrivals are facing considerable financial strain because of the unexpected extra costs that are built into suburban life: the need for two cars, for instance, or the unexpected rise in service costs that have caused property taxes to skyrocket. "When I bought my house seven years ago," he offers, "the property taxes were $3,000. They are now $6,000 . . . The reality is that a lot of people are unable to keep paying the taxes on their houses."

I see an eerie resemblance between the modern-day story Robert Navarretta tells and an earlier, sorrowful episode of local history. In his book *Unplanned Suburbs: Toronto's American Tragedy*, McMaster University geographer Richard Harris recounts the story of another wave of immigrants to Canada. They were poor industrial workers from the inner-city slums of northern England who, much like the Italian newcomers who began arriving in the 1950s, saw home-ownership as their best ticket to becoming middle-class. These English newcomers, who in the 1910s and 1920s settled in Toronto's suburban hinterlands (which are now considered part of the city), also shared with the later wave of Italian immigrants a willingness to make considerable sacrifices in their quest to own a piece of property. As Harris says, "the growth of blue-collar suburbs [in the 1920s] had depended upon extensive self-provisioning. Men saved money by building [their own] homes and walking to work, women by making clothes and baking bread. Together they grew vegetables, kept animals, drew water from wells, buried or burned their wastes."[3]

Building their own homes was certainly the most notable of these activities; Harris thinks it was the main factor explaining the apparent paradox of steeply rising rates of home-ownership occurring at a time when wages were not rising to the extent that would have suggested there'd been a mass migration from the labouring to the middle classes. Using their own ingenuity and scrounged building materials, the new immigrants built passable accommodation on cheap parcels of unserviced land in communities such as Mimico, Long Branch, Weston, and the later boroughs of York and East York (all since incorporated into the greater City of Toronto), where lax building codes permitted the practice.

But the economic costs of this primitive form of suburban sprawl became apparent when it came time to extend urban conveniences such as sewage and water services to these ad hoc, owner-built suburbs. "Laying pipes in already developed areas was expensive, especially in the outer suburbs where existing development was scattered," Harris writes. Thus arose a suburban crunch of a kind that was then common across North America. While in the United States municipalities financed new services through an increase in their average per capita debt load from $90 in 1922 to $138 in 1929, municipal debts and taxes were also becoming unbearable around Toronto, especially in the self-built blue-collar suburbs. York township's per capita annual debt for local improvements — which was $30 in 1925, roughly the same as it was in the city of Toronto — doubled to $60 by 1929. As tax bills rose, so did delinquencies. "In York Township in 1926," Harris describes, "almost 22 percent of taxes levied went unpaid, and by 1929 the figure reached 27 percent. Although most suburban workers saw their wages rise during the 1920s, the growing cost of suburban living left them no farther ahead."

Although by the late 1920s workers who were unable to keep up financially had already begun to lose the homes they had built, the trend accelerated sharply as the Great Depression brought with it a tidal wave of job loss. The mood in suburbia was ripe for a populist revolt — this time it was of the left-wing variety.

"In the early 1930s popular opposition to foreclosures, evictions and tax auctions became common," says Harris, who recalled several examples of "vigilante justice."

In August, 1932, for example, fifty members of the East York Workers' Association foiled the eviction of a family on Barrington Avenue. The association threatened "harsh measures" if other, planned evictions were carried out. Six months later, under the heading "Bailiff's Life is Not 'Appy One in Suburban Areas," the *Globe* reported that "as many as one hundred citizens" had

turned out to oppose bailiffs in several suburban areas, while
thirty police officers had been required to eject one family from a
house in North York.

Soon workers and residents' associations elected sympathetic
representatives. Township governments did what they could, even
to the point of joining the picket line. In May, 1936, for example,
a meeting of East York Council was adjourned when news was
brought of the imminent eviction of Mr. and Mrs. James Plunkett
and their son and daughter. In closing the meeting, Arthur
Williams, the township reeve, declared "our place is with the
family that's going to be put out on the street." When the township delegation arrived, the six policemen present backed off.
Even when evictions could not be prevented, township councils
did what they could to find alternate accommodation.[4]

This kind of intervention, however, could not halt the broader
process whereby many blue-collar families lost their homes and moved
into substandard lodgings in the city, and their owner-built suburban
houses "filtered up," as Harris describes it, into the hands of more
middle-class and professional people. This outcome led Harris to
question whether the immigrants' fixation on home ownership was
perhaps misguided — whether it actually might have worsened their
position during the Great Depression, as it might have done at other
times in the history of suburban expansion.

Families pushed themselves to the limit. In the long run, owning
their own home gave them some security; in the short run,
however, they had run down their small savings to zero. Even the
slightest setback made them destitute. The first hint of this was
the recession of 1907-8, when only a citywide campaign saved
scores of suburban immigrants from starvation or hypothermia.
Another crisis emerged after World War I, when unemployment
cast hundreds of suburbanites, most of them immigrants, onto

provincial relief. Had they been too thrifty, or, to ask the question in a different way, too single minded in their thrift?[5]

For the optimist, there are too many differences between the present and the past to make these previous examples of suburban calamities in any way useful as cautionary tales or as guides to current policy. There are too many safeguards built into today's modern economy, so some might reason, to allow for economic catastrophe on the same scale as occurred in the grim old days. And today's suburban pioneers are hardly the desperate shanty-dwellers of yesteryear; most of them are highly educated professionals — accountants, lawyers, doctors, high-tech wizards — who are at the top of the economic pyramid, who command a good portion of the economic rewards to be had today. Even the lower-end suburban émigrés whose plight is championed by Robert Navarretta bring more skills, entrepreneurship, and accumulated capital out to the new frontier than their predecessors ever could have dreamed of.

Still, the common traits seen both in past suburban crashes and in today's squeeze — large and unanticipated servicing bills placing vast upward pressure on municipal property taxes, the phenomenon of overextended property-owners living on the line between solvency and foreclosure, deflationary pressure on property values (which were artificially inflated by speculation), and nervousness about economic downturn and job loss — make some wonder how bad things could get if a real crisis hit. In the decidedly apocalyptic view of James Howard Kunstler, author of *The Geography of Nowhere*, a biting critique of the human-built American landscape, some major social and economic calamity in suburbia (spurred perhaps by a repeat of the 1970s oil crisis) is almost inevitable; and when it comes, its effects will be all the worse because the suburban plains that now cover much of North America were built with virtually no respect for either economic or environmental limitations.

Examining the high cost of providing services and highways, of accommodation for our cars and our large yards, the author insists that these factors have already had a significant impact on America's political and economic health since "there is a direct connection between suburban sprawl and the spiralling costs of government" (although most politicians still prefer to blame social-welfare programs rather than suburban-friendly highway programs as the source of government debt). Kunstler concludes that "the physical setting we dwell in exhausts our capital." Still, any moment of reckoning with the broader impacts of suburban colonization has been forestalled by the falling energy prices and vast infusion of capital, which fed the real estate boom of the 1980s — activity Kunstler refers to as "the mindless twitchings of a brain-dead culture, artificially sustained by the intravenous feeding of cheap oil."

Kunstler has some faith that this mess will be offset by the rise of new schools of design such as the one known as "the new urbanism," whose practitioners have been building suburban communities that embrace many of the urban-planning principles — the inclusion of back lanes and front porches, the scaling down of roadways and the revival of the row house — which are believed to encourage a sense of community and diminish reliance on the car. But he is also resigned to the prospect that some of the post–World War II suburban landscape will collapse under its own weight; he predicts that at least the most unsustainable of suburban projects (S&L-funded housing projects built in the Mojave Desert being an extreme example) will lose much of their value and in some cases have to be abandoned. "Today's posh suburbs could easily become tomorrow's slums," he advises. "If it seems unthinkable, go to Detroit and check out the square miles of mansions-turned-slums off Woodward Avenue."[6]

The decline need not be that dramatic, of course, to fuel public discontent and spur a political backlash. Still, any future suburban populist revolt unleashed by an economic downturn is unlikely to take the form it did in the 1930s. It's difficult to imagine today's suburbanites being torn away from their satellite TVs, or politicians adjourning a local council meeting to stand between the bailiff and an insolvent family.

Back at the NDP office in Woodbridge, Navarretta admits that the institutions of the left in Canada are now poorly positioned to take advantage of suburbia's smouldering sense of unease. The labour movement, for instance, may have done a good job in the past of raising skilled workers' living standards so that many of them could move out to upscale communities such as this, but it has failed miserably at sustaining a sense of social solidarity. It was unable to convince its more affluent members that as they achieve their material aims, they also should look beyond their backyards to see the wrongs that still need righting, the common good that needs to be protected.

"To me," Navarretta laments, "the labour movement has been almost self-destructive in the way it has been single-issue focused. What I have been preaching is that a union cannot be just an agency to negotiate wages. A union has to be a social movement, and I think people should join a union because it is a social movement which touches every aspect of their lives. What's been happening — and again it has been our fault — is that we have not been able to educate our membership to the importance, for instance, of having a social conscience."

Actually Navarretta didn't do as badly — here in the heartland of consumerism, where the ultimate expression of social conscience might be deciding to buy your shampoo from the Body Shop — as one might have expected. His 2,127 vote count, when expressed proportionally as part of a new and compressed riding, was equivalent to a doubling of support in this area since the 1993 federal contest.

Still, it's difficult to think of the left making serious inroads into suburbia without mounting a credible philosophical challenge to the ideas that are almost built into this landscape. The York Region that Navarretta found while canvassing is one where people seem almost incapable of conceiving of social problems that could be addressed by concerted and collective social action. Forget solidarity, or even common cause. For many, the problems of society can all be reduced to questions of individual consumer choice, or marketplace preferences.

"We are reaching the era now," says Navarretta, "where if you go to a lot of houses and talk about the environment, you say, 'Look at the contamination in the water,' and they say, 'Who cares? I'm going to buy bottled water. The guy comes every week. He drops off the cases of bottled water for me to drink. Why should I be concerned about that?' Now the young kids are saying, 'Hold on a minute. I can open the fridge and get a bottle of water too, but there is now contamination in there too. Where does it come from? You are ruining the whole world. It's becoming much bigger than we are.'"

Which leads him to a glimmer of optimism. Navarretta believes that, if the Canadian left is to hope for any kind of renaissance on this terrain, it must introduce a broader conception of the public good that embraces both quality-of-life and moral issues. And the natural constituency for this approach may not be blue-collar, unionized workers, he says, but educated young people who have grown weary of society's obsessive materialism, so evident out in suburbia.

"Whether it is the environment," predicts Navarretta, "or a system that has created so many poor people, that kind of thing is going to revolt the stomachs of people who, even though they have everything they want in life, say, 'It is not right that where I walk, there are people starving all over the place.'"

— — —

Of course, those right-wing populists — the federal Reformers who have intermarried with the reborn Ontario Conservative party — have established a solid presence around here by taking precisely the opposite approach. Their adherents are not young idealists convinced of the bankruptcy of materialism, but older people who believe they have not received enough of the material rewards that are supposed to abound in our great consumer society. Their nostalgia is not for a time when social solidarity, a sense of community, was believed to be the cure for injustice, but for the promise of the early post-war period of ever-escalating material wealth, a dream that began to grow dimmer as inflation, stagnating wages, and an increasing tax burden took hold in the 1970s. They don't want government to address the ills of environmental contamination or homelessness or even to dampen crime through gun control; instead, they seek deliverance from government's good intentions, confident that if freed from the dual yokes of taxation and regulation, they could find their own way to the promised land. As for those who are living in the streets, well, that's downtown, not here.

Given how rapidly this set of ideas has become a political force in suburban Ontario, I have the feeling as I visit Reform candidate Maralyn Hazelgrove's rustic HQ that I'm being given a rare opportunity to gauge a particularly potent aspect of the local *Zeitgeist*. That my visit here will reveal a lot about what's going on just below the surface in a lot of people's minds.

Action central for the Hazelgrove campaign is a vacant storefront in a strip mall in Nobleton, a community that still looks like a country crossroads, having not yet been absorbed into the suburban behemoth. Right next to the Reform office is a satellite-TV dealership; across the road and a little bit down is a bustling greasy spoon. Inside the campaign office, workers are pumped and indulging in a salubrious breakfast of coffee and sugar-dusted doughnuts. The candidate herself is tied up on the phone. At first she excuses herself by saying, "I've just got to make an important phone call," but then remains on the sidelines — with the exception of a few one-line interjections — throughout the conversation. Never mind. I've been left in good hands. Hazelgrove introduces me to her son and assistant campaign manager, Burton Harrison, a guy with the beginnings of a beard growing in around his moustache. It makes him look a bit like a hockey player during the NHL playoffs, an apt image perhaps, since shooting for political office and for the Stanley Cup probably require similar quantities of commitment and adrenalin.

Harrison begins by filling me in on the family history and his mother's introduction to politics, which began a few months earlier when Hazelgrove sought the Reform nomination in their home riding of Simcoe-Grey. Although she lost out to a prominent local lawyer, Hazelgrove did get to meet Reform's deputy leader Deborah Grey, who "decided that 'this is a woman we want in our party,'" as her son remembers it. So the party set her up in Vaughan-King-Aurora, where Reform had no candidate.

Harrison says the family was new to this game, apolitical until a short while earlier when "we read the [Reform] policies and realized that this is a party that thinks the way we think. We realized that this is a party that cares about people. They are real people." He insists that even now, in the midst of political battle, he and his mother don't behave like politicians. If one thing has handicapped them, he says, it's that they lack the killer instinct.

"In this campaign we were accused of taking down Bevilacqua's signs," he relates. "But what's really happened is that I've been putting up signs near his, or near Lara's or whatever, but if they're leaning over and I'm putting up a sign, I usually straighten their signs, I don't take them down. I believe everybody has a shot at this. Seriously. I know you're recording this, but like, that's just the type of person I am."

Their abiding concern for people, Harrison explains, stems from the family's background as small-business people. His mother ran a textile business but later became a restaurateur, while his father used to publish a men's fashion magazine called *Ego*. In the mid-1980s mother and son moved from Montreal to Toronto, where they opened a small restaurant in the Eaton Centre. Living at first in the Annex and then the Beaches — both trendy and expensive urban neighbourhoods — they soon got sick of the city and moved north, first to suburban Thornhill and later to rural Creemore. "We wanted a little hobby farm and so on and so forth, so we went a little farther north, and we have that now," he says.

Their time in the grittier surroundings of downtown Toronto seems to have left them with a negative impression of the evolving Canadian reality. Like other Reformers, much of their attention is focused on crime. "Everything is totally out of hand," declares Harrison. "Everybody has guns, everybody has knives, there's murders every day. There's robberies, there's assaults. The jails are overflowing with criminals. There's no correctional system in this country. They just sit there and when they get out, they're worse than when they went in. As far as I'm concerned there's no justice system in this country either. It's just a legal system."

When you move up to Creemore, however, he tells me, you don't see the crime problem being resolved by the federal government's proposed gun registry, which has won more support from nervous urbanites and even more nervous city police departments. But this, alas, is a difficult and emotional topic that will require rebalancing the chemistry a bit — especially after the sugar from the doughnuts has started to kick in — and so Harrison pauses to ask me if I mind if he smokes. When I tell him it's okay with me, his mother — who's between calls — intones, "Good. This is the only place we're allowed to these days." Fortified by the nicotine fix, Harrison rallies his strength for the task of restating Reform policy on gun control — that criminals will always be able to find a way around the law, while good people like his new neighbours will suffer — and in so doing he segues into Victimization Story Number One.

"Yesterday we met a gunsmith who works in King City," he begins. "The Liberal and Tory governments, their gun-control laws that they are passing, have been destroying his business. He doesn't make guns for criminals — I mean, these are law-abiding citizens. Sometimes you have a cow on your farm that is dying, or a dog that was run over by a car. You are better off to shoot these animals and put them out of their misery than to let them suffer. The government is saying, okay, we are going to let the criminals have guns, we'll penalize the law-abiding citizens, and we'll let animals and people suffer. I'm sorry I'm getting so worked up, but it bothers me."

Harrison is not the only person who will do a little venting this morning.

At some point in the conversation, Bill King walks into the office. When the candidate introduces him to me, she says that "Bill is the most wonderful volunteer anyone could possibly ask for." I recognize him immediately as the person who, at the all-candidates meeting a few nights earlier, had gotten up to the microphone and lobbed some kind of rhetorical bomb at Bevilacqua. Actually my tape of the event records that King began with the statement that "Quebec is blatantly, unilingual French," moved on to accuse the federal Liberals of being an agent of separatism, then asked Bevilacqua how he could justify such a stance.

Here in the Reform office, King confirms that it's the French-English issue that's got him "totally ticked off" and pushed him to work for the Reform party, this representing his first involvement with federal politics. His strong views on English-French relations, King explains, arise from personal experience. And that leads us to Victimization Story Number Two, in which King himself plays a prominent role.

"I've been living in this area for thirty-five years," begins King, a man with a droopy white moustache, a gentle Scottish brogue, and a generally mild demeanour that's eerily out of sync with the thrust of his words. "I've also done a lot of business up in Ottawa, and that all came to a crunching end when the francophones replaced the anglophones. I was supplying the Department of National Defence with automated systems to control the liquor in the messes — press a button here and your drink is recorded in the computer. In the first part they screwed me over for $24,000, and had I been a francophone it would have been rubber-stamped. So I had a personal vengeance against the top brass, and in particular against the francophones."

A pattern is emerging. All the people I've met here — the candidate, her son/assistant campaign manager, and one of her star volunteers — are relative newcomers to politics, are mad as hell about something, are well-disposed towards theories of conspiracy and systemic corruption (this explains the fixation on the Sigalov affair at the all-candidates meeting), and have backgrounds as small-business people.[7] They will eagerly debate the issues raised in the Reform platform, but their attention seems fleeting; issues ultimately appear less important to them than the conviction that their world once held a great promise that is now gone, and they are desparate to get that lost world back.

King, who has a bit more political experience than others in this room, converted his rising sense of social disquiet into political action in the Ontario provincial election of 1995. "I campaigned for Al Palladini," he recalls. "But it wasn't actually Al Palladini I was campaigning for. It was Mike Harris. It was the Mike Harris platform." His burning issue back then was taxation. King had attended a number of tax-revolt rallies promoted by the *Toronto Sun* and attended by Harris, "so I got to know a little about him," he says.

"Again, this is one of the atrocities that is happening in our society, that is, the high taxation. The days of slavery didn't end; they simply changed form. They went from physical enslavement to economic enslavement, and that is even more true today than ten, fifteen, twenty years ago, and it's getting worse."

Pressed to comment on his own situation, King responds that he earns about $80,000 a year, and out of that he believes 65 percent is taken away in taxes, although that figure becomes more fluid as the discussion rolls along. "If you take first of all your wage, you pay your tax, you pay your other benefits that are in there, then you go out and buy some clothing — there is more tax — it doesn't matter what, you buy some gasoline and there's more tax and more tax. So when you work in all the taxes you are paying, you really don't wind up with more than twenty to twenty-five cents out of the dollar. Not just myself personally but the population as a whole . . . If that's not economic enslavement, I don't know what is."

Okay, time for a reality check. For a start, there are the figures: the idea that the taxman grabs 65 to 80 percent of Canadians' paycheques seems a bit out of the ballpark, even the ballpark where committed right-wingers play. When I interviewed Jason Kenny, the Reform MP and former president of the anti-taxation Canadian Taxpayers' Federation, he cited figures from the Fraser Institute that claimed Canadians' total tax payments, including all hidden taxes, had ballooned from 23 percent of earnings in 1961 to 48 percent in 1996.[8] Even that figure, promoted by a right-wing think tank and drastically out of line with other assessments, leaves you a lot more than twenty-five cents on the dollar.

(Indeed, David Perry, the chief researcher at the Canadian Tax

Foundation, says the Fraser Institute figures are misleading in a number of ways. First, comparing 1961 with 1996 is mixing apples and oranges, he says, since many aspects of our modern, technological world were not in place in 1961. At that time only 5 percent of the population had university-entrance qualifications [compared with current figures showing 15 to 20 percent of the population benefitting from higher education], Toronto was the only city with even the beginning of a rapid transit system, there was no community college system in Canada, and citizens had to pay for their own medical insurance. All of those services are now funded from the public purse. On top of that, says Perry, the Fraser Institute confuses the issue by comparing the average family incomes in 1961 and 1996; this does not account for the fact that average incomes have risen dramatically during that period. Since the Canadian tax system is progressive, the average family in Canada is today paying a higher proportion of its income in taxes than in 1961, although its take-home pay is much higher. A more accurate portrait would be found, he says, by comparing taxation rates as a percentage of gross domestic product. Using this yardstick, taxes rose from 23.7 percent in 1960 to 36.6 percent in 1996, far less than the doubling of taxation claimed in the Fraser Institute study. Meanwhile, economic journalist Linda McQuaig cites Organization for Economic Co-operation and Development statistics indicating that, since 1974, Canadian taxes have risen only 3.1 percent — much less than the average 7.2-percent increase for other OECD countries during the same period.)

More generally, though, there is the question of whether a person who lives in middle-class comfort isn't being a bit excessive by characterizing himself as a slave. After all, he lives in a country where many people are sleeping in the streets, where many refugees in our midst have suffered torture and survived war, where the legacy of residential schools remains a daily reality for many aboriginal people — choose whatever injustice you like. In this particular case, we have a person who runs his own business, lives in one of the nicest areas of the country, has time to work on political campaigns, and has children (as he later tells me) who have been university-educated and found decent, professional jobs — and still he describes his life as one of "enslavement."

Isn't it just possible, as well, that King and his family have benefitted from taxation, rather than just being its victim? After all, those contracts with National Defence, of which he says he was unjustly deprived, had been funded from the public purse. And consider the lot of his offspring. King says he has one son who graduated as a marine biologist at the University of Guelph (a public institution), a daughter who works in the taxation department of a municipality (no comment), two daughters who work at Litton Systems (a prominent military producer whose survival and prosperity has been dependent on the notorious government gravy-train of weapons procurement), while another son, an electrician, was also likely educated at public expense. Despite the high taxes, doesn't all that government-paid income and education make this look like a net gain?

King responds that any previous dependency on government provides no reason not to cut government down to size. If smaller government and lower taxes were to result in his offspring's losing their jobs, then "that's all part of the game," he says. "When I came to this country, I worked in construction, and when the job came to an end you were out. So in less than six weeks you were gone. You accepted that. So you went on and found another job in construction . . . All my kids can think. They've been taught to work and not to complain. So if they had to move from one job to another, one position to another, that's okay."

But King does not reflexively rebuff my criticisms of his argument. He's willing to consider that there are pros and cons to having a socially and economically interventionist government. He also appears to pick up on the hint that, despite the heavy tax burden, his standard of living is probably better than that of most people across the planet, tacitly acknowledging that his "economic enslavement" has not forced him to miss any meals or sleep in the street. So the money itself, the actual numbers, King suggests, are really a distraction; in fact, taxation per se isn't that important to him.

"I'm not against high taxation," the volunteer declares, back-pedalling a bit. "I would be happy to maintain the same level of taxation if the money that was going to government was to be used intelligently." The real affront, he believes, is that politicians spend the money wantonly, stupidly, and without accountability. Ultimately it's not a dollars-and-cents issue, it's a matter of principle. That's where Reform offers some comfort, some balm for the feelings of people who feel they've been hoodwinked and betrayed. King says what he really likes about Reform's policy is its provisions for direct democracy — for instance, the promise that if MPs are doing a lousy job, constituents can organize a recall campaign and fire them.

"That's democracy," he says. "Under the current system, we have one day of democracy, and that's when you cast your ballot. Once these animals are put in place, you no longer have democracy. You have a dictatorship. Because there's nothing you can do — if they decide they want to do something, there's absolutely nothing the public can do about it."

Burton Harrison agrees that devices like the recall campaign represent the essence of Reform. When you take it down to a single issue, he says, getting past all the intricacies of policy formation, the party's fundamental mission is to bring government closer to the people.

"I called Jean Chrétien's office every week for two years," he relates, "because I wanted to speak with him. The prime minister of my country. Never called me back. All of his aides, we knew each other on a first-name basis, but I could not speak to the prime minister of my country. Called Lloyd Axworthy's office several times; never spoke to him. I called my local MP's office, Murray Caldwell of the Liberal party; never spoke to him. My local MP I couldn't even get to. Dictatorship. They're in government, you'll never ever speak to them. Our party, when you want to speak to your MP, you're damn well going to speak to your MP. That's the main difference."

And this leads us to Victimization Story Number Three, which is, in fact, the meta-narrative that has drawn the volunteers in this office into the political fray, and that is inevitably referred to and reinforced in the TV ads and campaign documents issued by Canada's right-wing populist parties. The story goes something like this: Ordinary people have been hurt and humiliated by governments that have become increasingly heartless and remote, aided by the "special interest groups," which have become their pets. In the Ontario Tories' landmark 1995 TV ads, for instance, these alleged accomplices of big government were the women and minorities who had benefitted from the province's employment equity laws; they were soon joined by unions, doctors, and civil servants, who were publicly vilified by the government once it came to power. Reform, meanwhile, used ads that targeted francophone politicians whom it accused of denying anglophone Canadians a political voice.

King has a few thoughts of his own on which particular "special interest groups" should be brought back into line. His analysis is, once again, aided by some creative arithmetic. Take the province's teachers. They have made an art of whining about a soft work schedule, he believes, that more-stoic Ontarians can only dream about.

"They complain about having a class of thirty-two," says King. "We had classes of forty and forty-two, and no one complained — it was a given. If we had a class when there were only thirty-two students in it, we'd think this class was empty. So these people are spoiled, they are spoiled brats, as far as I'm concerned. When they talk about their workweek, if you analyze things in terms of the time they put in, in actual teaching time, the school year is nine months and they are really teaching two and a half months out of that, when you take professional development days, weekends, holidays."

Maybe if King could follow the teachers at my kids' school through their workdays, he might change his mind. Still, for now he is adamant that the teachers are a prime example of the enemy within, that they are accessories to the hijacking of the political system and its deliverance into the hands of Big Government. But in this worldview even greater threats are lurking without. During our discussion about tax rates, King feels the need to shift the focus, saying there is a larger reality that should be considered.

And that brings us to Victimization Story Number Four, or The Great Conspiracy.

"I would like you to just consider something for a moment about something apart from the economics," King says. "And that is focusing on society and the value and purpose of a human being. It's actually been stated, globally, by the international bankers, that there will be two types of people in the world: useful eaters and useless eaters. And they classify the biggest population in Africa as useless eaters, and that brings us to another subject, and I could show you a tape [about this] that could actually destroy your faith in humanity. AIDS did not come from a monkey. AIDS was ordered, produced, and developed out of a laboratory in Maryland and then transported to Africa . . . I could show you a tape that proves unequivocally that AIDS was produced by man, and it didn't come from a green monkey. International bankers are responsible for everything that is happening globally."

I am vaguely familiar with this theory about the CIA developing the AIDS virus in Maryland and have no idea whether there is any truth to it. What surprises me about hearing it from King, however, is that I had thought such conspiracy theories involving the CIA and the international banking community to be the province of *leftist* populist fringe movements. This confusion offers some clue as to what's going on here; the crossover between populist mythology from the left and from the right — together with King's backpedalling when pressed on issues like taxation — leads me to think that conservative politics is only a peripheral aspect of Reform's popularity with certain segments of its supporters, that this is an attraction only at the surface level. The real appeal, it seems, is the populism; the identification of remote and oversize institutions as corrupt, uncontrollable, and ill-intentioned; and the promise that government (a surrogate for all big bureaucracies) will be brought closer to the individual, that someone will acknowledge the alienated citizen's anger and act on it.

Places like York Region strike me as fertile ground for such a movement to grow in. For as small and distinct quasi-rural communities continue to be subsumed into the spreading mass that is suburbia — places without focus, without identity, with little sense of place to offer their residents apart from the local shopping mall — it may be logical to expect that people will see the forces that control their destinies as increasingly remote, alien, and sinister. So a movement that proposes an antidote to this perceived reality is likely to find a secure place, particularly during a moment of economic stress, in the hearts and imaginations of these growing numbers of people whose lives sprout from the amorphous cultural mud of the suburbs.

The idea that Reform's identity is tied far more to populism than to economic or social conservatism is in line with at least one up-close portrait of the party's founder and leader, Preston Manning. In his book *Waiting for the Wave*, University of Calgary political scientist and former Manning adviser Tom Flanagan, a committed ideological conservative himself, laments that Manning is too concerned with keeping his finger on the pulse of public opinion to be able to take consistently conservative political stands. Manning's populist instincts may have led Reform to embrace the conservative policies that are popular today, he argues, but they may lead elsewhere in the future.

Proof of this is found in the fact that

Manning shows little interest in the revival of conservative thinking in Britain and the United States in the 1980s. Although he is an intellectual man who reads widely, he makes no reference in his own writings and conversation to leading neo-conservative authors such as Friedrich Hayek, Milton Friedman, Thomas Sowell, Irving Kristol, Nathan Glazer, Michael Novak, or the public-choice school. Neither in public nor in private does he ever refer to Margaret Thatcher or Ronald Reagan as models for what he would do if he became prime minister of Canada. He is fascinated with Vaclav Havel, who, like himself, claims to transcend ideology, but oddly uninterested in Vaclav Klaus, the prime minister of the Czech Republic and a self-professed conservative intellectual now leading a government.[9]

Flanagan even goes so far as to suggest that Manning, whose adversaries generally portray him as a tool of corporate interests, may actually be some kind of a closet socialist. "Manning has repeatedly described himself as wanting to save medicare and pensions by making them financially sustainable," complains Flanagan, "but he does not advocate privatizing them or even introducing an element of competition through quasi-markets backed by public funding. In his televised debate with Audrey McLaughlin during the Charlottetown referendum campaign, he said, 'I like the programs — all I say is you better figure out how to pay for them.'"

There are a couple of possible explanations for Manning's soft-peddling of Reform's conservative policies. His adversaries from the left and centre might assume that Manning is keeping quiet in order not to frighten off moderate Canadian voters who would warm to the party's common touch but not identify themselves as Thatcherites or Reaganites. Flanagan, on the other hand, believes that Manning's motivations are different: While he leads a party that has evolved as a hard-right conservative entity, simply because most of its members are right-wingers who were "deserted by the centrist leaders of the Progressive Conservative party," the leader himself thinks of Reform as a "trans-ideological populist movement" that may change over time.

Flanagan's description of Manning's populist mystique goes a long way towards explaining the character of the movement that's been formed in his shadow, and this explanation seems strikingly in sync with the atmosphere I found at the Reform campaign office in Nobleton. Manning's greatest attribute, says Flanagan, is that he is "a human barometer of political dissatisfaction lying beneath the surface. Time and again he has brought issues to the surface that other politicians were ignoring." Well, yes, dissatisfaction was clearly evident at Maralyn Hazelgrove's campaign HQ, although that may be far too mild a word for it. Related to his "human barometer" function, meanwhile, is Manning's "flair for what Murray Dobbin has called 'calculated ambiguity.' He is able to express politically incorrect sentiments, such as opposition to official bilingualism and multiculturalism, with carefully crafted statements that, while radically opposed to the conventional wisdom, steer clear of extremism." Or at least *almost* steer clear of extremism. There is no clearer example of this than the 1997 campaign ads urging Canadians not to elect another Québécois as prime minister. While denounced by many, the ad blitz did, nonetheless, light some fires in the bellies of grassroots supporters, as we have already seen.

— — —

Of course, the process of cultivating and corralling widespread public discontent into a wave of support for a populist political project is not something that can be accomplished solely by means of the leader's intuition. These days it is more a science than anything else. So while Juan Peron might have had some mystical link with his public, Preston Manning and Mike Harris have their coterie of pollsters, admen, and assorted stage managers, all of them master practitioners at their own arcane callings, professions that are equal parts computer science and the reading of entrails.

Which, as we contemplate how it is that the rumblings in riding associations across the country coalesce as political events with significant national impact, brings us to a new cast of characters. Our triad of commentators, heading into the final segment of this tale, are:

- *The strategist.* Rick Anderson is adviser to Preston Manning and a key member of the Reform Party brain trust. Eloquent and careful with his choice of words, Anderson is responsible for translating polling data into campaign strategies and sound bites. Never far from a cell phone, he likes to conduct meetings in restaurants, according to his secretary. But I interviewed him in the office of the leader of the opposition in Centre Block.
- *The politician.* Jason Kenny is a young Alberta MP whose permanent domicile is Mackenzietown, a "new urbanist" development in suburban Calgary. He's a former president and CEO of the western-based Canadian Taxpayers' Federation. One of his func-

tions as an MP has been to direct the party's United Alternative Campaign, which aims to forge a partnership between federal Tories and Reformers in Ontario. This likely explains his keen interest in probing what's on the minds of Ontario suburbanites. We talked in Kenny's office on the western edge of Parliament Hill.

- *The image maker.* Bryan Thomas runs an advertising firm called Thomas Crncich & Partners (formerly Thomas Watt Advertising Inc.), with offices in London, Ontario, and Toronto. His firm made those US-style attack ads for the Harris Tories in the 1995 campaign[10] and Reform's ads in the 1997 contest. (Harris's TV spots promised the tax cuts and, more memorably, attacked welfare recipients and employment equity programs that aimed to increase the ratio of women and minorities working in government; Manning's commercials included the ones that showed Québécois politicians with their faces crossed out.) More recently Thomas's firm has been responsible for part of the deluge of those upbeat, sunny promos that have been telling Ontarians how the government has been improving the health and education systems, not slashing and burning them into oblivion, as the public may otherwise believe. Thomas stopped by to be interviewed at the bar at Ottawa's Chateau Laurier hotel, before catching a plane back to home base in London.

I'll start with Thomas, whose most surprising characteristic is that he doesn't seem like the kind of guy who would create those hostility-laden ads for Harris and Manning. A tall, bespectacled fellow in his late forties, his most notable qualities are a mellow demeanour and an understated wit. If you opt for such adjectives as "clinical" or "serene" to describe the calm and fastidious fashion in which he discusses the use of public hostility as a political weapon, he might start to seem a bit scary, but that wasn't the way he struck me at the time. Thomas's ready supply of euphemisms keeps the tenor of discussion cool. Those ads for Harris and Manning, for instance, are of the "hard-hitting, comparative" genre. Comparative because they contrast one party's policies with its rivals'; hard-hitting because they have all the subtlety of a hammer-blow to the solar plexus.

While one might assume that the manufacturers of these sorts of agitprop projectiles would be committed political warriors, as are many political media consultants in the US, Thomas says he got into his line of work almost by accident after starting out (here's the second-biggest surprise) as an ordained minister preaching in an inter-denominational church. "I guess much of the communications skills I developed started there," he states flatly. Moving over to radio and media sales, Thomas eventually landed a job with an ad agency and then founded his own firm in 1982. The occasional political ads for groups of Tory candidates in southwestern Ontario, which supplemented the bread-and-butter work for clients such as a drugstore chain, led to a meeting with Harris campaign chair Tom Long sometime in the mid-1990s, "and we threw our lot in with them very early, I guess when other people thought they were going nowhere." Thomas's firm wound up as the "agency of record" for the 1995 Tory campaign;[11] later, the success of those ads landed Thomas a contract to produce all of Reform's promos heading into the 1997 federal contest.

But Thomas is careful not to take all the credit for the stunning success of those TV blitzes, the first of which helped Harris's party form a majority government after starting out in third place, and the second of which contributed to Reform's leap into the role of official Opposition, a feat requiring that it almost double its level of support between the pre-election period and election day. These things require teamwork, Thomas points out. So you can forget that sitcom image of how ad agencies work: creative geniuses brainstorming through the night, bringing their inspired storyboards to an astonished client the next morning.[12] It's not like that.

In the case of the Harris ads, says Thomas, the creative types did nothing before the market research firms had conducted their polls and focus groups to determine who the Tories' target constituency was, what they were thinking, what was important in their lives, and how the party could create a message that would appear to mirror their concerns. So by the time the ad agency was called in, campaigners knew what they wanted to say and to whom, and the role of Thomas's firm was simply to "boil it down to three simple memorable icons that were repeated over and over and over again."

And memorable they were. The saturation airing of the three sets of ads — targeting welfare recipients, opposing employment equity for women and minorities, and promising tax cuts — set a new standard for political advertising in Canada. The employment equity ads in particular, which Thomas classifies as "the main target" of the "three hot buttons" arising out of focus groups, were characterized by former NDP consumer minister Marilyn Churley, in the wake of the election, as "[opening] up a Pandora's box. That to me is frightening," she told the *Ottawa Citizen*. "It just leads one to think, What's the next step if it's okay to be racist and sexist? What after that?" Liberal leader Lyn McLeod opined similarly that the Tory campaign "legitimized resentment against newcomers and against people on welfare."[13] For his part, Thomas confirms that the market research had revealed a sour, resentful mood in the newly populous suburban fringes around Toronto, and that the Harris team had no reservations about exploiting that mood as a road to victory.

What the agency began to see through the research, the adman recalls, "was that the suburbanite became much more the mean kind of person, you know, like, 'Look, I'm in the car for an hour and a half, two hours a day, I pay high taxes, I live a stressful life, I want what gets done to benefit me and my family.' That kind of attitude. So some of the traditional value systems of universality and 'Let's take care of the poor first' seemed to move down the hierarchy of priorities, and that group wanted to seize control of their own lives, that was their objective. So issues like tax relief became big. They really weren't the issues of urban Canadians but of suburban Canadians."

All three strategists of the populist uprising with whom I consulted — Thomas, Anderson, and Kenny — agreed that this schism between urban and suburban value systems is now a national phenomenon. As an example, Reform — whose basic platform of lower taxes, reduced government, and less support for the poor mirrors that of the Harris Tories — made a clean sweep in the suburban Fraser Valley surrounding Vancouver in the last election but failed to elect any members in the city itself. In fact, with the exception of Calgary and Edmonton, Reform hasn't elected any members from urban Canada. Rick Anderson calls this, in the Ontario context, "the problem of the two towers . . . If you are standing at the base of either of the two towers that dominate Ontario — the CN Tower or the Peace Tower — we don't look like we are going anywhere. But if you go five miles out from either one of them, you start to feel a little life in Reform, and by the time you're fifty miles out from both of them, you're into pretty Reform-friendly country."

Anderson explains this peculiarity with the idea that Reform's economic approach doesn't mesh well with urban priorities. Cities, he believes, "at a certain point in their evolution become growth unfriendly. It becomes more a question of a 'making it work' rather than 'expanding it.' The dynamic in the suburbs is still about 'making it grow' versus 'making it work.'" This, he continues, suggests that the more "entrepreneurial" people targeted by Reform are more likely to settle in a community where it's still relatively easy to build a road or get a permit for a new factory, rather than in an established city where "putting an expressway through is physically very difficult, politically it's almost impossible, and financially it's very expensive." So since those entrepreneurial types — or the "people who are more on the self-reliant, self-initiative, individual responsibility side of the spectrum, versus, on the other side, people who think that government creates jobs or government manages pension programs," as Anderson says — tend to gravitate to the burbs, and since they are the type of people Reform is after, it stands to reason that the party has greater appeal in suburbia.

While there's general agreement that the urban/suburban split is now a fact of political life across the country, I found greater variance on the question of which particular group of suburbanites — out of the great diversity of people who find themselves, for any number of reasons, surrounded by grass and parking lots — would qualify as the core supporters of right-wing populists like Harris and Manning.

Jason Kenny, an earnest and evangelistic young conservative with short, slicked-back black hair and a traditional striped tie, believes that Reform is most at home amongst lower-income, possibly blue-collar voters in the older, more downscale suburbs, rather than in the gold-plated technoburbs built to accommodate the flood of urban exiles in the 1980s. This does, in fact, tend to be borne out by the 1997 election results, which saw Reform bomb in upscale Vaughan-King-Aurora but score quite well in longer-established, more modest-income suburbs in places like Oshawa and Mississauga.

"What I found consistently in my riding [in Calgary]," Kenny says, "is that the strongest, most visible and most visceral support comes from what could be characterized as lower-middle-class suburban areas. It was precisely the older suburbs in my riding — the suburbs with the $100,000 homes — where I found I could walk down the street and in ten homes I could get five lawn signs and eight commitments to vote. The only areas where I ever got called nasty names — racist, bigot, and some of the negative stereotypes we have — was in the highest-income newest suburban developments, which was presumably from double-income professional families well into the six-figure-income range."

The reason? Kenny thinks part of it is practical: those lower-end suburbanites are more in need of a tax break to provide some relief from the squeeze of declining salaries, a rising weekly workload, and increased tax burden. It also doesn't hurt that Reform's social conservatism might provide some comfort to people who are living in a world of rapid change, but who feel they have no control over how that change affects them.

"My theory," he proposes, "is that people in those older suburbs who are characterized as being more middle class are closer to reality. They suffer the slings and arrows of fortune more directly in their lives than do the higher-income middle class. They can't afford to live in a gated community; they can't afford a security system for their homes; their kids tend to go to schools in slightly rougher neighbourhoods and are therefore more exposed to youth crime and all other forms of social delinquency. The tax burden, while it may not be quite as high for them as it is for people [with] twice the income, they feel the bite more acutely. Every dollar out of their pocket is a dollar that counts. When you are dealing with the higher-middle-income family, sure they may be paying upwards of 55 percent marginal income taxes, but the actual effect on their lives isn't as acute. So in everything from crime, to education, to personal security issues, to the effects of stagnant income and higher taxes, it's the lower middle class generally, with the older houses, that are most directly affected."

The MP adds one other factor — the political predilections of ethnic minorities — as a hint of where Reform's future fortunes may lie in suburbia. Many established suburbs across the country are now largely non-white, and despite a trail of racist bloopers by Reform activists — as well as the general perception that Reformers are mostly pale, middle-aged guys who don't want Sikhs wearing turbans in Legion halls — Kenny feels that first- and second-generation immigrants are likely to see their values reflected in Reform's platform. This could, of course, be just a recruiting speech or wishful thinking, but *you'll* have to be the judge of that.

"These new Canadian voters in older suburban middle-, lower-middle-class ridings are an ideal constituency for us," Kenny states. "They are pro-family, they have traditional social values, respect for the traditional family, etc., low tolerance for crime and for any kind of general social disorder. Very growth-oriented, very entrepreneurial. Very uncomfortable with big interventionist government."

Adding ethnicity to a more lower-middle-class background, the MP finds himself looking at a "classic" conservative voter coalition which has helped create some historic sea changes in the past. "The Reagan Democrats," Kenny recalls, "were mostly suburban, blue-collar, first- or second-generation immigrant voters from places like Detroit and

Chicago, New York, New Jersey — from the northern rust belt. People who traditionally voted Democrat, had traditional family values and wanted a bit of an economic break. So it's a similar kind of dynamic going on there. Margaret Thatcher appealed to a similar constituency, the blue-collar tradesmen in suburban London — this is the swing vote that elected her, the swing vote that elected Reagan, and no party owns the loyalties of those kinds of voters."

But a significantly different portrait is emerging back at the Chateau Laurier, where Bryan Thomas prefers to segment the suburban electorate not by class or ethnic origin but by where they fall on the generational divide. The suburban baby boomers, who had returned to the burbs to raise their own children, voted en masse for Mike Harris in 1995. Although this is the generation that protested against the Vietnam war and once espoused the rather limp slogans of "flower power," today, says Thomas with a somewhat cynical chuckle, "they've got kids, dogs, and mortgages. Property to take care of and lawns to cut. I mean, this sobers all of us, does it not?"

Identifying this group as a prime core of support for Harris, and by extension, perhaps, for federal Reformers, puts a dent in the widely held notion that the most diehard Harrisites fit the blanket classification of males over fifty. The male part, Thomas says, is correct: "Females tend to be more communal, a little less willing to take the bull by the horns . . . [and less likely to warm to something] branded a 'Common Sense Revolution' — I mean, that's not mild stuff, right?" But Thomas says the "over fifty" part is only partly true; as you start to look at voters further past the half-century mark, say, into their sixties and beyond, they "are actually often a little frightened by these things. They're very used to government providing stuff, and frankly it has for most of their lives."

Boomers, on the other hand, have a less rosy view of what government can and will be able to do for them in the future. "If you were to poll that group," says Thomas, "there's not one out of ten that thinks the Canada Pension Plan will take care of them when they are sixty-five." This has led to a dog-eat-dog, every-man-for-himself attitude, where the best the government can do for you is "get out of your face" and not put up any roadblocks, such as taxes, to your efforts to forge your way on your own. As for the plight of others less fortunate, much of the ageing minivan crowd believes they should be left to make it on their own too.

"They [the boomers] perceive that they work their own asses off and can't get ahead; therefore they are less sympathetic to the argument about 'let's tax more, to help the have-not part of our society.' They say, 'Look, I've paid my dues, so don't ask me for more. I've reached my limits.' I'm not giving you moral judgment on this. I'm just telling you how people feel."

So, in summary, these suburban boomers feel (1) pessimistic about the role of government, (2) less sympathetic about the plight of the poor and disadvantaged, (3) stressed out because of the daily commute and the need for two high-pressure jobs to pay down the mortgage, and (4) lacking in control over their own lives. And all of this, Thomas adds, feels worse because the fast-moving treadmill the boomers now find themselves on materialized without warning.

"When they were in school, they were told about a world in which technology would make their lives simpler. There would be less of a workweek, a lot more leisure time. They find themselves, instead, in a global marketplace, not competing with someone in the next town, but competing with someone in Tokyo or Stuttgart or Buenos Aires. So they live in a pressure-cooker world that was never really anticipated, and they're fed up. They want change."

Whichever of these two subsets of suburbanites one considers to be the core constituency of the rising populist right — the struggling blue-collar/first- and second-generation immigrant crowd, or the flower-children-turned-born-again-materialists — the appeal of those "hard-hitting comparative" TV ads out on the suburban frontier says something about the species as a whole. These people are angry. They feel cheated out of something, and they are looking for someone to blame. The simmering hostility I found at Reform's campaign office in Vaughan-King-Aurora is, it seems, spread quite liberally across the suburban landscape. But is it socially responsible for politicians to pander to that resentment and to voters' need to find scapegoats by airing those attack ads? I see this as an important question, for as I write, NATO warplanes are bombing Yugoslavia, a country whose recent history tragically illustrates how tensions can escalate when politicians choose to use ethnic and group resentments to help build their political power bases. Once you let the genie out of the bottle, who knows what it will do? We need to ask, "Where is the line that separates a legitimate recognition of voters' grievances from a demagogic exercise that will inflame irrational and destructive hostilities?"

Ontario Tory pollster John Mykytyshyn found out where that line was after he had crossed it. In February 1999 he conducted a survey in the York Region community of Thornhill, in the course of which residents were quizzed about whether or not they would support a Jewish candidate or the son of a Holocaust survivor. (The Liberal candidate in the area, Dan Ronen, is both, leading some horrified observers to the logical conclusion that the Tories were planning on using Ronen's Jewishness against him.)[14] Party officials immediately moved to denounce the poll and distance themselves from Mykytyshyn, suggesting it was the pollster himself, employed by the riding association and acting without oversight, who was responsible for the question. Premier Harris insisted: "It wasn't done by me, nor was it the PC party, nor was it authorized by us."[15] Party chair Tom Long pledged that Mykytyshyn "will not be involved in the central campaign" and said that "my heart sank when I read those questions. This is not the kind of thing anyone wants to see happen."[16] Long also wrote a letter of apology to the Canadian Jewish Congress, saying that "the questions which were being asked in the survey were completely unacceptable to the Progressive Conservative Party of Ontario."[17]

It's not much of a leap, however, to see Mykytyshyn's racial focus in the Thornhill poll as an inappropriate extension of the well-established and fruitful Tory strategy of bad-mouthing welfare recipients and the beneficiaries of pay equity programs in order to appeal to "the mean kind of person" Bryan Thomas pegged as the target viewer of the

Tories' ads in the campaign of 1995. Certainly Mykytyshyn was steeped in the culture of Harris's public relations machine, and would have been intimately familiar with the standard approach and objectives of its polling and campaign advertising.

That much is clear, despite what *Toronto Star* reporter Joel Ruimy termed "a talking campaign [by party officials] suggesting that Mykytyshyn had never been a player anyway."[18] There are several printed references to the pollster as an influential insider in the 1995 Common Sense Revolution campaign and a close acquaintance of Mike Harris. *Toronto Sun* reporter Christina Blizzard writes in her book, *Right Turn: How the Tories Took Ontario*, that "Mykytyshyn had been with Mike Harris since 1990 and had worked on the Victoria-Haliburton by-election" won by the Tories in what Blizzard calls "a dry run for the 1995 election." Blizzard also refers to Mykytyshyn as being a member of the elite Bradgate Group, the team of high-level Tory strategists — which included Tom Long and other key members of Harris's inner circle — who designed the Common Sense Revolution during meetings at Toronto's Bradgate Hotel.[19] John Ibbitson's book *Promised Land: Inside the Mike Harris Revolution* also contains two separate references to Mykytyshyn as a Bradgate Group participant.[20]

So was that Thornhill poll an aberration or just an overzealous and indiscreet extension of business-as-usual? Clearly Mykytyshyn had violated a taboo by asking voters pointed questions about whether they liked or would vote for members of an ethnic minority — an historically persecuted ethnic minority, no less. The Tories' adversaries perceived the 1995 Common Sense Revolution ads, for instance, as lightning rods for resentment against welfare recipients and against the women and minorities hired by government under "job quotas," but their creators had enough room to argue that they were really legitimate commentaries on government policies, spending priorities, and issues of "fairness."

There was similar ambiguity surrounding the Reform ads showing Charest and Chrétien with their faces crossed out. Rick Anderson strenuously complains that they were misrepresented as being anti-Quebec or anti-francophone, insisting that their real message was that Quebec politicians have dominated the debate on national unity to the exclusion of Canadians from elsewhere. But, as Marshall McLuhan would have said, television is not about carefully chosen words and nuanced arguments; it's about impressions, created by sensory cues. And so it seems much more realistic to think that English-Canadians who harbour deep-seated anti-Québécois feelings — those folks who burnt the Quebec flag in Brockville, for instance — might get the impression that Reform supports their point of view and deserves their votes.

For Bryan Thomas, who created the Reform ads, the relevant question seems not to be whether they are socially divisive, but whether they deliver votes.

"We went into this knowing that it would be perceived as quite negative, and I guess we now feel that there's a lot of people who don't like it," he says. "But in this business it's not all of the people you are looking to appeal to. It's actually a fairly narrow target group that we are looking to influence. At any given moment in an election, at least two out of three, often three out of four people have made their minds up. So it's really just this much of the pie that you're out to try to appeal to."

And by most accounts, those "hard-hitting" spots about Quebec did snare enough uncommitted voters to spur a significant surge for Reform. According to Rick Anderson, the most reliable polls "showed that we did nothing but go up very dramatically during the three days the ads were running and for about three days afterwards — which is a pretty long after-effect for an ad." But at what price did this partisan gain come? Federal PC Leader Jean Charest, for instance, fumed that the ads had renewed hostilities and damaged the cause of national unity in the wake of a Quebec sovereignty referendum that federalist forces had won only by a hair's breadth.

"He's entitled to his opinion," responds Thomas, "but the ad did what it was intended to do." End of story.

But there's more to this than images. Canada's populist revolutionaries have responded to voters' sense of alienation not just with angry
campaign ads providing a temporary catharsis, but with a political
program that promises to put them back into the loop. According to
Bryan Thomas, in focus groups suburbanites have been delivering the
resounding message "We want to control our own destiny; give us a
political platform that returns control to us." In the US, these feelings
of personal disempowerment and frustration — a daily fact of life for
suburbanites who must wrestle with the traffic and the quest to pay
down that mortgage — have long been a potent political force. They
have also pushed many jurisdictions to adopt the mechanisms of
"direct democracy," which attempt to return to an alienated, atom-
ized population some feeling of control over government actions.

These ideas have been moving north. The Ontario Tories have
stepped gingerly onto this terrain by introducing legislation that
would compel future governments to balance their budgets, except
under abnormal circumstances, and to hold referendums before
raising taxes. Federal Reformers, on the other hand, almost define
themselves by their attachment to direct democracy. They propose an
expansive and interlocking set of reforms that would fundamentally
change the Canadian political system; among these are provisions for
referendums on major issues, MP recall campaigns, and a general and
sweeping devolution of powers from the federal level, to the provincial, right down to individual communities. Says Jason Kenny, "I
think most Reformers, as small-c conservatives, intuitively believe in
the principle of subsidiarity, that local governments should be given
authority to solve problems over more senior levels of government."

In fact, it's this issue of local control that some Reformers admit
causes them some discomfort in their alliance with the Ontario Tories.
For while the Harrisites have embraced the populist rhetoric about
making government closer and more responsive to the people, in
practice they have often moved in the opposite direction, amalgamat-
ing school boards and centralizing control over education, giving
additional powers to unelected bureaucrats at Queen's Park, creating

a new Toronto megacity with a larger and more remote political system (despite a municipal referendum vote that overwhelmingly rejected the plan).

Anderson says his party's philosophical allies at Queen's Park may redeem themselves if the community councils that are supposed to accompany the megacity structure are more than window-dressing. "If it turns out," he postulates, "that neighbourhood councils really have some authority — over the zoning or the garbage collection — if their advice is taken seriously and their influence is real, then I think it will probably work. But if it turns out the neighbourhood councils aren't real and it's just a councillor and 150,000 voters, so people can't get heard about the stop sign in the street or the kids' playground or the stuff that will matter to them, then I think they [the voters] will not like the set-up."

His choice of examples says a lot about how Anderson thinks people would use their new democratic implements. The shorthand to explain this view of the public interest might be "What's in it for me?", which includes the questions "What's going on in my neighbourhood?" and, of course, "How are the politicians spending my tax dollars?" Anderson confirms that Reform's proposed redesign of Canadian democracy is based on the assumption that while people want more control of the events that affect them personally, they are relatively content to relinquish control of issues that are deemed to be outside their personal sphere.

"My perception," he says, "is that the trends around government and politics are twofold and they are in opposite directions. At one level, the trend that people have generally accepted and generally support — although they are worried a little bit about some parts of it — is the trend towards globalization, the trend towards some of the more big-picture things getting determined at the supranational level. So it's not uncommon for people to think that our rules for financial services or something would be set in international treaties or negotiations, whether it's at the NAFTA level or the WTO . . . We have willingly ceded some sovereignty to these kind of things, both in the economic area and the diplomatic area."

And yet, Anderson continues, "I think the opposite thing that the public is pushing for is that the things that matter most in their daily lives be brought under local control, which is where you get into democratic accountability. Even as they are saying Look, I understand that our level of taxes and the way our currency moves, the big-picture things, are going to be set or influenced heavily by supranational agreements — the question of whether the park has swings in it, or whether the school has a computer lab, or whether to do French immersion here, or whether the hospital has a burn-treatment unit — these decisions that most people perceive to affect their daily lives they want under the most local authority possible. In that picture, governments like the federal government of Canada are under severe stress, because they [the voters] want those decisions not just brought to Queen's Park, but right into the neighbourhood."

Anderson concedes that one problem with this hypothesis is that it is not borne out by voting patterns. Turnout remains much higher in federal and provincial elections than in municipal contests, suggesting that voters are not uninterested in the "big picture" issues at all.

Other commentators might see a hidden agenda here, believing that devolution of political power simply uses the veneer of democratic reform to assure the achievement of right-wing economic policies that help the rich stay rich and the poor stay poor. Stripping higher levels of government of their power makes it much more difficult for the federal government to transfer payments to equalize regional economic disparities, or to impose national standards that guarantee medical, educational, or social services are of an equal calibre regardless of income levels in the communities where they are delivered. Certainly, in this decentralized, devolved political environment, all communities might be able to decide whether they want a swing set in the park or a burn unit in the hospital, but in the absence of strong federal and provincial governments to smooth out inequalities, only rich communities would be able to act on those decisions.

An equally troublesome aspect of the populist vision of direct democracy is that it requires of citizens two things that are in desperately short supply: time and attention. One would think that if voters assumed more direct control over decision-making — through referendums, for instance — they would need to be equipped for the task with more and deeper information. But things seem to be going in precisely the opposite direction. Anderson believes that the number of people who base their voting decisions solely on the TV ads they see is not a majority, "but it would be approaching it." Thomas, the commercial-maker, adds that while thirty-second political spots are the standard in Canada, "as lifestyles become more and more hectic for people, we may see a trend towards shorter messages." He adds that although Canadians feel strongly enough about exercising their franchise to pay fairly close attention during an election, "between elections, most people don't give a tinker's dam about this stuff [politics]."

This raises the spectre of the opinion professionals, now an apparently intractable part of the scene in the US, with their focus groups and high-powered advertising techniques, manufacturing "hot button" issues to distract voters from the real questions about how a party has performed while in office. It also raises concerns, often voiced in jurisdictions such as California, where referendums are a major feature of political life, that such plebiscites would merely be exercises in mass advertising, where issues are sold like soap, with empty slogans instead of reasoned debate.

Thomas is not about to apologize, however, for probing the dark recesses of voters' minds in those focus groups. In an era when people are too busy to congregate in church basements, he says, populist movements have to send the professionals out to monitor their psyches.

"I view it as the ultimate form of democracy," he says. "People ultimately decide in an election, right? So the party that best understands what they are looking for is more likely to win . . . Any successful marketing campaign, political or otherwise, is basically giving people what's important to them, what they want. If you don't, they buy something else, right?"

More cynical types might point to the less flattering portrait that has emerged in the United States, where pollsters and political advertisers have taken the concept of direct democracy and created a circus of advertising pyrotechnics — all heat and very little light, lots of emotion but little context — within which it has become increasingly difficult to decide the issues intelligently. In fact, it is instructive to look south, where referendums, vastly devolved political powers, and government by TV ads have in many cases become established facts of life.

Next stop, Southern California, where it all began; where the suburban-centred spin doctors first honed their craft; where the prototypical suburban rebellion swept a neophyte politician named Ronald Reagan into the governor's chair in 1966, paving the way for the nationwide Reagan revolution that gripped the U.S. in the 1980s; where the Proposition 13 tax revolt of the late 1970s created a new mould for several decades of bellicose anti-taxation, anti-government politicking.

Today the forces that have pushed Ontario into a suburban-driven, right-wing revolt are much the same as those that coalesced in sunny California thirty years ago. Like the sharp right turn taken in Ontario in the 1990s, the earlier rightward lurch in formerly liberal California was prompted by a massive real estate boom that sent housing prices to undreamed-of heights, unleashing tremors of greed and uncertainty across the landscape. In history and social approach as well, the two jurisdictions — Ontario and California — have some uncanny similarities. Both had advanced economic infrastructures, education, and social welfare systems, produced by massive public investments and resulting in positions of economic dominance within their respective nations. Both grew up under liberal political cultures, which remain popular in the urban centres, even after the right-wing slide in the burbs. And both were in key ways victims of their own success, with their economic dominance and desirability as places to live creating sprawl, overheated real estate markets, and increasingly onerous costs of living.

One primary difference between the two locales, however, is their position on the historical continuum. When I was undertaking my research, Ontario was at the beginning of its flirtation with the politics of suburban backlash; on the verge of turning a one-term experiment with the Common Sense Revolution into a two-term dynasty; seeking to quell suburban angst through a program of tax cuts, anti-urban service reductions, and the loud proclamation of traditional values. California, on the other hand — headed into the 1998 contests to elect a governor, state assembly, Congresspeople, and various local officials — had experienced thirty years of suburban backlash politics, had paid the price, and was to some extent poised to turn away from that path.

For Canadians, regardless of political stripe, the California experience with surburban-driven politics is highly instructive. For those who seek to entrench a suburbo-centric right-wing movement north of the border, the question is this: How did California's Republicans manage to wield their influence so effectively and for so long, placing the bungalow-dwelling middle classes in the political driver's seat and throwing the bulk of the state's economic resources their way? For those with a more traditionally Canadian outlook, however, the question is more ominous: How can we avoid the mistakes of California, with its deeply polarized social order, where urban wastelands stand a short distance from bucolic suburbs — pristine, prosperous, yet paranoid — mini-paradises that are guarded and sometimes walled-in, where luxury for the more fortunate members of society comes at the price of having to constantly look over your shoulder?

part 2 | # California Dreams and Nightmares

4 | The Lie of the Land, the Lot of the People

For Canadians touching down at the San Diego International Airport in early January, Southern California seems to be everything the sun-drenched mythology promises. It's a giant, animated, 3-D postcard of swaying palm trees, warm dry breezes, and cloudless blue skies. Something close to paradise — if you ignore the daily traffic gridlock, with its pervasive perfume of exhaust and the occasional impulse to commit homicide. Such were our first impressions at least, as my wife, Laura, and I led our two sons — six-year-old Ben and eighteen-month-old Matthew — out of an airplane cabin and into four and a half months of eagerly awaited exile in the promised land. Laura had taken an academic fellowship at the University of California at San Diego — this being her sabbatical year — while I was set to divide my time between oceanside child-care duty and the gathering of trenchant observations on Southern

California's sprawling suburban scene, a scene whose tranquil surfaces and angst-filled undercurrents had become familiar even to us northerners through films such as *The Graduate*, *The Swimmer*, and — my personal favourite — *Pump Up the Volume*. We dropped into this fabled milieu just days before our home in Ottawa, the world's coldest capital, was hammered by a massive ice storm that the press immediately dubbed "the storm of the century." It made us about as lucky as Jed Clampett when his errant rifle blast unleashed a gusher of "Texas tea" and propelled his ragged clan westward to this land of "swimming pools, movie stars."

California has always, in fact, been a magnet for people looking to change their luck, to find a better and an easier life, or just to experience nicer weather. And witnessing this sprawling state's charms up close and in technicolour, it's not difficult to understand why people from all parts of the world — rich or poor; people with graduate degrees in computer science or with only their own optimism and sweat to serve them — continue to flock to the Golden State, the Land of Dreams.

Of course, anyone who has seen footage of the LA riots in 1992, of the mayhem in Watts a generation before, or of one of the Immigration and Naturalization Service's regular roundups of the illegal immigrants who wait in groups on LA street corners for offers of work, will realize that for many people California's enticing dream is nothing but a cruel mirage, a broken promise.

These two sides of life in this land serve, to Canadians, as both a temptation and a validation of what we have left behind. Business commentators have been berating the Canadian government recently with the threat that if it doesn't lower taxes, our much courted computer professionals will pack up and head for California, where they can keep more of their paycheques. True enough, there are a lot of Canadians down here who drive expensive late-model cars and spend a lot of time in swimming pools. But it all comes at a price. It must have been a bit like this to live in apartheid South Africa: you get an uneasy feeling knowing that society is so divided, feel pain in the knowledge that there is so much misery on the flipside of the glowing California dream. In a way, life here is like a premonition of what Canada may turn out to be if Mike Harris and the other anti-tax crusaders get their way: the middle class might be able to buy a lot more stuff, but there's sure to be more social strife and more hardship at the bottom, more neighbourhoods where you don't want to walk.

It didn't take long for hints of the grittier side of the California reality to pierce — ever so gently — our fantasy of the California good life. Our taxi pulled to a stop in front of our new home, the El Dorado Hills apartment complex in San Diego's suburban Tierrasanta neighbourhood — "The Island in the Hills," as the neighbourhood association's customized licence plate covers proclaimed, with all the appropriate implications of insularity that the word "island" conveys. Our cabbie, an Afghani refugee, took a wistful, longing glance at the well-tended grounds, where tropical plants had been cut and shaped by members of one of this state's numerous private militias of gardeners, and given sustenance by one of those underground-sprinkler systems that seem to reach into California's remotest corners. "This is a good neighbourhood," he said. His intent was to be reassuring, but his voice held a tinge of envy: "There will be good schools here. You can get an apartment in San Diego for $450, but they are in neighbourhoods where you don't want to raise your kids. This is a very good place."

His words were a commentary on the two-tiered nature of California society. Here, access to a decent education and the ability to walk the streets in safety is determined largely by what neighbour-hood you can afford to live in. The message was driven home to me a day or so later as I went to sign up for phone service. For people who have good credit and a social security number, California, with its prototypical post-industrial economy, is perhaps the most convenient place in the world to do business. There are drive-through banking kiosks, and the middle classes pay most of their bills by personal computer. But I was a foreigner, without a social security number, so I had to apply for a telephone in person. This quirk of fate gave me my first glimpse of the underside of the sparkling California reality, where being allowed to use a debit card was about as remote a possibility as trading in that beat-up '68 Impala for one of those gleaming Mercedes-Benzes that crowd the streets in upscale La Jolla.

The Pacific Bell office, where our phone could be activated, is located on the fringes of working-class North Park, a neighbourhood of potholed streets, liquor stores with iron rails on the windows, discount clothing outlets, and run-down bars. This is a place where you can clearly see the other face of California — its smile considerably dimmer, with lines produced not just by too much sun but by worry and hard times. Almost all of the people here are black or Hispanic, a picture that reflects the obvious and well-known fact that non-whites make up a disproportionate share of the disadvantaged in this state. A few of the customers waiting in the long line that snaked through the cavernous PacBell office, advancing by a couple paces on the worn carpet each time one of a handful of tellers' green lights flashed on, had come, as I had, to present the ID or a deposit that would secure them a new phone line. But most were here to pay their phone bills with a small packet of cash.

To a naive Canadian, the scene was a little puzzling. Why so many people paying cash? The probable answer arose quite serendipitously a few weeks later when the newspapers reported on a trip by President Bill Clinton, Congresswoman Maxine Waters, and Federal Reserve Board chief Alan Greenspan to the notoriously troubled community of South Central Los Angeles, three or four hours' drive north of here. The high-level entourage sought to publicize the fact that most American banks refuse to do business in poor, inner-city neighbourhoods and to put pressure on the banking community to start opening branches and offering credit in neighbourhoods such as these. In this way Wall Street could be seen to offer at least some kind of minimal contribution towards rebuilding blighted America and empowering its forgotten people.

Which brings us back to the people standing patiently in the PacBell office. It's a fairly safe conjecture that many of them have found themselves here, waiting to unfurl a small roll of bills in front of a teller, because they couldn't get a chequing account; no bank would consider it worthwhile to deal with them.

Another near certainty is that many of those people in the PacBell line are employed "under the table" in California's booming underground economy. The untold legions of people living in California illegally and providing discount services on a strictly cash basis to wealthier citizens are proof that this economy is an accepted fact of life here. It only becomes news when someone can use it to make political hay, such as during the 1998 California gubernatorial contest when Democratic candidate Jane Harman was found to have knowingly hired a nanny who was living in California illegally, which allowed her opponents to pounce; or earlier in the campaign when Republicans floated a hotly debated citizen-ballot initiative, Proposition 187 (since struck down as unconstitutional by the US Supreme Court)[1] that would have outlawed the provision of services such as schooling and health care to illegal immigrants. Aside from isolated blips such as these, however, the parallel underground economy is not the stuff of headlines but rather an invisible backdrop that determines how the details of many people's daily lives will be played out: that phone bills will be paid in cash, that there will be no pension plan to pay into, that an injury at work will trigger no interest from the authorities, no promise of official compensation.

This kind of invisibility — that is, being invisible to the computers, bureaucracies, and data-management firms that constantly track participants in the above-ground economy — underscores the fact that the divide between the haves and have-nots in California is no longer just a question of physical geography, with the poor living in the old urban regions and the wealthy in the newer suburbs. That urban-suburban split is now overlaid by the question of who will be granted admittance to the ethereal terrain of cyberspace, an area colonized almost entirely by comfortable middle-class people who draw their diversion from satellite dishes and their money from ATMs, and who stand a good chance of making an excellent living from some aspect of this "knowledge economy." While these people conduct their business via high-speed modem, others who are poor or perhaps illegal must linger in that slow-moving queue, waiting for the teller's green light.

The kicker to this scene in the faded PacBell office in North Park came a few months later when the San Diego *Union-Tribune* ran a story reporting that Pacific Bell, aiming to lower expenses and presumably to reinvest in the more lucrative cell phone market, was preparing to close its neighbourhood offices, against the protests of the people who use them.[2] Thus, yet another barrier is erected on this strange, two-tiered landscape: getting and keeping a phone, a pretty rudimentary lifeline in the wired world, just got that much more difficult for those who don't have the right zip code or a social security number.

But back to the physical world. If I've given the impression that San Diego consists, as many American cities do, of a bloom of prosperous suburbs surrounding a neglected and rotting urban core, the real picture is far more nuanced than that. Unlike much of the suburban region that lies a short stretch north along the Southern California coast — an endless patchwork of subdivisions, shopping malls, and industrial parks, which have long since ceased to use urban Los Angeles as any kind of reference point — most of San Diego's suburbs are within a forty-five-minute drive of the city centre. It's a centre that has retained much of its earlier charm and, in many ways, is still waiting to realize its full potential.

The jewel at the heart of downtown San Diego is Balboa Park, site of the 1911 World's Exposition but now the permanent home of roughly two dozen museums. Its ornate, human-scale Spanish colonial architecture, Old World terraces, and shaded walkways, its Japanese garden, bandshell area, and unspoiled ravines create an involving sense of public space that seems almost antithetical to the spirit of Southern California. Sure, you'll get the same crowds and bustle at some of the bigger shopping malls, or at Disneyland or Seaworld, but Balboa Park brings together a more diverse crowd and lacks the raw jolt of a throng intent on seeing more, consuming more, on getting their money's worth before the long hike back to the parking lot. In short, what makes Balboa Park different from most things in this region is that its *raison d'être* is not just commerce.

The influence of Balboa Park over the surrounding cityscape is also buttressed by the impact of its neighbour, the San Diego Zoo. Home of some reticent panda bears and several hundred other species of animals, it's the main attraction for vast numbers of tourists who descend on this city each year from all corners of the globe. I'll vouch for its reputation as possibly the best zoo in the world, not because I've seen any other of the world's great zoos, but because I have witnessed its miraculously salutary effects on a six-year-old boy suffering inconsolably from the sharp pangs of homesickness. Like my son, the city itself seems to have had its spirits lifted by the presence of the zoo and the park. With these institutions serving as anchors, downtown San Diego was never completely written off when the middle classes began their migration to remote suburbs in the 1950s. Now, with comparatively strong life signs pulsing outward from the city centre, there is a new interest in recolonizing the downtown area. Both young pilgrims grown tired of socializing at the mall, and real estate interests, feeling the environmental and economic counter-pressures against continued expansion beyond the current suburban frontier, are playing a role.

Local politicians have also begun to realize that a downtown core, particularly one that does not resemble a battle zone, is a pretty rare commodity in these parts, and that it brings some advantages, economic and otherwise. Consider the annual tribal celebration of beer and bone-crunching known as the Superbowl. It was played out so successfully in San Diego in 1998 that NFL officials announced that they wanted to bring it back there, pronto. (City councillors, meanwhile, have balked at NFL demands for more investments in the football facilities.) Sure, the game itself took place at Qualcomm Stadium, out in the suburbs where parking is plentiful and three main freeways intersect. But for the pre- and post-game carousing,

131

revellers hopped on San Diego's new high-speed electric trolleys and headed down to the Gaslamp District, a newly gentrified enclave of downtown restaurants and bars close to Balboa Park, the zoo, and the waterfront. Although the 1984 LA Olympics proved that it was possible to hold a large public celebration in a decentralized, low-density region, the point the Superbowl celebrations made more than a decade later is this: It's far preferable to stage a public pageant in a real city, with streets that have sidewalks and storefronts so the crowds can mingle, with the kind of compactness and compression that creates a sense of community and amplifies the emotion of the event.

It's clear from recent proposals before San Diego's city council that the politicians have made a priority of investing in the kinds of public infrastructure they hope will ignite more sparks of excitement in the downtown core and attract more events like the Superbowl. During my stay, the council was considering approving hundreds of millions of dollars' worth of big-ticket projects, including a new library, an expansion of the waterfront convention centre, and a new downtown ballpark where the city's beloved Padres would play. One proposal would locate a $200-million-plus (all figures used here are in US dollars) ballpark in a shabby downtown warehouse district, with adjoining facilities such as a new $110-million tower with revolving restaurant.[3] Another scheme calls for $1 billion worth of construction (the ballpark, hotels, offices, retail, and entertainment facilities) on publicly owned waterfront land.[4] In both cases, the pitch made to taxpayers is that these public expenditures will provide a major impetus to the private building and renovation binge, which as well as drawing more tourists, has already begun to entice disaffected suburbanites back to the inner city.

In fact, for the past several years now, downtown San Diego has been undergoing the same step-by-step metamorphosis that's become familiar in many of the northern US centres, where downtowns have begun to be transformed from First World versions of Beirut to paragons of urban chic. First the artists and musicians move in, setting up their working and living spaces in empty warehouses, and adding funky flavour and a certain respectability to the area. Next small businesses — restaurateurs and retailers — set up shop in clusters nearby and invite tourists and adventurous suburbanites to soak in some of the slightly edgy, Bohemian ambiance. The next stage becomes evident when those same small businesses start to complain that their rents are shooting through the roof, making it difficult to resist the pressure to vacate their premises so the big chains, attracted by the scent of a new profit centre, can plant their corporate logos in this newly revitalized territory.

So far, the "white-painting" process that has unfolded in San Diego is patchy at best, and the result is a jarringly uneven cityscape that speaks with grim honesty of the promises and failures of the American dream. Horton Plaza, a determinedly cheerful pastel high-rise shopping mall, ablaze with neon advertising endless good times at the Hard Rock Café or an endless childhood at F.A.O. Schwartz, rises in the midst of downtown streets where storefronts signs flatly state "Liquor" and "Bail Bonds." New loft apartments, meanwhile, are advertised on street corners where practically no one walks at night, amidst acres of empty warehouses and potholed parking lots. Even the celebrated Gaslamp District, where those Superbowl fans came to drink Budweiser and shooters on the eve of the big game, is only a few short blocks of scrubbed concrete and brick, tightly cordoned off by an invisible wall of resignation and despair. Walk a few hundred paces from Croce's, the Gaslamp's flagship nightclub operated by the widow of singer Jim Croce, and you're sure to encounter homeless men pushing shopping carts down the sidewalk or sleeping in doorways. This is a side of San Diego that city fathers would just as soon forget. The same council that's looking to spend a bundle on a new ballpark voted recently to close down shower facilities for the homeless, which may explain why, on downtown San Diego streets at night, the ammonialike stench of unwashed and unwell human beings becomes evident half a block before you pass a cluster of them huddled under blankets in a storefront.

But this scene should not be taken as proof that California society is divided evenly between terrific wealth and abject destitution. There are plenty of working-class neighbourhoods in close proximity to the downtown core, where the signs of a daily struggle are evident but hope is clearly not lost. Some of these neighbourhoods, North Park, for example, have older cars in the driveways, smaller homes, and certainly a lot fewer hot tubs per capita than out in the middle-class burbs. Although residents of neighbourhoods like these have not fallen off the socio-economic ladder, they nonetheless must deal with high crime rates on their streets and with schools that are badly underfunded and often controlled by street gangs.

Still, the stark contrasts on display in deepest downtown San Diego are worth holding in mind because they provide a rare opportunity to see starkly different aspects of the California dream side by side. In a state where the biggest chunk of construction has taken place since World War II — most of it conforming to the model of the modern suburb, which shunned the heterogeneity of the pre-war metropolis — most communities tend to be uniform and highly self-selecting, according to income level, race, and even political preference. Many people can live and work entirely within their own social orbit in California and rarely be reminded that a whole other universe of human experience exists only a few freeway exits away.

Tierrasanta, the suburban community where my family and I lived for close to five months, is one of those places. If your working arrangements favour it, you can spend your life in the same kind of splendid isolation as the contented villager of bygone rural America, dividing your time between home and the local shopping centre, the equivalent of the old town square. Like almost all of San Diego's suburban enclaves, Tierrasanta is isolated from its sister communities not only by the wide swaths of freeway that serve much the same function as the walls around a medieval walled city, but also by the natural topography. Our relatively unspoiled corner of southern California is a roller-coaster ride of canyons and steep hillsides. This

means that individual communities have tended to be built in discrete chunks where the terrain favours human settlement, and that suburbs are generally prevented from bleeding into one another by the natural barriers. From atop the plateau where our apartment complex rested, for instance, you could clearly see the red bricks, green backyards, and blue swimming pools of the next-closest suburban outpost. The two communities were kept separate, however, by a several-hundred-foot drop, by countless acres of uncultivated terrain that was either too rocky or too jealously guarded by residents and environmentalists to have been developed, and by the extra miles it took for the freeways to snake around the base of hillsides and into the next community.

Even within neighbourhoods, the lie of the land has a powerful effect in separating individual patches of development. For suburban San Diegans, it is as if nature had conspired with California's development industry to bring to belated fruition the English planners' vision of the "new town." Strips of greenbelt have been virtually assured by a landscape largely comprising steep grades and rocky outcroppings. Driving down Tierrasanta's main drag to our home, for instance, what was visible from the road were not housing developments but the hiking trails that wind between the clusters of homes, and the canopy of trees that lean in from either side of the asphalt. The overall effect is the fulfilment of a standard advertising copy-writer's cliché — a cliché with an unusual ring of truth in this context: a place that feels more like a small settlement in the countryside than a greener, slightly less dense extension of the city.

The word "countryside," on second thought, is too genteel a term for this rugged landscape that human beings can make no credible claim to having conquered, despite the importation of sport utility vehicles and automatic sprinkler systems. That people have only a tenuous foothold on this wild terrain was driven home to me one Saturday morning as my two sons bounded out of our apartment and down the path that leads to the parking lot. I had forgotten something and gone inside for a moment. When I caught up with them, I found

that they were now part of a small crowd gathered around something making a loud hissing sound. I thought at first it was the buzz of a live electrical wire. Turned out it was a rattlesnake, and there was Steve, the maintenance man, wielding some kind of device with long pincers, trying to move this clearly vexed reptile away from the bushes under someone's window and over to an embankment where he could be tossed towards a new life in the secluded valley below. I'm pleased to report that, after dropping the rattler a couple of times, Steve succeeded in this task. His response when I asked him about this episode was nonchalant; apparently encounters with rattlesnakes are commonplace here. We were told by others, for instance, that local daycare centres check their sandboxes every morning because the snakes love to nest in sand.

Writer and academic Mike Davis, whose most recent book is *The Ecology of Fear: Los Angeles and the Imagination of Disaster*, has included in that volume a liberal helping of scary critter stories, to illustrate the tension and ambiguity underlying Californians' relationship with nature. Those tensions often come to the fore during periods when excessive development places pressure on animals' food supply. There was a surge of angst a few years back, for example, when coyotes began entering suburban-LA neighbourhoods and attacking children; in one case, the animals carried off a small girl from her yard and killed her. Davis also recounts a horror story from the early part of this century, when mountain lions, hawks, and coyotes in Kern County were exterminated by officials. The upshot was that twenty million mice, which had been food for the predators, invaded the town of Taft; the rodents were so plentiful that some of the townsfolk had mice in their hair, which quite literally drove some of them insane.[5]

But there are other, less dramatic reminders of suburban California's tenuous relationship with nature, especially in an El Niño year. Those brilliant skies that greeted us in early January gave way in a mere week or two to frequent bursts of torrential rain, and the signs of mortal humans trying to protect their possessions from the cruel

advance of the elements were everywhere. High above the freeways, the owners of multi-million-dollar hilltop properties had laid out fluorescent tarpaulins in an effort to halt the soil erosion that threatened to undermine homes and that might have, in time, sent them plunging to lower ground. On the nightly news were disaster shots that Hollywood FX artists would have been proud of: homes buried by landslides, swimming pools filled with oozing mud, an upscale restaurant now resting on a tennis court. We had our own souvenir of El Niño nearby. Five miles down Tierrasanta Boulevard, the Murphy Canyon freeway exit had been swallowed up by a gigantic sinkhole — a Biblical-scale opening-up of the earth — to which $5 million in repair money was immediately assigned, freeway exits being a high priority in these parts. Blazing klieg lights went up so that workers could patch the hole around the clock, and the Murphy Canyon sinkhole soon became a local tourist draw, with its own newsletter to keep enthusiasts up on repair details and with motorists flocking from miles around to gaze upon this Niagara Falls of potholes.

Disasters aside, the proximity to nature is generally considered a positive aspect of life in Southern California. Try to imagine, perched on a majestic ledge overlooking our apartment complex, a row of expensive houses, their mighty barbecue flames piercing the falling dusk each night after work. The most obvious selling point of these homes was their location and the view it afforded. It's natural then that the fronts of these dwellings, with their great big picture windows, were positioned to look out over the canyon, so occupants could soak in that lovely vista. But there was a displacement effect at work here. If you took a walk along the roadway that snaked up behind these homes, you'd see how the streetscape was nothing more than a utilitarian strip of garage doors and fenced-in back entrances. So forget about front-porch chatter or a kids' street-hockey game on the empty pavement. It was obvious that the kind of social life the design of these homes was meant to encourage was the private, by-invitation-only consumption of barbecued steaks and beer in front of that beautiful, starlit panorama

stretching out over the hilltops and into the blackened void of night.

But you work with what you've got, and in the case of Tierrasanta, natural surroundings were something it had in abundance. Built on the site of Camp Elliot, a former marine corps training camp, our adopted home showed few signs of its spartan past — except for the notices posted at the entrance to hiking trails warning of "unexploded ordnance," live ammunition that might get washed down onto the pathways during the rainy season, and instructing anyone who finds some to keep their hands off it, mark the spot with a stick or a stone, and call 911. Otherwise, the make-over had been complete. Old barracks had given way to pricey houses, some with orange trees in the front yard and nearly all with signs telling which of an array of competing electronic-security companies the occupants had signed on with. The trails, which once would have been the site of gruelling, mandatory marches, were now a place for joggers and hikers and the owners of thousand-dollar mountain bikes. Indeed, the pursuit of physical perfection seemed to be the prime off-hours occupation of people in this neighbourhood.

The El Dorado Hills apartment complex, where my brood and I put down our temporary stakes, was fully integrated into this neighbourhood motif of access to the great outdoors and abundant opportunity for recreation. For a monthly rent that was well beyond the mortgage payments on our World War I–vintage Ottawa duplex, we got a small two-bedroom apartment that smacked of hastily assembled plaster and plywood, with a kitchen that never saw natural light in the middle of the day. But who spends their days indoors in Southern California? "California living at its best," the phrase the pre-recorded Voice uttered when the rental office put me on hold, was not about interior space. It was about the "quiet parklike setting," as the Voice so convincingly put it. It was about waking up at seven each morning to the gentle ping of tennis balls striking the strings of rackets. It was about being able to take a few steps past the laundry room to where a heated pool and a spa — "hot tub" to us non-Californians — promised to vapourize your cares at the end of a day. Even a walk

to the mailbox in these lush surroundings was a strangely meditative exercise. You followed a winding path past sculpted bushes, the occasional cat, and the more occasional hummingbird; exchanged pleasantries with dog-walkers and with the maintenance staff who motored by on their white golf carts; opened your mailbox and then walked back again. The overall effect was like being at a summer camp or, when the golf carts were out in force, on the set of that old British TV show from the late 1960s, *The Prisoner*. Or maybe in some kind of secular monastery. Or perhaps some combination of all three.

During the course of our stay, I had the uneasy feeling that this picture of tranquility provided some kind of confirmation of the stereotype of Southern Californians' being a bunch of vacuous hedonists who are much more content to lie beside a swimming pool than to browse in a bookstore. This is an especially disturbing thought if you think of yourself as a modestly cerebral type but find yourself starting to enjoy this life. After a while, however, you've got no choice but to go native and shrug off these anxieties. Few people in Southland — the term the *Los Angeles Times* favours for Southern California — would deny that the California lifestyle is all about *dis*connecting the brain from the rest of human experience. It's about an enveloping sensation, best reflected by the landscape itself, where human structures and the bounties of nature are intertwined to the point where it seems that one cannot exist without the other.

All of this is to say, in a roundabout way, that the California lifestyle is probably far preferable to the daily grind endured by many people elsewhere; that if you've got a reasonable amount of money (okay, a *lot* of money), life in California can be pretty good. There are beautiful beaches to walk on and lush countryside to admire; most of the movie theatres have more than ten screens; and the shopping malls, unlike their counterparts in the industrial northeast, are open-air temples to the splendour of nature, most of them built in light-coloured stone and painted in pastels to reflect the sunlight. Even in spheres where human judgment, rather than a gift of nature, is the chief determinant of success or failure, Californians seem to be doing

better than people in other places. By the mid-1990s, for instance, a California economy that had been laid low by military cutbacks at the beginning of the decade had roared back to life, mostly due to a boom in civilian high-tech. Southern California's air quality, once considered amongst the worst in the world, has even shown a marked improvement, thanks to the state's strict anti-smog regulations.

— — —

But why, if California's middle classes have so much to enjoy, are they known around the world for having fostered some particularly mean-spirited political movements? Much of California's middle class has been in a state of revolt since at least the mid-1960s, when Ronald Reagan scored his massive victory over incumbent liberal Democratic governor Pat Brown, and jumpstarted the nascent Republican crusade against socially interventionist government that, by the 1980s, catapulted Reagan into the White House for two terms. Many of Reagan's policies, designed primarily to appeal to middle-class suburbanites, had a powerful influence on the programs of other politicians, such as Margaret Thatcher in the UK. Similarly, California's prototypical tax revolt of the late 1970s — which culminated with voter approval of Proposition 13, the landmark citizen-ballot initiative requiring that any local tax increases be approved by a "supermajority" of 66 percent of voters — set the stage for a slew of similar right-wing tax revolts throughout the United States and hints of the same in Canada.

That these successful right-wing experiments were hatched in California is ironic, given that this state historically had been a pioneer in creating and generously supporting social welfare programs, and since its urban areas have consistently elected liberal politicians to office, especially at the federal level. But since the 1950s, California has become increasingly suburbanized, and suburbanites clearly have come to embrace different political ideals than their city-dwelling cousins. The influence of this group on the national stage has remained into the late 1990s, when California's suburban populist revolt was thought by many to have played itself out; consider, for instance, that

by 1998 even outgoing Republican governor Pete Wilson was calling for massive reinvestment in education[6] to counteract the dramatic decline in education standards that resulted from decades of continual cutbacks. And yet, right-wing activists in California still showed the knack for floating incendiary little trial balloons that could capture the attention of politicians and the electorate at the national level. One example is Proposition 226 — a.k.a. the Campaign Reform Initiative, colloquially referred to as the Armageddon Initiative — a referendum question accompanying the 1998 state assembly vote that aimed to dramatically reduce the ability of labour unions to support political causes and candidates. This became the model for three similar initiatives introduced nationally in Congress, and for ballot initiatives in twelve other states that would likewise dramatically restrict campaign contributions from labour unions.[7]

But if Southern California is a raging cauldron of suburban-backlash politics and middle-class hostility — a germ-warfare laboratory overseen by the mad scientists of the political right — I could discern little of this from daily life in placid Tierrasanta. Oh, sure, the occasional bumper stickers gave me pause: "If they take away our guns, how will we shoot liberals?" was one; "Politicians want citizens unarmed and ignorant" was another. It is always wise to keep back a few car lengths when one of these comes into view. But their influence on the freeways and in the parking lots seemed to be offset by the more squishy liberal/New Age–type proclamations like "Hate is not a family value" and "Practice senseless beauty and random acts of kindness."

And let me state — as a further non-scientific and completely subjective measure of the public *Zeitgeist* — that none of our neighbours seemed to fit the profile of the uptight, resentful voter you think of as the prime target of the right-wing political-image machines. You'd expect some real, hard-core conservative support in our neighbourhood, since San Diego is the home of a huge naval base, and military families are generally pegged as conservative. We got to know one military family in our complex — their five-year-old son, Peter,

played with my older son Ben — but Peter's parents seemed more pragmatic than ideological. They were primarily concerned with the issues that affected their daily lives: the deterioration of the school system through underfunding, and the erosion of the health care system since the private health-management organizations (HMOs) began to order doctors to make medical decisions with cost foremost in mind. These were the kinds of areas where the right had clearly failed to deliver any tangible benefit to ordinary people, areas where the right could no longer expect reflexive support from the mainstream of American society. Our neighbours Jim and Amy, émigrés from Wyoming and Colorado, respectively, and the owners of two gigantic poodles, were also embittered about the state of the schools, not because they had kids but because they work as teachers. We also saw no evidence of the stereotypical suburban xenophobia or racism here. There was a fairly diverse racial mix among the apartment dwellers, including a number of mixed-race couples.

But California is surprisingly pluralistic, in a political sense, and so it's possible to stumble across pockets of liberalism or conservatism that may contradict the wider trends. I decided that, if I wanted to get a truer profile of suburban Southern California — the heart of modern conservatism, which gave the world Ronald Reagan and tax revolts — I'd have to go elsewhere. And what better place to go than Orange County, just an hour and a half north on Interstate 5? Orange County, or OC as it's known in the local shorthand, is renowned as one of the most conservative jurisdictions in the United States; it is one of only two "safe" areas for Republicans running at the state level, having been in the grip of a particularly militant segment of the GOP for as long as anyone can remember. And unlike suburban San Diego, Orange County wants nothing to do with the urban parent that spawned it. Most of its inhabitants moved there to get away from the problems of Los Angeles, and for them the idea of recapturing the urban bustle and romantic feel of a true downtown, as many San Diegans apparently wanted to do, seems positively nuts. It became obvious to me that only a few miles north you could expect both the

psychological and political climates to get noticeably hotter. Equally obvious was that it was time to fill up the gas tank, find a good radio station, and see how my reticent old rented Mazda 323 would do on a real stretch of pavement.

5 | Orange County and the Origins of the Middle-Class Revolt

For most outsiders, Orange County is Disneyland, the Anaheim Angels, and possibly the NHL's Mighty Ducks. Political junkies make an entirely different set of associations. To them, OC is safe territory for the most rightward faction of the Republican party, home to such fire-breathing crusaders as Congressman Bob Dornan. Orange County was also the stomping ground of cowboy screen legend John Wayne, whose tough-guy stance and menacing drawl were emblematic of the political and social outlook of these environs, and whose name now graces the county's airport. Orange County is also the site of the largest municipal bankruptcy in modern US history, caused not by hard times but by a blind and unwavering faith in the free market: squeezed by the conflicting pressures both to provide costly infrastructure and services and to keep

taxes low, the country administrator invested heavily in derivatives and other risky financial instruments that ultimately proved about as solid a platform for public financial planning as a Las Vegas roulette wheel.

All of these have cemented OC's reputation as the spiritual home of California's political right, a reputation that has developed over a surprisingly short period of time. As its name suggests, for much of its history Orange County was not known for people or politics but for its citrus fruits. And in an earlier era, if strong political convictions were to be associated with OC, they were more likely to be of the left-wing variety. Towards the end of the last century, for instance, a rump of thirty-nine "Bible Communists" from the disbanded Oneida community in New York State attempted to replant their Utopian ideals in Santa Ana, the seat of the Orange County government.[1] This is just one of a multitude of experimental religious and socialist communities that flourished in California before the landscape came to be dominated by freeways and strip malls.

But that was then and this is now. Much of the current conservative cast of Orange County is due, according to Rob Kling, Spencer Olin, and Mark Poster, authors of *Postsuburban California: The Transformation of Orange County Since World War II*, to the impact of that war, which saw large numbers of troops stationed in southern California before being sent off across the Pacific. At the same time, aircraft manufacturers such as Douglas and Lockheed experienced enormous growth as they met the demands of the US Air Force, which also positioned Southern California for a prominent role in the wave of aerospace-industry expansion that came with the Cold War. Many of those troops who had been stationed in California were Midwesterners who, after returning to civilian life, were reluctant to bid goodbye to this Pacific paradise of warm breezes, sunny skies, and open spaces, and so began to move permanently to California. The westward exodus by former prairie dwellers was so huge that the city of Long Beach, just south of LA, came to be known in jest as "Iowa's seaport."

As the boom continued into the 1950s, however, land immediately around LA became scarce and expensive. So both the aircraft industry and residential developers set their sights on Orange County, a territory of agricultural lands and rural towns and villages to the south of Los Angeles which had gained its independence from LA County in 1889. Migrants from the Midwest and elsewhere were attracted to OC not just because of lower housing prices but also, as Kling, Olin, and Poster recount, by the "Utopian images of a trouble-free, healthy life for families [which] included modern housing, rural open space, high-quality schools, superb amenities and a temperate climate that permitted an easy-going outdoor life year-round."

But as this trio of scholars points out, the suburban Utopia-to-be quickly morphed into something that would soon be barely recognizable to the first wave of post-war suburban migrants — the type of place Joel Garreau would call the Edge City. Originally envisaged as a collection of sleepy bedroom communities providing rest for the drones of LA, Orange County developed its own independent economic base, which ultimately blossomed into a "powerful sub-regional economy." It exceeded $60 billion in 1989, ranking among the top thirty economies in the world, on a par with those of Argentina, Austria, Denmark, and Egypt. Its population also multiplied tenfold, from 200,000 in 1950 to more than two million by 1987. Given this vast growth in the population and the economy, Orange County has become increasingly self-sufficient, with 80 percent of its workforce commuting to jobs within the county by 1985.

A corollary to these transformations in the scale of enterprise and settlement has been the change in the *character* of the place. While it once was almost homogeneously white and middle-class, Orange County today is highly diverse, with large Hispanic and Asian communities, and with poor neighbourhoods, which emerged in the 1970s to challenge the idea of suburbia as a refuge for the well-to-do. In fact, Kling, Olin, and Poster contend, Orange County can no longer legitimately be termed "suburban"; to them it is a "post-suburban" region, which blends the decentralized, low-density physical form of

the suburbs with the economic dynamism and social diversity of a
traditional urban area. It makes sense that the economic growth and
the broadening of the socio-economic range in Orange County are
linked. An economy this big is sure to have a huge low-end service
component — for example, people who work in restaurants and retail
stores — which makes it certain that a big chunk of the local population will be people who eke out their survival somewhere around the
minimum wage line.[2]

The vast changes that have taken place here in the past half-century
are written plainly on the landscape as you journey between San
Diego and the interlocking web of communities that make up most of
Orange County. Starting off from the northern fringe of San Diego,
the view from the freeway is classically suburban: lots of subdivisions
with acres of homes that all look more or less the same, shopping
malls at every freeway exit, and only the occasional office tower or
industrial park. All of this comes to an abrupt end as Interstate 5
begins to bisect Camp Pendleton, an unlikely combination of military
training base and nature preserve. Refreshing expanses of open green
space and arresting plateaus are disturbed only by the packs of Huey
helicopters practising the kind of low-altitude choreography that
appeared in *Apocalypse Now*. Emerging at the northern end of Camp
Pendleton, the traffic slows in anticipation of an INS checkpoint —
where immigration officials in Ray-Bans and trooper hats gaze into
the slow-moving automobiles in search of people whose skin colour
or clothes might suggest they are not legally in the United States.
For a mile or two in advance of the checkpoint, there are yellow,
diamond-shaped signs depicting a man, a woman, and two children
holding hands and leaning forward as if running; it warns drivers that
families fearing that they will be caught by the INS may get out of
their vehicles and attempt to cross the eighty-mile-an-hour current
of traffic. Recently these symbols have become popular adornments
on the front of T-shirts.

Once past the INS checkpoint, the freeway widens, the exits
become more frequent, the traffic becomes denser but simultaneously

faster-moving than farther south — all signs that you have crossed a magical threshold into the vast megalopolitan hinterlands surrounding Los Angeles. The view from this section of the I-5 holds many things familiar to suburbanites everywhere — those shopping malls and subdivisions — but there's also a pressurized, pulsing feel to the place that speaks of a big city, less green space by the roadside, and more office towers. The farther you travel into OC the more you get the sense of a place bursting at the seams as it tries to keep up with the pace of development. Around Anaheim, where Disneyland is, there is virtually no shoulder by the side of the freeway — certainly no grass. On the main thoroughfares leading off the I-5, traffic is perpetually backed up while construction crews implant new sewer and water pipes to replace an ageing infrastructure that can't keep up with the demands of ballooning local communities and the city of hotels that surround the Magic Kingdom.

— — —

In most of my research jaunts to the OC, however, I chose not to venture as far as Anaheim, but rather to bide my time in and around Irvine, a more recent settlement whose fortunes have been tied to the rise of the high-tech, information-centred economy. Although construction began in the 1960s, Irvine officially became a city in 1971, the same year that my temporary home of Tierrasanta was officially granted the status of a separate community within the city of San Diego. By the time the City of Irvine was incorporated, therefore, the conservative onslaught had already been launched, with Ronald Reagan having served a full term as governor of California and preparing his encore performance of another four years. The Proposition 13 tax revolt was still a few years off; the trigger would be a sudden, dramatic surge in real estate prices that would lead to wild increases in property tax assessments towards the end of the decade. In a more general way, Irvine was born at a time when Orange County was much more in line with the quiet, suburban Utopia those legions of ex-servicemen had imagined. It was still primarily residential, middle-

class, and white; the freeways weren't so busy and less of the land-scape had been paved over.

I was given a unique opportunity to see how much this corner of OC had changed in just a fraction more than a generation, when reporter Peggy Goetz invited me to come into the offices of the *Irvine World News*, a local community newspaper, to look through the paper's archives. (The "world" in *Irvine World News*, as Peggy explained to me, does not signify that the paper covers international affairs. Rather, it's a throwback to when the paper was the house organ for the Irvine Company, the corporation that built this planned community. The "world" on the paper's masthead is therefore the fig-urative "world" of the Irvine Company, as in "my world and welcome to it" or "this company is a world unto itself." Although they kept the name, Peggy says, the paper was long ago spun off as a separate entity and now has no ties to the real estate giant.)

There is probably no better way to get a sense of the vast societal changes that have swept over this terrain in the past three decades than to compare today's newspapers with those of the early 1970s. Some of the shifts in tone and news judgment, of course, arise from the fact that the *Irvine World News*, and its spinoff publications serving adjacent communities, is now a journalistic enterprise rather than an Irvine Company propaganda tool. Its job is to cover the good, the bad, and the ugly, rather than simply the aspects of life in this community that will persuade people to buy real estate. So today there's a grittier feel to the paper. Although it certainly isn't the *L.A. Times*, in which homicides and freeway gun battles are a daily staple, many of its stories do reflect a sense of creeping menace, the sense of some evil encroaching from the margins or perhaps working its way into the soul of this unguarded paradise like some drug-resistant bacterium. On the day I made my way down to the warehouselike structure where a handful of *News* reporters keep their fingers on the local pulse, a crime story headlined "Dental assistant suspected of molesting two patients" had made it to the front page; it was posi-tioned just below the report "Coyote attacks dog" — a confirmation

of Mike Davis's theory about Californians' nascent terror of the natural world surrounding them. Meanwhile, page one of the *Saddleback Valley Voice*, a sister publication of the *World News*, was divided evenly between a large photo of schoolchildren holding umbrellas, positioned under the headline "Damp Days," and a story headlined "Assault of boy underscores presence of street gangs in Saddleback Valley." The latter was about another brand of California angst, one that is arguably more pervasive and of greater immediate concern than that created by the wild kingdom.

Turning to the bound volumes sitting on a high shelf in a small, cluttered conference room that doubles as the papers' archives, I found no stories about street gangs, malfeasant dental assistants, or coyote attacks in the paper's first decade of publishing. To be fair, those early editions were not all puff pieces and advertorials; they did contain some hard news stories, including the lead article from the premiere issue of January 1970, which announced that "today, Irvine stands on the threshold of becoming the first major urban community to be built according to a master plan since the founding of our capital." The construction of an entirely new city of hundreds of thousands of people from scratch is, after all, a major news event, although the editors of the first *Irvine World News* were surely not at liberty to draw out the irony in the fact of a fully planned community — where Big Brother corporation retained the right to dictate to the citizenry what colours they could paint their shutters — being constructed deep in the heartland of the libertarian right wing. Throughout 1970 and 1971 there was also extensive coverage of the ongoing political epic of lobbying, referendum-signing, and chest-thumping that led to Irvine's incorporation as a city. Many of these stories relied heavily on quotes from William R. Mason, president of the Irvine Company. Although reported in factual style, they had the kind of triumphal, heroic tone that for many readers might conjure up the phantom strains of a marching band welcoming home a winning football team.

For the most part, however, politics was clearly something that was supposed to happen elsewhere. The stock-in-trade of the early *News*

was the folksy stuff — local sports, social events, and charity shindigs — the kind of goings-on that reinforced the sense of living in a close-knit, small town. Beauty contests ranked high among these events. They provided the perfect fodder for the writers of goofball headlines who had apprenticed in a world where men were men, women were girls, and sexism was somehow cute and wholesome. Each issue from the first volume of the *IWN* seemed to contain at least one weird little essay/photo package linking the grading of female flesh to some pseudo-exotic theme. To wit, from March 1970: a shot of the new Orange County Fair Princess who, with pitchfork in hand, "gets into the spirit of the 'country fun' theme . . . aided by helpful hints from fair board president CJ Marks." Or from June 3, 1971, news that "Miss Judy Tingum, 18, who represented the East Bluff Shopping Center in the recent Hawaii Week Celebrations, was crowned queen of the festivities at the pau party staged poolside at the Newporter Inn." And from June 24, 1971, the kind of headline that anyone would want to put on their resume: "Miss Newport Beach, Level Headed and Lovely."

When women went from "Miss" to "Mrs.", they apparently stopped entering beauty contests and turned to more reflective feminine pursuits to occupy them while their husbands brought home the bacon. To wit, the headline from April 1, 1971: "Mrs. Craig Parks Sews Winningly," a reference to a needlework contest. But while these sorts of events had a decidedly downscale, country fair quality about them — the Midwestern influence, perhaps — an equally important facet of the emerging Orange County persona was its affluence. OC had a respectable number of society wives, whose celebrity entitled them to more than the usual quantity of ink. Under the banner "Fall Fashions Glitter at Benefit" in its September 1970 edition, the *News* reported breathlessly on a charity fashion show where "five hundred of Newport Harbour-Irvine's leading ladies packed out the Balboa Bay club dining room during a recent Friday luncheon hour . . . and helped hostess Pilar Wayne raise more than $9,000 for the people of Peru, who are still digging out from the

disastrous earthquake that took the lives of 50,000 on May 31." Pilar Wayne, a Peruvian herself, was also the wife of actor John Wayne and, apparently, the one woman the paper did not refer to by putting "Mrs." in front of her husband's first and last names. In fact, the Duke was a featured speaker at the charity bash. Distinguished guests, including Mrs. Barry Goldwater and Mrs. Rod Laver, received their reward for sitting politely through the Peruvian ambassador's address when their favourite Hollywood icon advanced to the podium to deliver a rousing, high-spirited speech.

Only occasionally was this catalogue of fun and unfettered expectations punctured with some inescapable reference to the turbulence of the times. This regularly took the form of tragic news from across the Pacific: "Vietnam War Claims Irvine Youth," one headline reads; another story details a woman's efforts to discover more about her husband, an airforce major, who was missing in action. Aside from these personal references to the Vietnam War, there was no indication that the United States was in the midst of massive social and political upheaval. Irvine and its environs come across as one gigantic suburban rec room, well insulated against the inclement political weather outside. Life was good, money was plentiful, gas was cheap and the family car had an eight-cylinder engine — at least, you'd get that impression from the ads for the local Cadillac dealership that appeared in every issue (which, tellingly, had been replaced by the dawn of the 1980s with a new set of pitches from the local Mercedes dealership).

And lest you get the sense that only women were intended to bide their time in leisure in the Irvine of the early 1970s, you are set straight by an article from March 1970 entitled "Tired Businessman May Be Thing of the Past." Like many similar documents of its time, this mini-manifesto constructs a glowingly optimistic vision of the future in new communities such as Irvine, based upon the assumption that the gains of the recent past (increased leisure time and prosperity due to economic expansion and technologically induced productivity gains) will continue apace, while glitches in the current system (freeways clogged with cars, humans made anxious and weary by the hectic

pace of work and life) can simply be engineered out of existence by competent planners, which, in this case, meant architects.

The article says that the cause of the businessman's fatigue goes much deeper than "his routine work if his office is in the heart of one of the typical downtowns in America. There is, first of all, the long and wearisome drive from Suburbia where he lives, the blaring horns, congestion and architectural monotony, the never-ending search for a decent place to park or eat, and lastly, the eternal view from his office window of concrete, asphalt and full parking lots." These, of course, were manageable details which were sure to disappear if the businessman in question decided to work and live in Irvine, given that "the drive (or sometimes healthy walk) from one of the nine communities in Irvine takes only a few minutes." By checking into this new life, the businessman's malaise would dissolve. The view from his office window would be tranquil and soothing, and his work routine would often overlap with leisure: "In his own building or one of the seven high-rise structures planned for the Plaza," the article continues, "he will deal with brokerage houses, banks, insurance firms and professional men. A few steps down the tree-lined street is a medical center with all related facilities. In the center is Fashion Island, one of the largest and most beautiful shopping centers in the world. Here he has an opportunity to shop, get a haircut and shoeshine, and choose one of the fine restaurants for lunch or a snack." Then the kicker, speaking to a vision of labour-management relations that would strike most toilers of the 1990s as a science-fiction vision of life on another planet: "When he returns from lunch, he may decide to take the afternoon off and join a foursome on one of the two golf courses abounding his office building."

When I mention this article to Peggy Goetz, she hears the title — "Tired Businessman May Be Thing of the Past" — and bursts into unrestrained laughter, followed by an emphatic "I don't think so!" Well, yes, you can file this one away with those artists' drawings of the robot in the kitchen preparing breakfast for Future Family before they take their personal spacecraft to work and school. Tired

businessmen, to be sure, have no more receded into history than Irvinites have been delivered from the scourge of Southern California traffic jams. Still, the scene a few megablocks down the road from the *News*, at the shopping mall food court where Peggy and I have since relocated, is proof that things have turned out pretty well for most Californians since that glowing prophecy was penned in 1970. Brilliant sunlight is streaming onto the shopping mall's reflective stone terrace, the lunch crowd all look impeccably dressed and well-fed, and the restaurants appear to offer just about every type of cuisine known to humanity. Despite this, it's clear that many aspects of the good life that the pioneers of Irvine living took for granted are irretrievably lost. Consequently life has become, in some respects, a lot tougher even as material wealth has increased. Having one spouse stay home to look after domestic and family concerns is, of course, now economically impossible for many families with increasingly onerous mortgages. And while consumer goods seem to have become more plentiful and sophisticated, the leisure time to enjoy them has dropped; taking an afternoon off to play golf has become an almost unthinkable liberty for most white-collar workers. And so, having spent the morning filling my head with news reports from Irvine's early days, when the future was still young and optimism reigned, I can't shake this notion that the conservative backlash of the past three decades came about mostly because an older generation of Southern Californians were promised an enchanted life that could only get better, and when problems started to arise — the work/time crunch, increased crime, heavier traffic jams — they had to find somebody to blame for the loss of their perfect future. Even though the life of a middle-class Californian would be unimaginably bountiful to the bulk of the world's population — the shopping malls keep being built, filled with ever more wonderful techno-gadgets — you can still hear prosperous white folks speak of their sense of loss, betrayal, even victimization at what has happened to their lives.

When I ask Peggy about this idea that diminishing expectations are behind the conservative backlash in California, she accepts it only to

a point. In some respects, she believes, the Tired Businessman article got it right: life does become easier in these idyllic surroundings, and people here know it.

"Actually," she says, "I think people do enjoy the amenities here. If you're here on a weekend, you see people in the parks and hills; every night you see people jogging. And there's all these golfers. The part that hasn't worked out is related to the whole culture, not just to life here. The point is that to live anywhere now you have to have both spouses working. Life is just very, very busy when you have two people working in your family. In the 1980s, there was an economic downturn and a lot of companies downsized. They didn't downsize their task; they downsized their workforce. Life is very busy and I think it's tied to the economy."

But if you had a choice of anywhere in the world to bide your time through a post-downsizing decade, Peggy suggests that anywhere should be Irvine. Having moved here as a teenager in 1963, after her father took on the post of founding dean of the biology department at the new University of California at Irvine (UCI), she has remained, quite simply, nuts about the place. Ask Peggy about any aspect of life in Irvine, and the accolades will flow. "We really have excellent schools all around," she says in response to a question about how heated educational issues have become in California. But what about the lack of street life? Wouldn't she prefer a place that had, say, some kind of café scene? "No, because I think we have that. We have a coffee shop right across the street from our house. And we go over there, we see people we know." How about the arts? Don't urbanites have the advantage of easy access to art galleries and theatres? "We have that," she responds again. "The Berkeley Theatre is at UCI. Costa Mesa [just down the I-5], there is live theatre there, and a fine arts centre. I check the movies every week for Irvine, and there must be fifty screens going every week in this city. There are fascinating people — we may not have as many bums or colourful poor people, but you know, you just sit here for a day and you'll see people from all over the world. And if you are outgoing and you talk to

them, you'll find there are so many interesting people here."

The one thing they also have in abundance here that Peggy isn't so thrilled about is people whose politics, by her assessment, can be classified as extremist. When her parents moved here from funky, liberal Berkeley, she recounts, "they were the only Democrats in their precinct." The balance has shifted somewhat within Irvine, largely because of the influence of UCI, which has come to occupy a prominent place in the town. But this and the environs still provide a very comfortable home for a far-right fringe for whom the mainstream of the Republican party is almost too tame. Peggy says, for example, that down the road in the City of Orange where the school board is "way out there, way over the deep end in the reactionary area," teaching in any language but English has been outlawed, while the provision of school lunches has been prohibited, since lunch programs are federally funded and the board is philosophically opposed to taking federal money.

Peggy has done a lot of thinking about why such a cosmopolitan and in some ways avant-garde region — it has certainly been in the forefront of the technological revolution, even if the same can't be said about art or culture — should provide such fertile ground for a political movement whose agenda is rooted in the past. Her view is that the conservative machine has not so much been fuelled by fear of declining living standards, as I postulated, but rather by a desire to maintain a sense of personal identity in the midst of a society growing beyond recognition. Economic insecurity isn't a real motivator, she believes, since any economic pressure felt by the professional classes arises not because they don't have money to live, but because they don't have the money to buy everything they are expected to own. In this culture, "there's so much," she says, "so much to buy, so much to keep up with. People feel the need to keep up. I mean, your kids come home from school and they say, 'All the other kids have a certain kind of clothes,' and everybody responds to that to a certain degree."

It's clear that the neo-con economic program — the limits on government spending imposed by the tax revolt, for example — must

have shifted some of the burden for social spending off the shoulders of California's affluent, allowing them to keep up with their neighbours in the escalating consumer contest. This would account for all those Mercedes and Jaguars on the freeways, and for the preponderance of upmarket retailers in suburban shopping malls. According to author Peter Schrag, the effects of both tax policy and broader economic trends in improving the lot of the rich are also statistically quantifiable. In 1992, for instance, despite an ongoing recession, California's top-bracket incomes were higher than they had ever been, while the state's tax burden as a percentage of income had dropped. Overall the gap between the top and bottom 20 percent of income earners has been growing faster in California than most other places in the US. This has been exacerbated in the 1990s, as low-income tax breaks like the renter's tax credit were abolished, while corporate and business taxes were cut by $2.3 billion a year.[3]

Peggy Goetz believes, however, that the economic impacts of these policies are not as dramatic as they seem, and that most people are aware that they'll wind up paying, in one way or another, for much of what no longer comes out of government tax revenues. "What we saw after Proposition 13 was that every time you turn around you've got to pay for something for your kid at school, whereas before it was paid for out of your taxes," she says. While such user fees have hit everyone who uses basic services, the freeze on property taxes also reassigned the burden for municipal services to more recent homeowners through the creation of "Mello-Roos districts" — special taxation zones where the money to fund the infrastructural services needed for new homes is raised through development fees that are passed on to the new homeowners through a clause in their deeds. Thus, a two-tier tax system has arisen: those whose homes were built before Proposition 13 and those who bought after it.

But the question of who pays and how much is really almost beside the point, the reporter believes. The real purpose of the tax-cutting policies and anti-government rhetoric that have become sacred tenets of the political right is to reassure the individual that his or her voice

has not been lost as distinct communities are swallowed by suburban sprawl and governments have become increasingly remote and inaccessible. To Peggy Goetz, what's behind California's suburban conservatism is a desire to return to the days when individual citizens could ramble down to the local town council meeting, tell the politicians what they want their tax money spent on, and be heard and heeded. The only problem, she says, is that in a big-city context it can't possibly work.

"If you've got a little town of five hundred people you can probably co-operatively get together and do more things, but when you're dealing with a big population of 100,000, you can't do that. You could never come to an agreement. And I think sometimes people in this very idealistic way would like to have the freedom of a very small community, where you could know everyone, where you could all agree, you know what I mean? But it doesn't fit in a city, never has."

What makes this notion of returning to a small-scale, participatory democracy so compelling for so many people is that well within the lifespan of one generation of suburban émigrés, an entire way of life has disappeared, supplanted by something unknown and alien. But during the years this transition was taking place, so Peggy believes, the memory of that former life back in the Midwest (or wherever) has become blurred and distorted. The result is that many people cling to a romantic vision of a lost era that is about as realistic as John Wayne's cinematic portrayals of the Wild West.

"America used to be — like Canada used to be — a nation of small towns. It's really different to live in a small town. I think that people are really nostalgic about the good things in a small town, but they've kind of forgotten what the bad things are. And there are lots of them. Everybody knows your business. There's a lot of pressure — it's a lot easier to be different in a city. If you're in a minority, I think it's probably better to be in a minority in a city than a small town. [But] I do think people have a kind of nostalgia for the control you would feel over your life in a small town. I even have that nostalgia for Irvine when it was small. I used to feel it was really nice that you know the

mayor lives on your street, or that you run into your councillor in the grocery store. I mean, that is a sort of nice idea."

Peggy believes that the need to recapture this lost, human-scale past is expressed through more than right-wing economic programs, which speak of a pitched battle between big government and the downtrodden individual. Other important parts of the package are the cultural labels — fundamentalist Christian, private school supporter, and so on — that suburbanites use to identify themselves as part of the populist revolt. These are the necessary tools for building a strong personal identity, which in turn will attract people of similar persuasions into your orbit, she says. Doing this is part of a survival strategy; if you don't have a pre-formed, cohesive community on the street where you live, you've got to build a more virtual one to surround you, assembling the pieces from wherever you find people of like mind.

"I think the popularity of fundamentalist churches is part of the need for community," she says. "It's part of living in a place where you don't know your neighbours anymore. You look for a community. My own personal theory is that you can only deal with a certain size community; as a human being, there are only a certain number of people you can deal with in your life. So you search for people who are like you, who will support who you are, who will complement you in some way. People used to do that by moving to a place, to a small town, where the people would be like them. Now people have to accumulate that for themselves. You might do that by going to church. You might do it in your job. You might do it by choosing to send your child to a more strict school, so the other parents in that school would agree with your parenting techniques. So your community becomes a lot smaller and more supportive."

Is this quest to return to an idealized past — say, by restating one's commitment to "traditional morality" or "family values" by joining a fundamentalist church — a part of suburban life everywhere, or is it more specfic to this particular landscape?

Certainly the scale and intensity of change in California's post-suburban pastures are likely to create a stronger desire to turn the

clock back. Population growth has been massive here, creating conditions of overcrowding and alienation that are sure to drive people to seek shelter in smaller, more supportive social groups. And while the United States is said to have a much more mobile population than Canada, this is especially evident in California, where the number of out-of-state licence plates on the highways indicated that large numbers of people had been drawn towards economically robust California in search of work.

The state's ominous undercurrent of racial animosity is another factor that would reinforce the seige mentality among affluent, white suburbanites in places like Orange County, causing them to seek comfort in the company of people just like them, and to idealize the notion of a lost golden age when their values were the values of the majority. But there's a simpler and more pragmatic reason the social lives of many SoCal suburbanites now centre, for instance, on fundamentalist churches. These institutions have become major social-service providers, jumping in to fill the void left by a retreating public sector. Of the four daycare centres we observed close to our suburban San Diego apartment, for instance, all were church-run.

Still, that nostalgic impulse, the revival of social conservatism that Peggy Goetz observes in Irvine, would not be out of place in most suburbs — even those far to the northeast in the 905 fringe surrounding Toronto. The TV preachers who transmit their conservative messages from vast churches-cum-studios on the outskirts of Dallas or Anaheim have counterparts broadcasting from vast TV temples near the Toronto airport, while fringe religious parties now field candidates during elections. Of course the Christian right is much more powerful in the US than in Canada, where the desire to re-create a more traditional social order is mostly a secular quest. The conditions that support this nostalgic movement are certainly evident in the 905 belt. To wit, as was indicated earlier, growth in places like York Region has proceeded at a dizzying pace, and the ubiquitous, panic-inducing managerial-class grind of spending too much time on highways and at work, and too little time with family and friends, is

long established. Also, as the Tory adman Bryan Thomas told me, although many 905ers are ex-urbanites, another significant chunk of them are people who grew up in rural areas but migrated to take advantage of the big city's economic machine; despite making daily trips to the city, their values are still those of the small town.

6 | Ballot-Box Gunslingers and the Fight for the New West

Although suburb dwellers have had to be content, as reporter Peggy Goetz suggests, with re-creating merely the psychological dimensions of small-town life, this longing for the past has recently found a more concrete expression. A change in the approach of town planners has revived the option of finding small-town values in the *physical* form of a . . . well, a small town. So-called neo-traditional housing developments, as pioneered by the architectural firm of Plater-Zyberk — at first along a stretch of the Florida coast known as the "redneck Riviera," then in California and other states caught in a land/population squeeze[1] — have attracted considerable attention mostly for the way they use traditional planning techniques to mitigate the effects of suburban development on the natural environment and on resource-consumption levels. Houses are built taller on narrower lots, so as to house more people

on less land. Similarly the integration of residential and commercial building functions and the resurrection of the back laneway for parking and deliveries are attempts to dislodge the car from its central place on the streetscape and to discourage automobile use. Cumulatively the lifestyle these neo-traditional developments aim to stimulate, as a kind of antidote to the typical post-war suburban existence centred on cars, shopping malls, and television, is one where neighbours will feel inclined to walk the streets, use public parks, and get to know one another. Neo-traditional developments therefore tend to be seen by people in some jurisdictions, such as Toronto, as a response to the success of urban revival, with its Victorian architecture and colourful streetscapes, and a repudiation of the low-density, privatized post-war suburban dream. A new development in suburban Markham, for instance, called Cornell, promises the same bustling urban compactness and similar architectural styles to what exists in downtown neighbourhoods like the Annex.

Yet when University of Wisconsin geographer Karen Till examined the neo-traditional town in the context of California's persistent conditions of social anomie and suburban paranoia, she saw the effects of this new design wave as consistent with the social impact of older styles of suburbanization. Focusing not on building design and planning principles but on the promotional materials used to sell the neo-traditional community of Rancho Santa Margarita (just a few miles inland from Irvine), Till discovered that what the developers were really selling was a sense of identity and belonging, membership in a group that would choose to define itself by the values and cultural background of the family that had owned the land since 1882.

In its promotional campaign, the Santa Margarita Company had obviously applied a lot of its creative energy to crafting a community mythology, a sense of familial lineage, that members of its target market would feel comfortable buying into. Through its regular newsletters, "printed with brown ink and Western-style fonts" on "textured and tan pages," the company advanced the legend of Richard O'Neill Sr., the "banty-legged Irish cattleman" whom fate brought

from County Cork to Orange County in the 1800s and whose descendants today control the development company that is turning a portion of his original ranch into this neo-trad subdivision. The O'Neill family patriarch's story runs completely in step with the familiar mythology of the taming of the West. The newsletters, according to Till's précis, recount how the pioneer "imported Texas shorthorns, put in feed lots and crops, 'waged war on squatters and wild hogs in the San Mateo,' and welcomed the arrival of the Santa Fe Railroad line." Lest one discount the importance of this sort of myth-making, writing it off as some kind of frill or make-work project for unemployed PR artists, Till points out that in other cases where no such community memory accompanies a piece of developable land, the builders sometimes feel the need to make one up. The developers of the neo-traditional town of Montgomery Village, New Jersey, for instance, created a completely fictional tale. It told of a hard-working Dutch family who settled in the current-day Somerset County and whose rise to prosperity preceded and perhaps foreshadowed the arrival of Montgomery Village, a mass-produced subdivision whose "historic" architecture is as bogus as anything at Disney World or Canada's Wonderland.

These family histories act as a magnet to attract potential residents with similar social outlooks, thereby diminishing the possibility that chance would populate these close-packed, higher-density villages with people whose political views or social values might lead them to fisticuffs or fire-bombing. Generally the stories are designed to appeal to people whose social perspective can be summed up in the word "conservative." Central to these stories, whether fictional or true, is the inescapable idea that a strong work ethic is the key to success. This is a convenient and reassuring message for the average middle-class denizen of California's conservative heartland, who is likely to believe in abolishing welfare and cutting taxes in order to spur private initiative. The company stories also address the ambivalence of many Californians on ecological issues: The settler O'Neill tamed wild lands for human use, but the newsletters also assure the public that the

Santa Margarita Company will live up to the O'Neill family commitment to "caring for the land." The family saga also embodies a
pre-feminist worldview, a comfort to many Californians who turn to
conservative Christianity for their road map on family relations. As
Till writes, "the only female in the O'Neill story is described in terms
of her European ancestry and ability to reproduce: 'a descendent of
Spanish stock which arrived in California in 1781, Marguerite also
brought Rancho Mission Viejo's heritage full circle.'" Perhaps the
most disturbing implication in the O'Neill script, however, concerns
race. Beyond the fact that this story is told solely from the perspective
of a white European during the conquest of the West, Till wonders
what to make of that statement about Richard O'Neill waging war on
squatters. Who were these squatters? Indians? Mexicans? Chinese?
Blacks? Written in an era when many whites in Los Angeles and the
surrounding communities are feeling besieged, perhaps even at war,
with non-white populations, the story of the great patriarch O'Neill
could easily be taken as a codified commitment that Rancho Santa
Margarita will remain a bastion and defender of white culture and
traditions, on guard against invasion by non-white "squatters" or
interlopers from LA — and as a signal to non-whites that they are not
welcome here.[2]

Of course, attempts to keep blacks and other minorities out of
white neighbourhoods are nothing new to Southern California, and in
the past they have been undertaken with considerably less subtlety.
An appreciation of the tangled and tragic history of race relations
in this sometimes treacherous paradise is key to understanding the
convulsive political events — from the rise of Reagan to the battle
over Proposition 13 to the present — that have shaken the social landscape like a sudden shifting of tectonic plates.

On the face of it California is a highly pluralistic society, with
only 40 percent of its population now being white. And Southland
(to revert to that *L.A. Times*-ism) is a region that has rarely been
controlled by a WASP elite. Instead, power has routinely shifted from
one group to another, with old-stock Mexicans, an established Anglo-

Californian elite, an early influx of German-Jewish merchants, and newer waves of Japanese, British, and even Canadian investors, all taking turns exerting their influence within LA's shifting, multi-polar power class. Even so, there is a history of racist legislation and restriction in these parts that seems more characteristic of the Deep South.

As Mike Davis recounts in his landmark book *City of Quartz*, deed restrictions — specifying that particular properties must remain in white hands — were an important means of maintaining a "white wall" that restrained the growth of black neighbourhoods in Los Angeles, from the second decade in this century until the US Supreme Court outlawed them in 1948. At the same time, in neighbourhoods where racial ownership restrictions had not been written into property deeds, homeowners' associations — some of them with names such as the Anti-African Housing Association and the White Home Owners' Protective Association — sprang up to keep blacks and other non-whites from buying homes in white neighbourhoods. Such homeowners' organizations, which choose their names much more carefully now than in the 1920s, have since become ubiquitous on Southern California's political scene. They are particularly active in affluent suburbs, where they played a key role in mobilizing support for the Proposition 13 tax revolt in the 1970s, and where they now routinely perform quasi-governmental regulatory functions, often with greater funding and more political clout than downsized, tax-starved local governments. Although the racist origins of these organizations are often forgotten, Davis recounts that enforcing segregation was their primary purpose before the 1950s. White homeowner groups successfully filed hundreds of lawsuits prohibiting blacks, Filipinos, and Native Americans from occupying homes in their neighbourhoods, thanks in part to numerous racist state laws that remained in place even after racial deed restrictions had been struck down.[3]

When, around the time of the Korean War, minorities were finally able to buy into neighbourhoods such as South Central Los Angeles, they found that much of the tax base of these neighbourhoods, along with many of the employment opportunities, were in the process of

migrating to the suburbs along with departing white residents. Davis describes how the development industry engineered a new means of subsidizing "white flight" to the new 1950s suburbs, through a scheme first put into practice in the new community of Lakewood, just north of Long Beach, which contained the United States' first regional shopping centre. The "Lakewood Plan" called first for the incorporation of these "minimal cities" as separate political entities, so as to avoid absorption into the larger metropolitan region. The point of this was to avoid paying taxes that would be equalized across the region and applied to services delivered to older city neighbourhoods, and also to give suburban residents the legal framework to practise the "fiscal zoning" that would screen out renters and lower-income housing and compel developers to "gold-plate" their housing, thereby guaranteeing continued rises in suburban property values.

The second aspect of the Lakewood Plan was for the new cities to avoid the usual costs of running separate municipal governments by contracting, at cutrate prices, services from LA County — an arrangement that amounted to an outright subsidization of services for upper-income suburbanites by poorer residents in older neighbourhoods. While the Lakewood Plan was replicated throughout the suburban frontiers of LA, another big break was granted to this wave of suburban exiles. The state government in Sacramento passed the Bradley-Burns Act in 1956, allowing local governments to fund municipal services through one percent of the sales tax collected within their jurisdiction. Since sales taxes are said to be "regressive" and property taxes "progressive" — progressive meaning it's a tax levied according to the ability to pay, and regressive the reverse — suburbanites had again won at the expense of poorer city-dwellers. Affluent suburbanites who had more money to spend on consumer goods would consequently have better-funded local services than city folk on tighter budgets.

According to Davis, "Lakewoodization" and Bradley-Burns both provided the impetus for "the sorting out of [LA] county's population between zones of single-family homeowners (the majority in low-

tax-rate minimal cities) and renters (the increasing majority in higher-tax older cities)," thereby "producing widening income and racial divides." All of this precipitated a rapid downward spiral where the increasingly impoverished, overtaxed, and underserviced core areas of Los Angeles saw their tax base further eroded when, in competition with the ascendent suburbs, they became less able to attract and keep businesses and taxpaying residents. Writes Davis:

> The affluent enclaves with their gold-plated, ever-rising property values tend to steal higher income taxpayers as well as shopping malls from primate cities and needier suburbs . . . The huge magnet of fiscal zoning has also sucked hundreds of industries out of the heart of Los Angeles. In 1977 the *Times* reported that the city was losing up to 50 firms a year to the suburbs and Orange County, a trend that only increased in the 1980s with the flight of industry and warehousing to the Inland Empire. Not surprisingly black workers, less mobile than their jobs because of de facto residential segregation, have suffered disproportionately from this relocation of industry.[4]

It's against this backdrop of racial tension and deepening social polarization that the momentous events in California's recent political past have been played out. The rise of Ronald Reagan and the Proposition 13 tax revolt are both seen as bellwethers of a new era across the United States and even beyond — turning points that marked the end of the New Deal epoch of enlightened government intervention and its replacement with the rule of the New Right. Both Reagan and the anti-tax movement enjoyed their first glimmers of political success in the restless suburban hinterlands that had mushroomed around LA. This was entirely logical, given that it was on this terrain that a very conservative middle class was coming face-to-face with the harbingers of a very alien future: vast population growth that was changing the shape and scope of communities, immigration patterns and

demographic shifts that were altering the complexion of the state, student unrest on campus, and the rise of feminism. So white, affluent conservatives began to dig in, trying to re-create the ambiance of the small town in their sheltered suburban valleys and subdivisions, fighting to preserve traditional American values either celebrated openly or furtively acknowledged in whispers and winks: love of home and family, individual enterprise, and more ominously, racial discrimination. The more the Gomorrah of Los Angeles descended into poverty, despair, and crime — conditions caused largely by the white suburban exodus and the associated pilfering of public resources — the more many white suburbanites' racist notions were confirmed: "Look what happens when those people take over the old neighbourhood." Deepening social unrest made any kind of rapprochement a more remote possibility. It also confirmed the views of an increasing number of privileged southern Californians who had rejected the policies of FDR's New Deal and LBJ's Great Society, both of which had directed government might against the burdens of poverty, social injustice, and racial inequity. Distrust was solidified, fears compounded, and battle lines were drawn in cement.

But if the American right-wing renaissance has sprung in large measure from the conservative, traditional mindset of a big chunk of the population in Southern California, it also owes much of its success to the more futuristic, cutting-edge aspects of life here. The success of this movement is attributable not just to a new ideology, which spoke to the concerns of the suburban middle-class, but also to the movement's pioneering work in redesigning the mechanics of politicking — so that a new breed of conservative spokesmen would be able to aim their message more directly into the living rooms of their constituents. It's no surprise that this should happen on this landscape. Since so much of its growth took place in the post–World War II years, Southern California has served as an early predictor of the way much of the population of North America would wind up living; the constant expansion of low-density, sprawling suburbs, for instance,

diminished the role of the public gathering place — convention centre, town squares — as a nexus for social interaction, increasing the power of television.

This has exerted a tremendous influence on the practice of politics. Fast-forwarding three decades to the late 1990s, we can see that the dominance of TV has created an almost entirely new relationship between aspirants to public office and the voting public. It is the centrality of television, says pundit Joe Klein, that had, by the time of the 1998 California gubernatorial race, made the state's politics almost entirely captive to "the limitless grotesqueries of money politics." In that contest, all previous spending restraints were shattered when a new and unknown candidate — former airline executive Al Checchi, a Democratic contender — attempted to establish a political profile for himself and convince the electorate that he was a serious candidate. Given the geographic constraints, the only way this feat could be accomplished was by buying huge amounts of television-ad time. "The state, it is said, is just too enormous [and spread out] for old-fashioned electoral ceremonies, like speeches, rallies and handshakes; campaigns for statewide office are exercises in tele-marketing," according to Klein.[5]

Checchi spent $18 million buying TV time before the first day of spring for an election campaign that would run till October. One effect of his massive spending spree was that TV stations began to raise the price of their spots; this inflation in turn made it difficult for Checchi's lesser-funded rivals to compete in the battle of the thirty-second spot. (Despite his deep pockets, Checchi did not become governor; the victor was lesser-funded fellow Democrat Gray Davis.)

But back to the beginning. The conditions that precipitated the rise of this big-bucks, telecentric style of politics — primarily the growth of those scattered, low-density suburban settlements — have been well established in California for decades. And so, in retrospect, it's not surprising that the New Right's breakthrough candidate in the mid-1960s, Ronald Reagan (derided by his political opponents of the time for his lack of political experience), would be, first of all, a

product of this peculiar landscape, and second, someone with a ready-made television image. Reagan has often been characterized as a Hollywood B-movie actor, famous for a cinematic oeuvre that included such classics as *Bedtime for Bonzo*. In reality, the actor's film career, which was ancient history by the 1966 California gubernatorial race, had little to do with his political success; it was Reagan's later work in television, as the congenial host of CBS's *General Electric Theater*, that established the candidate as a welcomed guest in the living rooms of middle America. "Reagan as host," writes presidential biographer Garry Wills, "was given a vehicle for becoming familiar to a whole new generation of young people who would later vote for him. They were the first television generation, being introduced to the man who would use television better than any other politician."[6] In fact, Reagan is a key historical figure in shaping not just television-era politics but television itself; for it was Reagan who, as president of the Screen Actors' Guild (SAG) in the early 1950s, signed a confidential waiver allowing the Music Corporation of America (MCA) to act both as a talent agent and as a producer of television programs, a dual role hitherto considered a conflict of interest. By engineering the secret deal (which was later cause for Reagan to be investigated by federal authorities, although the Justice Department decided not to indict the actor), the future American president helped craft a new structure for the US entertainment industry. Television production would be centred in both New York and Los Angeles, as opposed to being based solely in New York, as it had been in the early 1950s; and talent agencies such as MCA would wield as much clout in Hollywood as the old studio bosses, partly by virtue of being able to increase their revenues through the kind of "vertically integrated" corporate structure that allowed them to both represent talent and own the production companies hiring the talent, an arrangement that made it possible for such conglomerates to collect a percentage on both ends of a single deal.[7]

Reagan was not the first politician, of course, to use TV to good effect. In the early 1950s Republican presidential candidate Dwight D. Eisenhower's resounding victory over Democrat Adlai Stevenson

— recognized as a far superior stump speaker — was credited largely to the pioneering television ads created for Eisenhower by Rosser Reeves, the advertising legend responsible for stocking middle America's medicine cabinets with large quantities of Listerine and Bayer Aspirin.[8] A decade later the smooth performance of John F. Kennedy in a televised debate with Richard Nixon was cited as the deciding factor in ending the Eisenhower era and bringing a Democrat back into the White House.

Yet Reagan's watershed first campaign for California governor differed from those efforts in that it did not merely use television as an adjunct to a traditional campaign. Rather, it led to a reconfiguration of political campaigning, with TV addresses displacing more traditional means of politicking and requiring the recruitment of a new class of campaign professionals with entirely new job descriptions. "Reagan was the first politician to ignore the traditional pageantry of the political campaign — the long rallies, handshaking tours, dawn-to-midnight rallies — and rely so heavily on television," writes Bill Boyarsky, another Reagan biographer, referring to Reagan's first run at the office of governor in California.[9] Paradoxically, although this sort of television-centred campaign required special qualities on the part of the candidate, it was also introduced — in Reagan's case — within the context of a professionalization of political campaigning that required a coterie of handlers, spin doctors, and manipulators. Eventually this would mutate into the brand of specialist–directed "hot button" campaigns — as frenetic, as technologized, as responsive to minute trends as the contemporary practice of stock trading — which have risen to the fore in most First World electoral contests. Canadians will recognize much of this in our own recent political history: Pierre Trudeau, an avowed student of Marshall McLuhan's ruminations on media, used television to enormous effect, while sophisticated polling and opinion manipulation have become standard features of politics both federally and provincially.

Two archetypal figures in the new politics, forerunners of the current breed of political manipulators, were clinical psychologists Dr. Stanley Plog and Dr. Kenneth Holden. Partners in the Behavior Sciences Corporation (BASICO), they were hired by the Republicans to mould citizen Reagan into a functional political candidate. Their primary tasks were to prime the candidate for question-and-answer sessions and to massage his moods. Plog and Holden set up shop with Reagan in a beach house in Malibu, where, using flash cards, they trained the actor to think about California politics thematically — in line with the campaign slogan of "the creative society," a phrase that had been borrowed from a far-right preacher named W.S. McBirnie. The psychologists also devised a schedule for Reagan that allowed for regular periods of rest, part of a regime that aimed to keep the candidate in peak form and to avoid straying from the campaign script or from his own bright, affirmative persona.

The irony in all this is that Reagan was the candidate of a right-wing, populist groundswell that had vehemently rejected mass advertising techniques and psychological conditioning as underhanded and un-American. Their suspicions inflamed by ideas put forth in Vance Packard's book *The Hidden Persuaders*, these far-right Republican partisans had blamed Barry Goldwater's defeat in the 1964 presidential election on the Democrats' use of psychological manipulation. Writes Garry Wills: "Social engineering was a swearword on the right. Yet Reagan was the first candidate to be engineered by professionals at that arcane calling." Wills also cites Herbert Baus, who wrote that "a major innovation, of clinical interest as a breakthrough in political technology, was the role played in the Reagan campaign by Behavior Sciences Corporation."[10]

Reagan's basic platform, calling for less government, lower taxation, a paring down of the welfare state, and more incentives for private initiative, was not new; these same ideas had drawn suburban warriors to Barry Goldwater's campaign. What *was* new, however, was that these ideas were being uttered by a political cyborg of sorts, a creation of "behavioural science."

Other hallmarks of the modern electoral machine would make their appearance after Reagan had won his first gubernatorial election. According to Boyarsky,

> Reagan's successful campaign for re-election in 1970 was note-worthy for its use of highly refined polling techniques that now dominate American politics. The crude briefing books used by Reagan in 1966 were abandoned in favor of a much more sophisticated system developed by his campaign managers . . . [who] had included all of the important ingredients of computer-ized politics. Among them were the results of public opinion polls; studies of political behavior in thousands of election precincts; histories of voting patterns; all the small details of the census, such as income, race, sex, education, family size, number of television sets in households. From that he [pollster Richard Wirthlin] made up a political profile of the state, which was kept timely with daily telephone pools of several hundred people. This permitted the campaign to shift to meet new issues.[11]

There is no shortage of irony here either: The Reagan campaign, built around the candidate's rousing rhetoric about revaluing personal initiative (designed to appeal to rugged individualists), was being directed by a priestlike class of political technocrats who saw voters merely as impersonal chunks of data to be moulded and manipulated to serve their own ends. Ironies aside, the point is that it worked. The fusion of populist sermonizing and precision psycho-manipulation assured the success of a new breed of right-wing politician throughout the following three decades and enabled this New Right movement to transform itself from the Republican party's lunatic fringe to a defining force in American politics.

It's possible that this durable new political alloy might never have been discovered had it not been for the proximity of specialized talent — television producers, University of California psychologists, a charismatic and ambitious Hollywood star — to the boiling cauldron

of discontent that was suburban Southern California in the early to mid-1960s. This region was so closely identified with right-wing radicalism that, according to Wills, when Goldwater clinched the California nomination in his bid to become the Republican presidential candidate in 1964, it was widely taken as confirmation that Goldwater was an "extremist" candidate. California in the early 1960s was also fertile ground for the racist, anti-government John Birch Society, founded by the conspiracy-minded Robert Welsh, which had become increasingly influential in the new suburbs surrounding LA. Within the Republican party itself, the swelling ranks of so-called "Taft Republicans" in California, who felt the nomination of Eisenhower as presidential candidate in 1952 had been a sellout to the party's "eastern establishment" and a surrender to the New Deal view of government that Eisenhower willingly upheld, were increasingly vocal in their denunciations of other "establishment" Republicans such as Nelson Rockefeller. This faction had become ardent supporters of Goldwater, but following that candidate's crushing defeat in the 1964 presidential election, it was Reagan who was to become their new saviour.

Reagan had the perfect political pedigree to appeal to this increasingly vocal fringe. Previously, as a spokesperson for General Electric, Reagan had toured the nation, visiting GE plants and delivering The Speech — a standardized address about the evils of communism and the threat that burgeoning government bureaucracies in the US would erode individual liberties and sap private initiative. The product of Reagan's own political conversion, The Speech did not always reflect the agenda of his corporate sponsors. At one point, he had to drop a negative reference to the Tennessee Valley Authority, a massive government-run electricity producer, since GE was the beneficiary of lucrative TVA contracts. Still, The Speech was influential in helping establish the climate in which a grassroots right-wing revolt began to flourish, and it won Reagan the support of its growing legions of zealots.

However, where Reagan differed from previous right-wing candidates — thanks in part to the sophisticated political packaging — was

in his ability to ford the gap between this hard-core base of support and a more timid mainstream. Barry Goldwater had embraced Southern California's right-wing militants at the expense of support by more moderate voters. Nixon, by contrast, had denounced the John Birch Society in the 1962 race for the governor's office and found that he couldn't win without the support of the far right. But Reagan, while careful not to alienate his extreme-right core of supporters, paid special attention to appearing rational and reasonable to the mainstream electorate. His rough edges had been filed down by his BASICO handlers, and his all-important, carefully choreographed television addresses had taken a much more prominent place than the traditional campaign appearances, where candidates risk making a spontaneous gaffe. This new style of campaigning hit like a U-2 bomb and the rest, as they say, is history. After his two decisive victories in 1966 and 1970, Reagan expected to be the Republican presidential candidate in 1976, but he lost to Gerald Ford and had to postpone his leap into national politics until 1980. At time Reagan repeated the trick he had performed in California: unseating the incumbent and then overseeing two terms of deregulation, Cold War weapons buildup, and the dismantling of large parts of the welfare state.

— — —

Who would have guessed that the sleepy suburbs of LA could have produced all this? After all, before the turmoil of the 1960s, the state's political parties were led by liberals or moderates — Republicans Earl Warren and Goodwin Knight, Democrat Pat Brown — while the state government oversaw one of the most generous social-welfare programs in the US. But something began to happen as white conservatives regrouped in their new suburban lairs. Bill Boyarsky recalls that it was at Lakewood Shopping Center (the same community that gave its name to the Lakewood Plan, which served as a model for suburban political reorganization throughout SoCal) that Ronald Reagan got one of his warmest receptions during a rare in-person

stop; it was also where Governor Pat Brown and Senator Robert Kennedy were, on separate occasions, shouted down by teenage members of a right-wing political group.[12] Boyarsky noted that these blue-collar suburbanites were, on the face of it, cheering for the wrong team, since many of them depended on government contracts for work and would likely suffer if state services were dismantled. This only underscores a much broader paradox about the rise of the right in the suburbs of California. As Wills says, the California activists who railed against government intervention in their lives and economy were actually living in a state whose very existence was predicated on government initiative and massive government spending. In fact, the condition of dependency fostered by government spending would only increase during Reagan's presidency, as the supposedly anti-government chief executive granted billions upon billions of dollars in military contracts to California aerospace firms. This, however, was part of a tradition so well established that it had become virtually invisible. Writes Wills:

[California], like the West in general, was born of dependence
on the federal government. In other states, federal troops had to
take land only from the Indians. California was also taken from
Mexico. Then it was developed by federal outlay on railroads,
naval operations and water projects. Ronald Reagan has several
times recalled how he mused on what he would put into a time
capsule while riding the highway along California's magnificent
coast. The freeway system, which is one of California's most
characteristic features, was heavily subsidized with federal money.
And the state draws even more government money for defense
contracts, especially in the realm of aeronautics and microcom-
puters. In 1980, California alone received a quarter of the
Defense Department's prime contracts (44 percent of NASA's) . . .
As Donald Worster has argued: "The West, more than any other
American region, was built by state power, state expertise, state
technology and state bureaucracy."[13]

The separation of image from reality, however, is a hallmark of the television era, and it would be accomplished with equal mastery a decade after Reagan's first election as California governor. Using the same formula of populist sloganeering and slick TV advertising that the Reagan campaigns had used (supplemented by a brilliant direct-mail campaign), the backers of the 1978 anti-tax ballot initiative Proposition 13 scored an impressive 2:1 victory, which is now considered a landmark in the rise of the political right and the reversal of New Deal ideals. The campaign's front man was Howard Jarvis, a well-known political maverick who had been dismissed by most politicians, even ultra-conservatives, as a crank. A one-time inventor — the first push-button radio, an odourless gas heater, and a proto-typical garbage disposal were among the gizmos he created — Jarvis had also founded the short-lived Conservative party in the early 1960s and had campaigned to have communists banned from seeking public office. But during his colourful political career, he had made enemies of more than just communists. Goldwater, for instance, sued Jarvis after postal inspectors confirmed that of $115,000 that had been raised by "Businessmen for Goldwater," an unauthorized campaign committee Jarvis co-founded, none of that money had reached the candidate. Jarvis and an associate later repeated this act with a "Friends of Hayakawa" committee, which likewise solicited contributions for Samuel Hayakawa's senate campaign but was sued by Hayakawa for allegedly pocketing the proceeds.[14]

Despite these black marks on his resumé, by the time of the Proposition 13 campaign Jarvis clearly possessed a remarkable ability to read the public mood and to communicate empathetically with angst-ridden Southern Californians. By the mid-1970s a sense of panic had settled on this lush landscape because of a sudden and dramatic leap in property tax assessments. According to Robert Kuttner, author of *Revolt of the Haves* (a detailed reconstruction of the California tax revolt), the jump in rates was primarily due to a requirement of a state tax-reform package, passed in 1967, that all properties be regularly reassessed at a set fraction of their current value. This meant that, as housing prices skyrocketed in the mid-1970s, property taxes rose in lockstep. In Kuttner's recounting, this inflation of property values was created by an interwoven conspiracy of circumstances: the unleashing of pent-up market demand as California recovered from the recession of 1973-74 and from a period of tight money; the realization that undeveloped land close to LA was running out, and the reticence of newly energy-conscious homebuyers to roam too far afield (given the recent experience with the early '70s oil shock); and a downturn in the stock market, which drove many investors into real estate, because it promised higher returns. Given these factors, the Southern California property market became a bizarre circus where hordes of desperate buyers, undeterred by prices that would have seemed ridiculous a short time before, fuelled a frenzied buying spree. Half of the new houses constructed in Orange County were bought by speculators, and many houses were sold and resold before construction was even completed. Homes traditionally valued at $25,000 were suddenly selling for over $100,000. Across Orange County, only 31 percent of single-family homes had been valued at over $70,000 in December 1975, but that number jumped to 87 percent just eighteen months later. In the four years between April 1974 and April 1978, the average price of a single-family home in LA rose from $37,800 to $83,200, a leap of 120 percent, as compared with a national rise of only 48 percent.[15]

There are differences of opinion about what the overall impact of this sudden rise in property values meant for California's middle class. Calling this period of land revaluation "one of the largest mass windfalls of wealth in history," Mike Davis comments that "if the infamous German inflation of 1920-23 ruined the Weimar middle class, this Southern California land inflation of 1975-79 by contrast enriched many tens of thousands of middle-class families beyond their wildest expectations." According to Davis, many of those families began to look at property primarily as an investment, rather than as shelter, and entered the speculation game, while some began to finance a more lavish lifestyle by accessing the new equity in their homes.[16]

Yet at the same time, for other homeowners who didn't do those things, the rise in property values was a purely abstract advance. If they didn't sell, they saw no profit, and the mere knowledge that their homes were suddenly worth more on paper meant nothing to them. On the other hand, property taxes that suddenly double or triple to match the wild ways of the real estate market are a real expense. For many Californians, then, this imposed a tangible burden that was particularly galling given that the state government, with corollary and equally unexpected rises in income and sales taxes, was amassing a huge budget surplus. (Kuttner considers it a huge political mistake that the state let the surplus pile up, rather than passing some of it along to the municipalities to offset the rise in property taxes.) The higher tax bills drove home to many Californians that the sudden upward lurch of the real estate market had made them feel poorer, not richer. New homeowners were already struggling to make the payments on overpriced homes, which they had felt compelled to buy as a hedge against future inflation, and the sudden rise in taxes compounded their woe. This is a situation that would be repeated many times in other locales, such as around Toronto during the real estate boom of the 1980s.

It is out of this ferment of rising expectations, fears, frustrations, injured feelings, and uncertainty about the future that Jarvis was able to rally a political movement that allowed him to take on virtually the entire California political establishment and win. Unlike other failed ballot initiatives, which had been written in the convoluted language of tax law, Jarvis made sure that Prop 13 was simple and direct. Using paid canvassers, he collected an impressive million and a half signatures to have the initiative put on California's June 1978 primary ballot. What it called for was a rollback of property assessments to 1975-76 levels, with a 2 percent annual increase to cover inflation (which at that time was well beyond 2 percent), although new and newly bought homes could be assessed at current market values. All properties would be taxed at a flat one percent of these values, and state and local governments would not be able to levy new taxes without the approval of two-thirds of voters. The rollback of property assessments meant that an owner paying $2,200 tax on a $70,000 home in 1977 would have those taxes reduced to $700 a year after Proposition 13 passed.[17]

Jarvis and his cohorts sold Proposition 13 as the best means both of providing relief to cash-strapped homeowners (particularly retirees on fixed incomes, for whom the tax increases could have meant losing their homes) and also of delivering a swift kick to the posteriors of the politicians who presided over swelling state coffers. While there was general agreement that Jarvis's movement was addressing a legitimate grievance, a large range of interested parties soon began to see his ballot initiative as rife with hidden consequences. For one, it would open up a huge intergenerational rift: While older people who had bought their homes in the '50s and '60s at bargain prices were guaranteed low property taxes, new homebuyers entering the market after 1978 had neither advantage. And while the loss of around $5.5 billion in taxes threatened to deprive local governments of close to a quarter of their revenues, the biggest chunk of that — $3.5 billion — would go not to pinched homeowners but to landlords and businesses, including out-of-state corporate shareholders. Since Jarvis was employed by a landlords' association, it was widely believed that this was an intended, though unstated, aim of Proposition 13. As Kuttner writes, the ballot initiative that was marketed as a tool for achieving justice for poor retirees who had little more than the homes they had struggled to buy, in reality wound up socking it to the poor in a variety of ways. Prop 13, Kuttner recounts,

> gave the bulk of the tax relief to those who needed it least. The cuts in public services typically reduced programs that served the needy. And when far more ordinary conservatives than Howard Jarvis seized the momentum of his tax protest to assure that the biggest tax cuts went to the well-off, then the tax revolt truly became a revolt of the haves . . . The inheritors of Jarvis's

momentum, unfortunately, are mostly Fortune 500 corporations, nimble trade associations, and well-off investors — not the sort of people being driven from their homes by property tax excesses.[18]

When the likely impact of Jarvis's proposition became apparent, a counter-initiative was put forth by a bipartisan group of legislators, supported by labour unions, consumer advocates, and even the Chamber of Commerce and prominent businesses who, although they stood to gain financially from Proposition 13, feared the measure would undermine the state's economy. Proposition 8, the head-to-head competitor of Prop 13, would use only $1.4 billion to provide substantially the same property tax relief as its rival (a 30 percent across-the-board cut), as well as special rebates directed at the elderly and renters, who had been left out of Proposition 13. Despite wide support for Proposition 8 from every imaginable segment of California society, the coalition that supported it was too unwieldy and ideologically riven to be able to present a coherent or convincing message.

Jarvis, by contrast, was at the helm of a streamlined organization directing the work of a fleet-footed advertising agency that hadn't forgotten how Reagan's gubernatorial campaigns had played on public mistrust of the "professional politicians." The Newport Beach–based Butcher-Forde agency had decided, against the conventional wisdom that saw Jarvis as a nutbar with no political credibility, to put the renegade crusader and one-time fraudster front and centre in its TV spots, based on the correct assumption that the average citizen would identify with him and appreciate his anti-politician appeal. Butcher-Forde also astutely divined the potential for milking the populist assumption that if most state politicians and such a wide set of interest groups were supporting Prop 8, there must be something wrong with it. Why, after all, would business giants like the electrical utility Southern California Edison be backing the counter-proposal unless it upheld corporate interests at the expense of the little guy? It was said that Proposition 8 had the backing of "everyone except the people," and although Prop 8 forces had raised enough questions as the campaign wore on to almost eliminate its rivals' lead in the opinion polls, ultimately the little people who had donated $10 or $25 to Jarvis's campaign rallied to produce a decisive and historic victory.

For Canadians, the Butcher-Forde strategy may recall the manoeuvres of another right-wing populist movement, the Reform Party. It scored big in public opinion by opposing the Charlottetown constitutional accord of 1992, which had the backing of all other political parties in English Canada, as well as almost all other major advocacy organizations routinely cited in the Canadian press. In this way Reform advanced its brand recognition as the political party that opposes conventional wisdom and entrenched interests, choosing instead to embrace the scepticism of the average, voiceless citizen.

Indeed, right-wing populist uprisings in a variety of places have tended to follow the basic script that was written during those heady days of revolutionary myth-making in 1970s California. A requisite ingredient of any such local rebellion is a leader who fits the mould — as defined by Reagan or Jarvis — of the "citizen politician," or perhaps the anti-politician politician, those who, no matter how well connected or powerful they become, can remain outsiders, with a common touch and a lack of pretention. Britain had Margaret Thatcher, the shopkeeper's daughter; Michigan had John Engler, the son of immigrants; and in Ontario there is Mike Harris, small-town guy from North Bay, who says he hasn't read much besides Mr. Silly and the Hardy Boys, who's never smoked pot but is rather partial to beer.

Behind these leaders are invariably the legions of pollsters, spin doctors, and political engineers, although in most places today, with succeeding generations having grown up within the all-enveloping cocoon of the mass media, this is much less a cause for embarrassment for right-wing rebels than it was in the aftermath of Barry Goldwater's 1964 shoot-from-the-hip, what-you-see-is-what-you-get run at the US presidency.

Post-Reagan/Jarvis populist rebellions have also raised much the same juxtaposition of ideas, pitting the same predictable partisan assertions against one another. The right-wing populists will claim to have the common person's interests at heart, promising average workers lower taxes and pledging to represent them directly, despite the lobbying for privileges by "special interest groups." Liberal opponents will say, as they did with some prescience during the Proposition 13 tax revolt, that it is the poor who will suffer most from these policies and the rich who are the hidden beneficiaries. Identical criticisms have been made of Ontario tax cuts, where naysayers feel that a few extra dollars in pocket money for average workers have come at the price of tattered services and a windfall for higher income taxpayers. But today, as in the 1970s, the latter arguments are more difficult to make on TV.

Many feel that the standard repertoire of images, promises, and tricks put forth by the right-wing, revolutionary variety of anti-politicians have taken on the musty scent of cliché in the time since they were first unleashed in suburban SoCal in the '70s. This schtick has become, perhaps, like one of those evangelical road shows that blow through a series of small towns over the course of a summer. A little faith healing, a little confession, some prayers and some songs — slick and impressive if you haven't seen it before, but wearing and suspicion-provoking if you've seen it too much.

Has this archetypal style of proselytizing populist politics outlived its effectiveness? Ironically, just at a time when Ontarians were about to decide whether to have more than a brief stroll down the revolutionary path first marked out by Messrs. Reagan and Jarvis, Californians were on the verge of choosing to break with their revolutionary past.

⁷ Keeping the Sacred Flame Burning

Victory. Success. Triumph. That sweet taste still lingers in the mouths of legions of California conservatives who remember the time, not too many TV seasons ago, that Sam and Suzy Suburbanite put down their barbecue tongs, turned off the power mower, and rose up in revolt. Those warm, wondrous memories — of how average Californians shocked the political/media elite by electing Ronald Reagan as governor; of how they told the taxman to take a hike when Prop 13 appeared on the ballot — provide sustenance in these trying times when, for the first time since Jimmy Carter, there's a Democrat in the White House, and all those day-to-day battles must be fought against the creeping forces of liberalism that would boost government budgets and untie the meddling hands of the state while no one is looking.

Twenty years after the vote on Proposition 13 and more than thirty years after Reagan's election as governor, I attend a meeting of the Republican Central Committee of Orange County, a group that has kept faith with the heroes of its revolution and, as a consequence, has won the lion's share of the political spoils here throughout that period.

The venue is a conference room in the Westin South Coast Plaza, a hotel adjoining the South Coast Plaza shopping mall, which just happens to register the highest sales receipts of any mall in the US and, probably, in the world.[1] The South Coast complex is located in Costa Mesa, one of those peculiar mock-downtown areas that appear occasionally like mirages above the low-rise suburban-California landscape. The streetscape surrounding the Westin looks like a real downtown given its wide, imperial-style boulevards surrounded by marble-clad skyscrapers, but what's weird is that it's all executed in a uniform style. Rather than having buildings of different aesthetics or eras lining its streets as in real downtowns where different developers compete to occupy different parcels of land, "downtown" Costa Mesa has been done in one solid, master-planned, corporate-imposed look, just like those low-rise suburban subdivisions where it's illegal to paint your shutters an unsanctioned hue.

But enough about architecture. The point here is that the Republican Central Committee members milling about on the plush broadloom of the Westin have an important purpose before them. Tonight, as at the past few central committee meetings, they will be considering the worthiness of candidates standing for various offices in the statewide elections in October. The candidates will attempt to explain to party activists why they deserve their votes, campaign donations, and volunteer time, and all of them will do so by situating their own candidacy within the illustrious California tradition of middle-class, populist revolt for which the Republican party has been the standard-bearer for the past generation. Here you don't just get to call yourself a Republican and have your name put on the ballot; you have to prove that you've got the right stuff to carry the torch, that there's something acidic in your blood that connects you to the rest of the tribe. It will become obvious to me as the night wears on that each person who rises to the podium has much of his or her self-image tied up in this political movement. This is clear from the evangelical, sometimes ferocious tone the speakers will adopt. Being a devoted Republican, as one of them will say, "is not just a political philosophy, it's a way of life."

Time was when this militant fervour could sweep away most of the middle class in this state like a flash flood rushing through a suburban canyon. Is this still true today? A quarter-century is a long time for a political movement to stay vital, especially in a culture and a place where a year or two can make what was a cutting-edge technology obsolete, where fashions change as quickly as you can say, "Master-Card, please." This question of how accurately Republican rhetoric represents the current public mood will stick with me as I listen this evening to continual homages to California's rightist revolution. I can't help wondering if all this revolutionary triumphalism is in essence a kind of nostalgia — like Fidel Castro delivering one of his famous four-hour rants to a Cuban public mostly too young to remember the former regime and the indignities of American dominance — or if, instead, it shows how schizoid Californians really are: trend-setting hipsters on the outside, button-down conservatives within. I won't bother to venture an opinion on that, since Californians will provide the definitive answer at the ballot box a few months after this meeting. What I will say is that there's a sense of something ritualized, something formalized here that strikes me as akin to a figure-skating contest: the candidates all deliver speeches that have standard, requisite elements, and the more of these the better. Squeeze more triple lutzes and loops, maybe a quadruple salchow into your program, and you'll do better than your competitors. In this political contest, the hurdles seem to be: What kind of tribute do the candidates pay to their revolutionary forebears? To Reagan? To Howard Jarvis? Do they give the right answers to questions on abortion? On their voting records on spending and taxing issues? The more vigorous the applause for a candidate's responses, the heartier the laughter after a candidate has told a joke, indicates how well the contestants have mastered the obligatory moves.

It all begins a few minutes after the official seven-thirty start time, as a call to order calms the rattling of coffee cups and dims the collegial hum of conversation. We launch into the proceedings with a recitation of the Pledge of Allegiance. The Lord's Prayer is next, and no one seems to notice any irony in the fact that the narrative segue linking these two solemn oaths was a dirty joke about Bill Clinton's sex life, a sneering barb that elicits a kind of laughter containing both disdain and a certain adrenalized delight. Then vice-chair Jo Ellen Allen makes a few announcements — one is about another meeting taking place on this same night just down the road at the Nixon Library in San Clemente about the fate of POWs from the Vietnam War — after which she hands the proceedings over to central committee chairman Tom Fuentes. A thoroughly bald man with a dapper appearance and an easy, hail-fellow-well-met demeanour, Fuentes is a longtime political powerhouse in these parts whose opinions are routinely solicited by the *L.A. Times* and other important West Coast media. His chairman's report is a recitation of all the ambitious initiatives the local GOP is currently undertaking. He mentions that former presidential candidate Steve Forbes will be in OC later in the month (which demonstrates how important it is for Republican politicians who aspire to create a national powerbase to cultivate a following in Orange County). He also says that he himself will be travelling to Korea the next day for the twinning of Anaheim with the Korean city of Chunchon (which indicates just how many miles Republicans are willing to travel to court Orange County's growing Korean community, made up largely of merchants who fled from LA after the "O.J." riots).

Although the first speaker Fuentes introduces will be the only one tonight not running for office, former OC state senator Ollie Speraw's presence here provides a symbolic link with the past. Speraw is hailed by Fuentes as a man who had no reason to interrupt a successful career in business to serve in government, but who "did it because he believed in the Reagan revolution, he believed in our movement, and he went there to carry those values to the state senate." Speraw himself gives a nod to the notion, implicit in the chairman's remarks, that his status derives mostly from his career as a businessman rather than as a legislator when he recalls that "for three years when we were starting up Century 21 [the real estate giant] this was the room where we brought in our franchisees from all over the United States to give them four days of training in sales management. This exact room." Making this discovery when he walked in this evening makes it "a true homecoming," says Speraw. If this observation establishes a certain continuity between the past and the present, then so too does Speraw's repertoire of jokes, which can't have changed much in thirty years. An innocent line — about how, when people ask him about his time as a politician, he answers that he remembers it "with strong mixed emotions" — turns out to be a set-up for a wisecrack. "Now when I was a kid," the ex-politician elaborates, "the definition of mixed emotions was your mother-in-law going over a cliff in your new Cadillac." The audience laughs appreciatively. "However, I repeated that to someone once and they said there's a new definition today: mixed emotions is when your seventeen-year-old daughter comes home at one in the morning with a Gideon Bible under her arm." But the former state senator, having learned "in a [Dale] Carnegie class that it's impossible to be brief and bad at the same time," moves quickly out of his stand-up act and into the meat of his address: the need to revise the means by which the state government redraws the electoral boundaries.

Since this process of "reapportionment" helped Speraw lose his own seat after serving one term, it is an issue dear to his heart. Essentially what he is asking the Republican party faithful to consider is pushing for a non-partisan committee that would redraw the electoral map solely with the purpose of ensuring districts are numerically even, thus fulfilling the constitutional dictate that each vote should carry equal weight. The current system, by contrast, assigns responsibility for reapportionment to the majority party in the

California legislature, and in so doing violates the common-sense edict that "you never make the madam of the bawdy house the chief of police." Since Democrats have controlled the legislative branch, although not the governorship, for most of thirty years, Speraw says, it's inevitable that the Republicans have come out on the losing end. But breaking with the tone of partisan jingoism that will dominate this evening, he remarks that Republicans must own up to their own role in creating this situation, for it was a Republican-controlled legislature that first started gerrymandering electoral boundaries to their own advantage in 1950.

If Speraw's speech suggests a style of political discourse that was last popular when the Ed Sullivan show was still on the air, the next act has likely been placed on the roster to inject an air of youth into the proceedings. It's time for the Volunteer of the Month presentation, and this month the honour goes to a college student named Bobby Zimmel. His service to the cause, according to the presenters of the award, has included a stint working as an intern for a conservative congressman in Washington.

Although this presentation may be a way of saying that the GOP welcomes and appreciates youth, Bobby appears totally unlike 98 percent of California's youth: he carries himself as if he's never been within ten feet of a skateboard and wouldn't be caught dead at a Pearl Jam concert. After the presentation has started Bobby seems a bit flummoxed — although not really, I think. It's more of a mock-flummox, a theatrical flummox perhaps (he's probably seen lots of videos of Ronald Reagan), and this adds a self-deprecating quality to his words when he walks up to the podium and announces, "I had no idea that this was going to happen. I guess that's why my Dad brought my sport coat in from the car." He concludes his deferentially short address with a Boy Scout–like pledge: "I strive every day to further the conservative cause, which is something I hold very dear and is implicit in every action of mine." In exchange for this, Bobby receives a set of cufflinks, a "short syllabus from Chapman University . . . entitled "The Leftist Leanings of the Political Science Faculty," and a warm round of applause from the members of the central committee.

While youthfulness may not be automatically equated with a reformist attitude, a couple of speakers on the program tonight hint, in an ever-so-guarded, highly codified fashion, at the need to remake Republican policies to appeal to changing public concerns. One of them is Steve Apodaca, who's seeking the nomination to run for assemblyman in the Seventy-third Assembly District. Steve has left his book of one-liners at home tonight; instead, he delivers an earnest, inspirational speech in a relentless, machine-gun cadence that goes on just long enough to piss off a significant chunk of the audience. The tone of the address is captured by Apodaca's statement "I'd like to offer you today a vision for the twenty-first century, a vision that I hope you don't wait till the year 2000 to embrace," as if he were a kind of Martin Luther King Jr., only with an entirely different political frame of reference. And what is this vision for the next century? A perplexing question. In attempting to marry the appearance of being forward-looking and innovative with constant reminders that his prophetic design is solidly based on conservative values, this speech makes one wonder just who Apodaca is trying to fool. Is he trying to sneak some truly reformist policy past a reactionary crowd by couching it in the familiar language of Republican conservatism? Or is he suggesting that Republicans, if they co-opt the language that progressives have successfully deployed, could repackage the old Reagan revolution shtick as some shiny new product?

This puzzle looms large as Apodaca talks about the need for Republicans to get out in front on environmental issues. He says his vision for twenty-first-century California begins "with the air we breathe, the water we drink, and the food we eat. Close your eyes and imagine, if you will, California's giant redwoods, the beautiful Yosemite Valley, the Camino Reál, and our marvellous and magnificent coastline. Is there anyone among us who would deprive our children of these great natural treasures? Of course not." As nature-loving as Republicans are, however, they have been victims of a vicious campaign to portray them as "despoilers of the earth who would clear-cut the forests, feed contaminated food to our children, poison the rivers, and pollute the air. All in the name of profit." This leads very nicely into an attack on the environmentalists who have spread these dastardly lies.

A neat trick, this: begin your list of policy issues by saying that the environment should be a top concern for the next century, and then bash the environmentalists, a favourite target of US conservatives these days, especially those of the Christian Right, who are fond of characterizing eco-agitators as a heathen bunch who worship Nature and reject that biblical edict about humanity having dominion over the Earth.

Continues Apodaca, putting the boots to this familiar target, "We let the radical environmentalists set the rhetorical trap and we, being defenders of the constitution, allow ourselves to be defined by their words rather than by our actions. It was a Republican, Teddy Roosevelt, who was America's first real environmentalist. It was Republican Congresses who set aside the great national parks for all of us to enjoy. And it is the magic of our free-enterprise system that has created the cleanest and healthiest environment on this planet."

Leaving aside that dubious last statement about capitalism and clean environments — you may remember it was "our free-enterprise system" that gave LA probably the worst air quality in the world, and remedial government intervention that has forced some improvement — it's a pretty long stretch to use Teddy Roosevelt, who occupied the White House way back in the early years of this century, as an emblem of Republicans' environmental commitment. Hasn't this legacy been undone by Reagan's interior secretary, James Watt, who opened up the national parks to corporate exploitation? Or by California's current Republican candidate for governor, Dan Lungren, who has been roundly criticized (as the state's attorney-general) for failing to punish corporations who break environmental laws?[2] In fact, at this very meeting Republican candidates will denounce the idea that government money be used to create a rapid-transit system in Orange County, while the party as a whole has made clear during this campaign its rejection of the proposed vehicle-registration fees that would discourage automobile use. But Apodaca does not mention these specific policies, opting instead to advance a more abstract notion of environmental stewardship where, by placing the appetites and interests of humanity at the top of the priorities list, the environment will automatically benefit — a redeployment, it seems, of Ayn Rand's exaltation of greed as an economic instrument into the area of environmental policy.

Ultimately it's not clear what the candidate is advocating. Is he calling for a new PR campaign to recast Republicans as saviours of the Earth? Or is he suggesting that Republicans start to take a deeper interest in environmental issues to meet new public expectations?

A similar ambiguity cloaks the other issues the candidate addresses. Declaring that "every son and daughter of California deserves an education that will adequately prepare them for the challenges of the future," Apodaca cites a statistic that California's fourth-graders rank dead last in American states in reading, tied with poor, backward Louisiana. What's interesting about this reference is that it entered the political lexicon after being used in Peter Schrag's recent book *Paradise Lost: California's Experience, America's Future*, a decidedly liberal tome, the main thesis of which is that public services such as education have deteriorated disastrously in California as a direct consequence of funding cuts and restrictions on taxation. This suggests that Apodaca wants to address the widespread public sentiment that critical services have been starved and need rebuilding. But again he tries to avoid looking like a liberal by blaming these falling education standards, *à la* the traditional conservative refrain, on today's educators' lack of emphasis on "the basics" and discipline. Ditto, when the candidate tackles multiculturalism and the explosive question of languages other than English (that is Spanish) being taught in schools, he makes a similar attempt to play both sides of the fence by stating that "California is like a quilt made up of many beautiful cultures, bound together by the common thread we call English." So what does this mean? The statement seems to suggest that he is in favour of English only in schools, but once more he's left plenty of room to manoeuvre, left open the opportunity for interpretation.

Apodaca employs his fanciest footwork, however, when he talks about his personal life. Republican activists, particularly those with overlapping memberships in zealot organizations like the Christian Coalition, want their candidates to be able to demonstrate an upward trajectory in their business lives and a straight-arrow approach to home and family. Turns out Apodaca falls a little short on both counts. But rather than leave himself open to sneak attack, he decides to face these issues head-on, borrowing a time-honoured trick from the travelling preachers and televangelists who tell the flock that their past indiscretions have allowed them to know better God's mercy, that their mistakes have made them more God-fearing and humble, more understanding of the sin that surrounds us. "When I had personal difficulties in my first marriage and later severe financial difficulties forcing me to declare bankruptcy," the candidate confesses, "I was ready to give up. At that point, I asked to be given a chance, a chance to make a difference. Well, I can tell you that my prayers were answered. My life is a living example of His gift, and the unlimited opportunity called America. My story is an American tale, one of perseverance and adversity overcome. I hope that you're not uncomfortable with these personal feelings, and if sharing them with you means that I'm out of step with the mainstream political philosophy in California, then so be it."

In reality the candidate seems to be very much a part of the California mainstream — personal bankruptcies are as common as car loans in California, while divorce seems so common that you expect every citizen over twenty-five and not gay to have gone through at least one. But in front of this crowd, it would be suicidal to acknowledge divorce, for instance, as something normal or routine. The religious right has become so influential within Republican ranks that issues of personal morality and "personal responsibility," as they call it, are at least as important as economic policy. All candidates must run a gauntlet of questions about their views on sex education in the schools, gay rights, abortion . . .

This last is the area where Steve Apodaca really gets tripped up. A bald, grey-haired man in a denim jacket, the only male in the room not wearing a dark business suit, asks Apodaca (as he will ask every candidate this evening) for a detailed accounting of his position on abortion. Apodaca responds that "quite simply, I oppose abortion, but I will not impose my will upon others. And I resent government's involvement in any aspect of that issue." Nice try. Steve has just attempted to justify his position against outlawing abortion by appealing to another principle deeply embedded in the hearts of Republican rightists: that government should be smaller and less intrusive, that it shouldn't interfere in the lives of individuals. There is tepid applause from some members of the audience, but the denim-clad pro-lifer is having none of it. He yells back in a voice sharp enough to shatter glass, "That's what you call pro-choice." There is no censure from the chair, only a moment of frozen silence and the rising flush of humiliation on Apodaca's face.

Jim Lacey, who's also standing for nomination in the Seventy-third Assembly District, sticks to a much more traditional script and has a far smoother ride. "I'm a consultant to the Howard Jarvis taxpayers' association," he announces in mock self-introduction, causing the room to explode into a chorus of cheers and whistles. Then he asks the crowd, "Wasn't Ronald Reagan a great president?" to stoke the fires a little more. The bulk of Lacey's brief speech is devoted to recounting his political career: how, as a delegate to the Republican national convention in 1976, he cast his vote for Reagan, making him a supporter at a time when the national party turned its back on the Gipper; how his first job after graduating from Pepperdine Law School in 1978 "was working for a crusty old man from Los Angeles named Howard Jarvis, who had this crazy idea that you could lower property taxes by two-thirds and the sun would still come up the next day"; and how he served in Reagan's federal administrations for the full eight years, first as a liaison dealing with corporations — "I learned that the best thing you can do in government to help business is to get out of the way" — and then as general counsel to the US Consumer Product Safety Commission "where we fought the [Ralph] Naderites, and where we brought reason into government regulation," by which Lacey means that cost/ benefit analyses were introduced so that product-safety improvements would be considered only within the context of their economic impacts.

Given these credentials it's not surprising that Lacey's nomination bid has received the endorsement of a slew of Republican office-holders and political action committees. The candidate makes clear that, in contrast to Apodaca, any vision he has for the twenty-first century comes not from a crystal ball but straight from the rear-view mirror. "I ask you to consider the future of the Reagan legacy," he appeals. "I think that looking to individuals that we can depend upon and trust to support lower taxes, less government spending, and traditional moral values is something that made us get involved as activists in the Republican party in the first place." This unambiguous message, unclouded by references to new challenges or new policy choices to consider, is clearly what this crowd wants to hear. When Lacey thanks the central committee for its time, he receives much more applause than his rival did.

The question-and-answer session that follows extends the theme of who, exactly, is fit to carry the revolutionary staff handed down by Reagan, Jarvis, *et al.* Under interrogation, Lacey confirms he's been endorsed by an anti-abortion group and that he voted against emergency tax measures in the wake of the OC bankruptcy; Apodaca, meanwhile, wavers on both of these.

The puzzle about who is the genuine article, who has the mettle to carry on the revolution, will re-emerge throughout the evening, occupying an even more prominent place in what might seem to outsiders' lesser contests — for school-board seats, for instance. Yet these have become the most conspicuously bloody theatres of war in

California's protracted ideological struggle. School issues, in fact, were a central plank in the platform of California's New Right even before there *was* a New Right. As Peter Schrag recounts in *Paradise Lost*, while liberal Democrat governor Pat Brown managed a convincing victory over challenger Richard Nixon in 1962, an early warning of an impending right-wing revolt was the election, as part of the same contest, of a hard-line conservative named Max Rafferty to the post of state superintendent of public instruction. "Rafferty ran on a platform of phonics, fundamentals, and patriotism, replacing Dick and Jane with *McGuffey's Readers*; 'indoctrinating' (his word) California's children against Communism — and cleaning up their behaviour and cutting their hair," writes Shrag. "And while the job to which he was elected had almost no real power, it was nonetheless a platform, and the election a sign that something out there was not quite right."[3]

Tonight at the Westin, there are strong echoes of Rafferty's prototypical platform against the hip curriculum in the words of Alexandria Coronado. She introduces her candidacy for a position on the county school board by warning that there is a counterfeit conservative on the ballot. According to Coronado, the incumbent, Sheila Myers (who is not present tonight), is unfit for office because she voted in favour of investing in the derivatives schemes that bankrupted the county, and because of a liberal policy drift that the challenger hints at but does not support with specific references to her voting record. Now, however, the camouflaged liberal "has been approaching many of our highly esteemed elected officials in this county and telling them that she is a good conservative Republican" — an impression Coronado wastes no time in correcting. "Ladies and gentlemen," she proclaims, "let there be no mistake about it: I am the true conservative in this race. I am pro-life. I am against abortion counselling in the schools. I am against any program that will predisposition [sic] our children and make sure they do not get an adequate education. I am for back-to-basics education, which means phonics, traditional math programs, and an account of American history our founding fathers would be proud of. I am for reducing bureaucracy and waste at the county board of education."

Normally, such a direct statement of what a candidate stands for would be welcomed by anyone who wants to see honesty and clarity in contenders for public office. But what is disquieting and unexpected in Coronado's presentation is that she has gotten to this point only after a prolonged, vitriolic attack on her rival. It's as if that rival, by expressing a view that differs from the conservative canon, were guilty of some contemptible, criminal act that makes her worthy of being run out of town; as if this race for a school-board seat were some kind of jihad. Even more off-putting is her audience's habit of punctuating Coronado's speech, whenever she jabs at her rival, with hisses and jeering laughter.

Coronado does even better fielding the audience's questions. First, one that's *de rigueur*: The jean-jacketed representative of the pro-life inquisition weighs in with the comment "I believe that your husband takes exceptions on abortion for rape and incest. I hope that's not your position." The phrasing of the question provides a lucky break for Coronado, who pre-empts further discussion with a simple "I'm not married." This unleashes a torrent of laughter from the crowd and prompts chairman Fuentes to quip, "Well, Ken, I think you've evened the score with that one."

The next question is about the candidate's stand on whether the state should continue to pay for the children of illegal immigrants to go to school. The issue of what services should be provided to illegals has been one of the most emotional questions during this whole electoral period. Earlier, a firestorm erupted over the Republican-sponsored ballot initiative that would have stopped the state from paying for prenatal care for women living in California illegally. The initiative raised the horrific, Dickensian scenario of poorly paid domestics, or, say, the wives of the workers who provide cheap gardening services to the rich, giving birth in unsafe and unsanitary conditions, some of them dying, many more having their babies harmed. For critics, the issue is emblematic of the right's moral hypocrisy: Here is the conservative, pro-life crowd exhibiting the most callous disregard possible for the health of mothers and their babies.[4] But Coronado has no such qualms. She takes the hard line, stating, "I do not wish to pay for illegal aliens to be educated in this county, nor do I wish to pay to have them get health services or anything else. They may become citizens of the United States before they ever receive any benefits from this great country of ours." After these words, there is thunderous applause.

Running in an adjacent school district — partnered with Coronado as part of a unified slate that hopes to overturn the 3:2 advantage held by alleged liberals on the Orange County school board — is Don Wagner, a heavy-hitter among the conservative political community, with credentials that make him seem overqualified for the job of school-board trustee. Wagner is an attorney whose clients include such conservative luminaries as national phone-in shrink Dr. Laura Schlessinger, who is "doing some of the finest work on the radio next to, perhaps, Rush Limbaugh or Michael Reagan" by each day regaling callers with the conservative refrain that they should stop blaming society for their problems and realize that the answers lie in "personal responsibility" and self-reliance. Wagner also represents the company that makes the "hooked on phonics" tapes, as well as Tom Fuentes's wife, whose hobby, apparently, is filing lawsuits against liberals. It seems less unusual to have a highly credentialled candidate like Wagner in this school-board race, however, when one considers how much money these contests can attract from both rich right-wing sponsors and, on the opposing side, from the teachers' union. As Schrag details, "In places like Orange County, the organized Christian conservatives, backed by deep-pockets contributors like billionaire (Home Savings and Loan) banking heir Howard F. Ahmanson Jr., and local affiliates of the CTA [California Teachers Association] are often the sole combatants in school-board elections. They can generate campaign funds, running into the tens of thousands of dollars, even in small suburban districts, that make the old-fashioned volunteer-based, door-bell-ringing school board campaign a thing of the past."⁵

At first Wagner's approach seems conciliatory. With three children in local schools, he thinks that in some ways the system provides "good, quality public education like my wife and I had received." So things have gotten off on a positive note. But soon he launches into an increasingly irate recitation of heresies committed by the "educrats" in charge of the schools. Wagner first cottoned onto one such violation when he took his first-grade son to a Republican function. He thought it odd that the boy hesitated before sitting down after the Pledge of Allegiance. He found out why a little later during a parent-teacher meeting in his son's classroom, where an unauthorized second verse was posted on the walls. "Anyone know the second verse of the Pledge of Allegiance?" Wagner asks the crowd. He proceeds to fill them in on the details: "'I pledge allegiance to the world,' and then it goes on to say how 'I promise to recycle and throw away my trash and be nice to things that crawl.'" Wagner pauses before delivering a leering, topical ad lib that qualifies the phrase 'things that crawl': "It didn't mention presidential interns. It may now — it didn't then."

It is only natural, Wagner says, that an educational system that would pollute a sacred American oath with weirdo environmental stuff would also be peddling revisionist American history. He recounts seeing his ten-year-old daughter's school play. Her classmates recited famous speeches from American history — passages from Jefferson and Lincoln and the like — "fine things for children to learn," he concedes. But why did they spend so much time on Kennedy while leaving out Ronald Reagan altogether? "They didn't even mention him, there was no 'shining city on a hill,' nothing," he muses incredulously. What really irked him, however, was the role played by his daughter, whom liberal educators had obviously been trying to turn into one of those zombies from *Night of the Living Dead*. "My daughter played a '60s radical at some bacchanalia," he recalls, who "traipses on stage and starts talking about how wonderful [Lyndon Johnson's] 'Great Society' is." (This is truly revisionist history on somebody's part, portraying '60s radicals and LBJ as soulmates and co-conspirators.)

The result of the night's performance: a reflection of American history that doesn't give conservative Republicans their due. The reason: "long-serving education bureaucrats have simply taken parents [who presumably would want to vet the script of the class pageant] out of the loop." The same holds true in the area of reading and writing, argues Wagner. A recent uproar arose over the adoption of a reading text that doesn't use phonics because "the parents have been taken out of the loop by the educators, the educrats, the folks who simply say, 'We know better.'"

This last issue probably sounds familiar to parents who haven't been within 4,000 miles of this room at the Westin South Coast Plaza. School boards across North America, probably around the world, have been grappling with the issue of whether whole language or phonics is the best way to teach the two R's; recently much of the emphasis in teaching reading has shifted back to the traditional, phonics-based methods. But listening tonight to how differences over teaching styles are being used to ignite outrage — as a political rallying cry — it strikes me how differently people would approach these matters, say, back home in Ottawa. Here pumped-up crusaders have forfeited the chance to have a calm discussion about the way different kids' brains are wired and the relative merits of the various teaching methods. They've written off the option of trying to reach a compromise, of hammering out a practical consensus. In this context of a continual populist revolt against those perceived to belong to entrenched, self-interested groups, which include teachers' unions, school-board experts, or anyone who feeds from the public trough, there can no longer be a rational back-and-forth. Any problems parents have with the school system are seen not as mechanical failures, but as further evidence of a vast liberal conspiracy, which requires a holy crusade to fix. Candidates for the school board therefore have to prove themselves not as administrators or arbitrators, but as warriors.

So, it seems, does everyone else who rises to the podium tonight. James Bone — "That's like James Bond, only one better," he quips — tries to tell this stalwart crowd that there are some offices, in contrast to school board seats, for which ideological fervour is not needed. One such office is county assessor, for which Bone is running. Since the assessor has no role in setting taxes, the primary requirements for the job are competence, fairness, and technical knowledge. "To carry out the job, the assessor has to find a million units, understand them, appraise them, and enter their value on the roll," he says. If the assessor does a good job of this, he will avoid unnecessary appeals and therefore save the county and its taxpayers the time and expense of appealing the assessor's judgments. And Bone is convinced that — with his thirty-two years of experience as a CPA specializing in California tax law, as well as stints as a controller with companies such as Jack LaLanne's European Health Spas — his credentials fit that job description. Add to this the fact that he has written a book on property tax and a paper on the Orange County assessment appeals process, as well as the impression that he's the nitpicky, anal-retentive type — one of his hobbies, for example, is studying the tectonic history of Orange County — and it seems as if his bid for the nomination is unassailable.

That is, until challenger Bruce Piotr steps up to the plate and challenges this characterization of county assessor as a non-partisan position. Piotr is a real estate lawyer, not an accountant, so while his background gives him a general expertise that would be useful as assessor, it's not a perfect fit. But never mind. Piotr's pitch is much more in line with the general tenor of the evening, as he tells the meeting it's political commitment that counts the most.

"The main thing we need is someone with a vision for the assessor's office, and that vision is that it's the taxpayers' money, not the government's money," he says. "Some candidates in the race are saying, 'I'm not pro-taxpayer or pro-government, anti-taxpayer or anti-government,' but I can tell you, 'I'm pro-taxpayer.'" He maintains that assessors always have flexibility in how they assess properties, and that if he were elected to the position, he would use that flexibility to subvert the grasping politicians' plans by lowering citizens' taxes.

And so it goes. Throughout the evening, only a few sparks fly up around non-ideological issues. One is the proposed construction of the El Toro airport, just south of Irvine, which John Hedges, a candidate for county supervisor who currently works as a commercial airline pilot, vehemently endorses against the protests of people who live nearby. Another issue that resists the simple left-right categorization is the school-voucher idea. Most candidates reluctantly support the proposal that citizens be allowed to use public funds, in the form of a voucher, to pay for private education. The exception is Pat Bates, another contender hoping to represent the Republicans in the race for the Seventy-third Assembly District (and the candidate who will snare the nomination, beating both Apodaca and Lacey, and go on to capture the seat with 66 percent of the vote). Bates worries that no proposal she's heard has provided the guarantees that those public monies would not be used to support schools run by dangerous cults. Remember, this is a society where militiamen, the Branch Davidians, or the Heaven's Gate cult could be living just down the street from you. Overall though, this gathering does not stray far from the tone of a religious revival meeting, with established articles of faith being reaffirmed for the moral comfort of the long-since converted. Those sacred tenets are few but frequently stated: We promise to cut taxes, to take a hard line on crime, to cut government down to size, to return to traditional morality. Amen.

And now comes the fun part of the service . . . I mean meeting. The psalm-singing and sermonizing are all done, so chairman Tom Fuentes switches gears by introducing a little cinematic fossil that's been unearthed at Republican party headquarters. "You're going to see bits of Orange County in all of this," he foretells, "and you're going to see two guys that all of us Orange Countyans have come to esteem and love over the years. So lights, camera, action, and enjoy." When the room plunges into darkness, there's a familiar face on the video screen, with an even more familiar voice hailing, "Fellow Republicans, hello. I'm real glad to be able to talk to you folks today about the elections. I'm sure we all agree on the candidate — couldn't have a better one. And now we've got to make sure he gets elected."

That unmistakable drawl belongs to the eminently imitable John Wayne, dead these many years, who addresses the camera in front of the Pacific coastline outside his family homestead at Newport Beach. In fact, the waterfront itself becomes a prop the Duke uses to explain, through a succession of single-clause sentences that he hammers out like nails into a board, how ferrying one or two extra voters to the polls in each precinct can mean the difference between victory and defeat. The total vote is "like that bay out there," he says, with an over-the-shoulder nod. "Pretty big body of water. But it's just a lot of drops put together. And that's what an election is."

Which brings him to the point of this flick. Republican activists need to try their darnedest to corral those drops into a big pool of votes. They can do this, he says, by joining the Victory Squad, a collection of volunteers who are asked to donate six hours of their time on election day to make sure registered Republicans get to the polls. And who should be on hand to guide our tour through the busy day of two Victory Squad volunteers? None other than the Republican candidate for governor, "my good friend Ronald Reagan" — the second esteemed character Fuentes promised.

The crowd here at the Westin reacts to this film with the warmth of a person meeting a long-lost relative at a family reunion. A contented hum settles over the room, interrupted at several points by spontaneous laughter. Mostly it's the anachronisms that provoke this response. In the first instance, there's a rising chorus of titters and guffaws as the camera provides an aerial view of the steno pool at Victory Squad HQ — a brigade of innocent-looking young women whose blond beehive hairdos tower over the manual typewriters and up into the stratosphere. More chuckles as the camera follows volunteer John Bennet door-to-door; the crowd picks up on the double entendre as an attractive young woman answers the knock and Reagan's voice-over intones, "John's hit pay dirt on his first try." Slightly more nervous, ironic laughter as Reagan, describing the strategy of possibly mythical but pleasingly alliterative volunteer Mary Myers, comments, "Mary's chosen a part of the city she doesn't know well. That's a good idea. That's an enjoyable aspect of this job: you get to meet new people in neighbourhoods you've never stopped to look at before." A short spasm of silence, then knowing chuckles when the significance of the last line sinks in: you might not want to try Mary's method in the '90s, not in the age of crack houses and drive-by shootings and paranoid suburbanites who limit their excursions to the local shopping mall.

Yet none of these outbursts of mirth tonight seems derisive. On the contrary, there is a flat, respectful silence during the serious parts for instance, the closing montage in which Reagan quotes Winston Churchill: "The destiny of mankind is not decided by material computation. When great causes are on the move in the world, we learn that we are spirits, not animals, and that something is going on in space and time, and beyond space and time which, whether we like it or not, spells duty." Reagan delivers this kicker as the two most famous bars from Beethoven's Fifth Symphony swell in the background. With that last rousing invocation, it appears that the troops here at the Westin have been rallied. No question that the basic message in the film, despite the comic nostalgia, still holds sway with this crowd, that they share that Churchillian sense of destiny and duty to keep fighting the good fight. For many battle-weary Republican activists in this room tonight — most of them over 50, to be sure — there has no doubt been a reconnection with the past; a reminder of the wholesome values this suburban playground once represented, of why they moved out here in the first place.

After the two legends have faded from the screen, there's a weary sense of denouement that the final presenters must struggle against as they draw attention to the various fundraisers, breakfasts, and celebrity appearances that accompany this frantic electoral season. But one of the speakers is up against more than just the hour and the

inertia of the crowd. Tim Whittaker makes a couple of announcements on behalf of the Republican National Hispanic Assembly,
asking attendees to patronize a Hispanic-owned restaurant that
has supported Republican events, and also to turn out for a cigar
night featuring some high-calibre smokes from Nicaragua. Once the
embodiment of evil for former president Ronald Reagan, this country,
it seems, is very much in favour with this crowd ever since it came to
its senses and voted a right-wing president into office. Whittaker's
impassioned pitch, selling Hispanic Californians as potential GOP
stalwarts by virtue of their ingrained family values and strong sense
of enterprise, bucks the conventional wisdom, from both within
and without the Republican party. For Latinos have been hopelessly
alienated from the GOP, pushed squarely into the Democrat camp.
"One on one — that's what it's all about," says Whittaker, swimming
hard against that fatalistic current, "as we reach out to individuals,
regardless of ethnicity, to join our party."

A few moments later, after the meeting has been adjourned and
most participants have bolted for their cars, I get the sense of how
hard it will be for activists like Whittaker to make that line stick. I
turn on my tape recorder to gather some observations from the grassroots. Obliging me with some words of reflection is the congressman's
father — a short, grey-haired man with a Clark Gable moustache,
who shares both first and last names with his politician son and who
himself is running for a seat on the central committee. When I ask
what amongst the body of policy proposals we have heard this
evening makes the strongest connection with the everyday concerns of
voters in Orange County — what accounts for the Republicans' historical strength amongst their solid core of Orange County supporters
— he fingers immigration as the key concern, turning his six-guns
with sudden fury on the recent waves of newcomers who have transformed this formerly white bastion into a polyglot metropolis.

"Well, I guess a lot of the people who live here are refugees
from LA County, that's one thing," he begins, with a laugh. "I'm one
of those. I came to Orange County in 1954. LA used to be a nice town

when I was a kid. You know the immigration has absolutely messed up LA County, and now it's doing the same to Orange County. We have so many immigrants coming in here and most of them are aligned with the Democrats. So the demographics are changing in Orange County. You go down to Santa Ana, down on Fourth Street, and you'd think you're in old Mexico."

Somewhere in the midst of his remarks, the politician's father takes note of the fact that he has given me his name, and asks me, for the sake of prudence, not to use it. "What I'm telling you now is not something I want broadcast around," he explains. "Not that I'm ashamed of what I'm saying, but my son is a congressman and I don't want my remarks attached to him. He's one man and I'm another. Not that we disagree," he continues, "but there again he might not put things in exactly the same words that I do." And the congressman's father is probably right; it's only his forthright tone that separates him from the Republican Party officials, including Governor Pete Wilson, who have backed ballot propositions to deny medical and educational services to illegal immigrants and to outlaw bilingual education in schools (the latter measure, Proposition 227, was voted into law in June 1998). But party officials, unlike the candid rank-and-filer I'm speaking with, try to avoid the impression that their support of these measures stems from racism, from a fear of more California towns becoming like "old Mexico"; instead they insist that they are motivated by a simple concern over cost. Having strayed from the official script, the congressman's father picks up on that pecuniary theme with renewed gusto.

"In spite of the baloney they give us that these people pay for themselves, it's just not true," he says. "Taxpayers pay for their medical care, their emergency care, their babies, their education — all of these things are paid for by taxpayers. Some of them [illegal immigrants] pay some taxes, but not anywhere near the costs. In LA County, it costs $6,000 a year to educate one child." Of course, this contention that immigrants are more economic liabilities than contributors is, as Peter Schrag notes in *Paradise Lost*, "a matter of endless dispute;

there are studies proving almost any argument." Schrag reports that "one Los Angeles County study, published in 1992, indicated that while immigrants, legal and illegal, paid more in taxes than the county's costs in providing education, health and other public services, most of those taxes went to the federal government . . . Another report, projected from a San Diego County study, concluded that statewide local and state agencies were spending $3 billion more in taxes than they were receiving from those groups."[6]

Regardless of what the true statistical picture is, however, at a visceral level you feel something is amiss. You're standing in a hotel meeting room abutting one of the most prosperous shopping centres in the world, at the conclusion of a meeting composed mostly of people who drive away in BMWs, and listening to one of those people decry the public expenditure of $6,000 to educate a child. This sum, chump change to many in this room tonight, could mean for a poor immigrant child the difference between the chance of a future and oblivion. If the presence of illegal immigrants has made established Californians poorer, you wouldn't notice it here.

Consider the income differential that exists within Orange County alone. Santa Ana, which is now over 74 percent Latino, has a per capita income of $10,813, while Newport, which is over 90 percent white, has a per capita income of $56,000.[7] In addition, it is generally accepted that new immigrants most often provide cheap labour for landscaping firms and restaurants patronized by affluent Californians. Thus the economic relationship that exists between recent immigrants and the wealthy ensures that the rich will be able to make those exponentially higher earnings stretch a lot further than could be expected in many other jurisdictions. In effect, they are getting more value for those extra dollars, because poor, and especially illegal, immigrants work harder for less pay.

But who will get the last laugh? While a hard line on immigration issues may have shored up the Republicans' support amongst conservative (and mostly white) voters, in the long run, it may spell political disaster for the GOP. With a greater proportion of California's growing Asian and Latino populations becoming eligible to vote, Republicans have real reason to fear that yesterday's immigrant-bashing policies will provide an electoral windfall for rival Democrats. Latinos and Asians have been prodded into the political arena, says Steve Scott, editor of the policy magazine *California Journal*, primarily by Governor Pete Wilson. In his 1994 re-election campaign Wilson identified himself strongly with Proposition 187, the initiative aimed at cutting off medical, educational, and other services for illegal immigrants. Writes Scott:

> While Wilson insisted he had no quarrel with legal immigrants, the tenor of his campaign advertising left many Latino and Asian immigrants feeling under attack, regardless of citizenship or socio-economic status. The alienation from Wilson and his party deepened two years later, when Wilson embraced Proposition 209, another racially charged initiative which sought to ban those aspects of affirmative action conferring racial and gender preferences.

Though many Republican activists believe they can heal the rift, party adviser and former Reagan adviser Stuart Spencer — he had hired the BASICO psychologists to work on Reagan's first gubernatorial campaign — has warned that if Asians and Latinos are not brought into the fold, the Republican party in California will descend into "permanent minority status."[8]

In the short run the Republicans may have scored a victory, if their goal was indeed to use such legislation to retrench white dominance in state-funded institutions and workplaces. The removal of racial quotas from state-funded universities, for instance, has resulted in a 61 percent drop in minority admissions at UC Berkeley, a 36 percent drop at UCLA, and a 40 percent drop at UC San Diego.[9] But the GOP soon felt the corresponding sting of ballot-box backlash in response to anti-immigrant initiatives. In Orange County, one of the first solid indications that an electoral sea change was in the works came in the November 1996 federal election with the defeat of longtime Republican congressman Robert Dornan by Democratic contender Loretta Sanchez. The racial subtext of that contest was not fully brought into public view, however, until after the election. Then, two separate probes were conducted into Dornan's allegations that a "massive criminal conspiracy" involving widespread voting by illegal immigrants was responsible for his loss to Sanchez.

The Republican incumbent, who had represented Orange County's Forty-sixth District for nine terms, had been a local icon of the Christian right. Dubbed "one of Congress's most colorful and confrontational members" by the Associated Press,[10] Dornan is known for his flamboyant rhetorical style. When asked a question by a reporter from the OCWeekly, the countywide alternative newsmagazine, for example, he asserted that the paper is "Satan's instrument" and "an evil paper spreading infected bodily fluids all over."[11]

Yet bluster, bombast, and biblical curses were of no avail to Dornan in his post-electoral brawl with Sanchez. At the federal level, a Republican-led task force recommended that Dornan's challenge be dropped, after finding that only 750 non-citizens voted in the election — far fewer than the 2,500 illegal voters Dornan had claimed to know about, and fewer than the 984 votes by which Sanchez had won the election.[12] Meanwhile a "nearly all white, all-Republican Orange County grand jury," as the OCWeekly described it, concluded that 442 votes had been cast by illegals countywide in the 1996 elections, a figure that then became fodder for partisan newspaper ads decrying "intentional voter fraud" in the Sanchez-Dornan race. The ads had been bought with public funds by California secretary of state Bill Jones, an ally of Dornan. However, according to OCWeekly writer R. Scott Moxley, what the ads failed to mention is that the 442 votes were spread across the county, not confined to the Forty-sixth District; that they would have gone to both Democrats and Republicans; and that many of those votes were cast by people who had applied for citizenship and were genuinely confused about whether the law allowed them to exercise an electoral franchise. In any case, whatever fraction of those 442 votes were cast for Sanchez in the Forty-sixth District, their absence would not have kept Dornan in office.[13]

On the other hand, Dornan's crusade to regain his seat — so thoroughly motivated by the assumption that Hispanic votes must somehow be tainted by illegality and so clear in its message that Latino voters constitute an illegitimate segment of the state's society, unworthy of the rights of citizenship — has surely gone a long way to making lifelong Democrats out of growing numbers of Latinos who are about to have their first encounters with a US ballot box. After the congressional committee dropped the Dornan complaint, high-profile California Democrats like Senator Barbara Boxer wasted no time in publicly embracing Sanchez as a symbol of Democratic inclusiveness. Sanchez's press conference, in the wake of the committee decision, was broadcast nationally on C-SPAN, the US political cable channel, an indication that her victory ranked as a national landmark and, quite possibly, historic turning point.

Fulminations like those that emerged from the Sanchez-Dornan fight are an exotic sight for the political tourist. And for a visiting Canadian, who still remembers the determinedly bland, inoffensive leadership of politicians like longtime Ontario premier Bill Davis, who remembers the not-too-distant day when Canadian politicos appeared to agree on everything from the need for socialized medicine to official bilingualism, scenes like the fearsome freak show at the Westin in Costa Mesa are proof, on a surface level at least, of how different Canadians are from Americans. Indeed, many of the most heated debates at the Westin seemed to be unmistakably American in nature, springing from the peculiarities of the local landscape. The obsession with immigration is a good example; so are the pivotol influences of fundamentalist Christian churches and the fierce nationalism, bordering on a religion itself, that could lead to prolonged harangues over the Pledge of Allegiance and the portrayal of American history in a school play.

Yet a closer examination reveals that many of these elements of US politics are creeping into our debates back home. This became especially evident as Mike Harris's Tories sought a second mandate in Ontario, less than a year after Californians were beckoned to the polls in November 1998. Right-wing commentators such as David Frum or the crew at *Alberta Report* magazine have for some time been urging Canada's rightist parties to move beyond their fiscal conservatism and embrace the conservative social agenda — rejecting gay rights, for example, or making things tougher for single-parent families, ideas that have become front and centre for the US political right.

Harris may not have taken up these specific suggestions, but he was clearly headed down a parallel path during the 1999 election campaign, taking aim at groups that could be portrayed as lacking in moral character, playing on social hostilities and the sense that some old and comforting social values had been lost. So while he didn't go after immigrants, he attacked welfare recipients: People would now have to submit to mandatory drug testing if they hoped to receive social assistance. Meanwhile, that sense of nationalism, while more low-key in Canada, was also appealed to: Harris announced that his government would compel students to rise each morning to sing the national anthem. Of course, throughout their first term, Harris's Tories attempted to play the education issue in precisely the same way as it had been played in California — by denouncing teachers' unions and school-board employees ("educrats") and promising to give parents direct control over their children's education. At the same time, however, their actual policies were to centralize power over schools and to cut huge sums from the education budget. It's clear, given polls showing Ontarians' ongoing concern about the handling of education, that many people in this province, who already enjoyed a system that was open to parental involvement, were sceptical of the government's line that the closing of hundreds of schools could be blamed on entrenched "interest groups" such as teachers' unions.

Overall, this style of politics has been established in the cooler north with much less of the theatrical, evangelical flamboyance that was on display in Orange County. Canucks are generally more retiring people; we make less of a show of ourselves. Still, it's logical to ponder — if Canada's right-wing revolutionaries continue to look south for inspiration — how long it will be before we all start bellowing like Rush Limbaughs.

— — —

Back at the Westin South Coast Plaza hotel in Costa Mesa, however, the Republican congressman's father is sanguine about the prospect that vast demographic changes could interfere with his party's enduring dominion over Orange County. As Doris Day sang, *que sera, sera*; Latinos have become a majority in several parts of the south county, and there's probably not much the party can do to stop them from resenting many long-standing Republican policies. But where my source does smell trouble — which he believes the party has the power to avoid — is in that business about "family values."

"Abortion is a losing issue," he says bluntly when I ask him if there is difficulty ahead for Republicans. "I know Republican women who even give money to Democrats, just because of that one issue. Abortion is the most divisive issue in the Republican party . . . I think the Orange County voters have a lot of enthusiasm for most of the ideas [tonight's sampling of candidates] were talking about, and most Republicans are against abortions, but there are different degrees of it. If you say you are against abortion for any reason, that's a loser. But a lot of these people, that's part of their platform, and in fact that's about 17 percent of the people who don't want abortion for any reason. That's less than one in five people."

I ask him if Orange County voters may be moving away from their traditional conservatism — if Republican dominance will be challenged by non-white immigration, the liability of radical anti-abortionists within Republican ranks, and the emergence of what pundit Joe Klein predicts will be California's new social coalition of women voters and soft-hearted computer professionals (who, he says, are likely to reject hard-line ideologies in favour of a more conciliatory "digital" approach to politics).[14] The congressman's father responds with an answer that tonight's meeting has not prepared me for. After three and a half hours of thunderingly unequivocal pronouncements, at the end of the evening I'm suddenly hearing words with an unmistakable ring of uncertainty — one bordering on pessimism.

"Well, it's hard to say. I don't know," he says before introducing, without prompting, a scenario that often arises for parties that savour the bitter taste of defeat after a long run of landslide victories. The party may splinter, falling prey to internal dissension and single-interest crusades. "The next election is going to tell us a lot about whether the party goes off in all directions. You know, the people who think that abortion is not that bad; the people who think you've got to have absolutely no abortions whatsoever. Then we've got people who go off in [Ross Perot's] Reform Party and, of course, the Libertarians. All of these groups want less government and less interference in their lives, and we can do a lot more if we band together. You know, united we stand."

— — —

As it turned out, the November 1998 election did not provide an encouraging sign for Republicans, and its supporters may indeed form splinter groups. In what the *L.A. Times* described as "the best showing for their party since 1958," Democrats seized control of both the state assembly and the governor's office, with Democrat Gray Davis defeating Republican Dan Lungren by an impressive twenty-point margin. "If my election says anything," said Davis, "it's that people want problem-solvers, not ideologues." As predicted, a strong minority turnout contributed to the Democratic landslide, with Latinos increasing their share of the vote to 13 percent from 8 percent in 1994, and blacks rising to 13 percent of the electorate from 5 percent in 1994. In their grudge match at the congressional level, Sanchez scored a more decisive victory, beating Dornan by roughly 40,000 votes to 28,000. In Orange County, at the state assembly level, Republicans lost their hold on Anaheim but kept much of the rest of the county — including District 73, which was captured for the GOP by Patricia Bates.

For some time Orange County's conservatives have had the feeling that the curtain may soon close on them. Many hard-core right-wingers in the county, sensing the irresistible tide of liberalism and multi-ethnicity waiting to wash over them, have chosen to build them-selves an ark to head for higher ground. For many of them that higher ground, quite literally, is Colorado Springs, Colorado, a new mecca of conservatism in the mountain state that created national headlines in 1992 when its electorate passed the anti-gay ballot initiative known as Amendment 2. LA journalist Marc Cooper recounts, in a riveting profile that appeared in the *Nation*, how an already conservative town — which got that way partly because it is home to four military installations, including the Air Force Academy and the NORAD control centre — became much more conservative when a local economic development committee began to encourage conservative Christian organizations to move their headquarters to Colorado Springs. "Colorado had just liberalized its tax code to accommodate religious groups as California was tightening up its regulations," he writes. "After a local business foundation sweetened the pot with a $4 million grant to buy land, Los Angeles–based Focus on the Family took the bait and relocated to the Springs, leading what would become a stampede of like-minded brethren."[15]

So a city that had been laid desperately low in the early 1990s as military budget-trimming shut down local aerospace industries was suddenly reborn as a boom town. More than seventy "evangelical and para-church groups" moved in, along with 2,500 employees and their families. Next came a steady stream of unaffiliated refugees, most of them from decaying urban and suburban communities in Southern California, who found that the substantial equity in their homes back on the Coast would buy them a massive spread in the undervalued real estate market of Colorado Springs. Their trek was a replay of the great exodus that had brought all those Midwestern ex-servicemen to Orange County in search of quiet family life, fresh air, and a culturally homogeneous community back in the 1950s — only this time the pilgrims were heading back inland, since you can't move any farther west of OC without falling into the Pacific. Cooper describes the suburban pastures mushrooming around Colorado Springs in a way that would seem familiar to those who had, in earlier years, rushed to OC to escape the turmoil that is LA. New subdivisions, he wrote, are built on "lopped, topped and slabbed hillsides covered with a thin crust of pre-planned, Southern California–style gated communities with overblown names seemingly lifted from $6 bottles of Zinfandel: Raven's Crest, Sable Chase, Briargate, Rock Rimmon, Black Forest, Summer Fields." Migrants to Colorado Springs from Orange County can even read a local newspaper just like the one back home. That's because part of the shared heritage of the two regions includes the presence of Harry Hoiles, the outspoken, libertarian former president of Freedom Communications, a company that publishes both the *Orange County Register* (whose editorial line, as one wag describes it, is "guns good/government bad") and the *Colorado Springs Gazette Telegraph*.[16]

This new exodus is sure to change both locales. For Colorado Springs, the eastbound pipeline has restored the mountain city's flagging economy and established its reputation as the worldwide capital of the Christian political right. But what about Orange County? Will the departure of some of the most zealous members of its conservative vanguard create some kind of a vacuum? Will this combine with changing demographics, new political challenges, and a softening outlook amongst info-age "knowledge workers" to instal a new, more pragmatic brand of politicking behind the invisible barricades of suburbia?

There's a strange new breed in these parts — they call themselves liberals — who are betting that the answer is yes.

8 | A Liberal Renaissance?

It is one of those typically luminous Southern California days. On the grounds of the University of California at Irvine (UCI), sunshine is everywhere, bouncing in shimmering waves off the rounded, white concrete contours of the buildings, penetrating the deep green, sculpted shrubbery, cut into abstract shapes like living versions of Henry Moore.

It is into this radiant scene — which the locals probably take for granted but which creates a kind of reverie for me, aware as I am that it is March but there is no snow, not even a chill in the air — that a parade of distinguished visitors strides, heading from campus auditorium to a quarantined picnic ground. A quick visual survey suggests these guests are almost all white, over sixty, and know how to dress for a special occasion. (Later, the crush of Mercedes and Jaguars leaving the parking garage will also suggest that they are loaded.) At the picnic ground, serving staff in white shirts and black bow ties will hand them their box lunches, small containers of moulded clear plastic filled, it would be safe to assume, with something other than Big Macs and fries.

I am not part of this crowd so I keep walking, past the VIP section, to the little commercial area where students line up in front of hamburger franchises, pizza outlets, and — yes, for this is California the Hip — a sushi joint. I grab a slice of pizza and head for the nearby tuck shop to buy a newspaper and check out the wide assortment of ginseng-enhanced "power" refreshments, then plant myself at an outdoor table to sample the campus culture. There is a pleasant buzz here; it feels enlivening to be in a place where people from a variety of backgrounds have this kind of casual, friendly engagement. Some walk together, some talk, some read. At the table across from me, a student gets hit on by two wandering proselytizers, one a tall, hefty white guy and the other a slight, short Asian fellow. "Hi, I'm Andrew and this is Wade. We're Christians," says one of them. But the student sitting at the table responds that he's not interested and so the apprentice Billy Grahams quickly move on.

When I glance around, the difference between the students who mill about on this terrace and the visitors cordoned off farther up becomes immediately and strikingly apparent: about 50 percent of the students are non-white — Asian, Latino, and black, in descending order. Here on this little parcel of green splendor, in fact, is a clear representation of the changing of the guard. That procession of older, white visitors have the money and the power today. Meanwhile, the polyglot student body is awaiting its turn — if not for the money then at least for some of the power.

When it's time to head back to the Bren Events Center the parade line forms anew. The visitors stream across a grassy embankment, through a field, across a street. At the corner a white Honda sports car sits with engine idling, waiting for a break in the human traffic. The tinted passenger window is rolled down, and a young man inside calls out to no one in particular, "Who's here today?"

"Al Gore," one of the guests responds.

"Al Gore?" the kid in the Honda says. "Cool."

Well, probably half cool, which in Orange County is a lot better than being totally cool in the outlaw sense of, say, Jack Nicholson or Christian Slater. On the one hand the vice-president has his relative youth and his film-star looks and his Hollywood connections. These, combined with the perception that the Democratic party he represents is less likely to give sanctuary to racist wackos than the Republicans, tend to give him a certain amount of sway with hip, young, educated Orange Countyans, who may resent being governed by people who still live in the 1950s. Cool — yes, in a way, he is. But on the other hand he is family-values Al, a southern-bred graduate of divinity school, son of longtime federal senator Albert Gore and husband of Tipper Gore, who led the congressional fight to clean up rock and roll by requiring parental-warning stickers on albums containing "explicit" lyrics. In Orange County, however, the risk of alienating Marilyn Manson fans is probably outweighed by the advantage of appealing to those older, more conservative folk who, although they would never join the Christian Coalition, may want reassurance that a future president will conduct himself with a greater sense of personal decorum than Gore's current boss.

Not that Gore is — officially, at least — here to campaign. The stated purpose of his visit is to cap a day-long academic conference by delivering a speech on "reinventing government" — an otherwise somnolence-inducing topic that has apparently become a passionate obsession of the VP's — and also to mark the endowment of a new chair in public management at UCI by Gore's personal friends Roger and Janice Johnson. The crowd is eagerly awaiting that speech and there's plenty of time for the anticipation to build. First the slow trek back into the Bren, with everyone having to pass through a metal detector and media types getting searched by Secret Service agents. Then the veep's motorcade is late. So for an hour and a half we react like Pavlovian dogs and bolt upright in our seats each time there is a sudden motion on or around the stage.

When the vice-president and his entourage do finally step into the spotlight, they launch into a presentation that has a casual, ad libbed quality, but that has obviously been meticulously calculated to hit all the right buttons. It demonstrates that while Gore and his team are in sync with the challenges of life in the '90s, they will not stray too far from the "traditional values" and free-enterprise spirit that tend to get people elected around these parts. That Gore is sharing the stage with Roger Johnson — a corporate heavy-hitter and longtime Republican who in recent years moved into the Democratic camp — in itself makes a powerful statement. Johnson is the former chairman and CEO of Western Digital Corporation, a Fortune 500 high-tech outfit based in Irvine, and he has also worked in executive capacities at such companies as Burroughs, Memorex, Singer, and General Electric. In 1993, however, he hauled his accumulated corporate cachet over to the public sector where, as UCI chancellor Laurel Wilkening tells the crowd, "he was the first Republican to hold a top post in the Clinton administration." His job was to assist Al Gore in the task of overhauling the federal public service by streamlining, redesigning, and paring down government operations and processes.

Despite Gore's laudatory remarks about his pal Roger's accomplishments during this time, Johnson's own assessment is that his attempts to make the federal bureaucracy function more efficiently were hampered by the fact that "we were dealing with a subject — professional management — that really had no constituency." Unlike housing or health or education, he says, "there was no political force that could sustain this effort over the long run . . . That's why the vice-president and I decided to put the concept of professional management into an independent academic body. Put aside the partisanship and deal with it in a place where you could research and analyze." And that's the genesis of the Roger W. and Janice M. Johnson Endowed Chair in Civic Governance and the Social Ecology of Public Management, the creation of which is being celebrated here today.

It's worth noting that Janice's name also rings some bells with this crowd. During a recitation of her local philanthropic endeavours comes a burst of applause when Chancellor Wilkening mentions Janice's work on the board of the AIDS Services Foundation and as co-chair of AIDS Walk, Orange County — associations which may partly explain why the couple is no longer comfortable in a Republican party that has become beholden to anti-gay, fundamentalist-Christian storm troopers. Later, Gore will invite some other featured guests to come under the PR umbrella of Roger and Janice, who project a perfect combination of hard-edged fiscal conservatism and a commitment to progressive social values, as he announces the names of several notables who are today travelling in their caravan. One is Loretta Sanchez, vanquisher of the homophobe Robert Dornan. Gore introduces Sanchez as a person who "actually comes out of a business background and has the same devotion to the new ideas of reinventing government that Roger and Janice and I share."

When Gore is at the podium, he is, in fact, fighting two battles simultaneously. One is the battle of Orange County, wherein the vice-president must persuade the public that the lessons of tax revolt and conservative backlash have been learned, that his crew are spending-choppers and waste-busters who have a commitment to making governments cheaper and more responsive to the needs of the average angry voter. The other is the battle of Hollywood, which requires that Gore neutralize the potency of that old cinematic iconography (the association of John Wayne and Ronald Reagan with a set of right-wing libertarian political ideas) by establishing a new set of associations of his own. This is why Gore quickly moves into the first of what will turn out be numerous references to the movies.

"It's an exciting time, of course — the Academy Awards are coming up," he announces out of the blue to the befuddled amusement of the audience. Then quickly into a chatty moment of personal reflection, "Last year, my wife, Tipper, and I were watching the Academy Awards on television, propped up on pillows on the bed. Billy Crystal came up — he was the host — and he had an Oscar on the podium. He looked up at the camera — and this is a true story, probably it didn't leave an impression on you; I guarantee it left an impression on me — and he noted how many people had been nominated for Academy Awards and how very few are going to win and that a lot of people are going to be disappointed. And he said, 'Remember, the only person who is guaranteed to wake up with a statue in the morning is Tipper Gore.'"

As the laughter rises, Gore begins to mug for the audience, turning sideways in profile and standing frozen like a statue before delivering the coup de grace: "As Groucho Marx once said, 'I resemble that remark.'"

It's a clever little anecdote, tossed into the crowd casually, with an endearing awkwardness, but it's filled with positive messages. In one thirty-second digression, Gore has managed to associate himself with a glamorous Hollywood elite — they obviously think Gore is important enough to make jokes about — yet has maintaind the impression that he is self-effacing, humble, and, given that he spends his free time watching TV in bed with his wife, a contented family man living in an island of domestic tranquillity.

There are plenty more humorous stories this afternoon, although Gore steers clear of any mother-in-law jokes or references to "the madam of the bawdy house." Instead, there are more self-deprecating jabs, as well as many more references to pop culture. A highlight among these is Gore's recounting of his appearance on the David Letterman show, where he delivered the top ten list and broke an ashtray. Then there are more references to the Academy Awards, all delivered in the same extemporaneous, stream-of-consciousness style of an average guy sharing his remarks with a close pal over coffee and doughnuts at the local mall. Gore wants people to feel they know him, and the guy he wants them to know is someone who's conservative but contemporary, an aficionado of the latest Hollywood blockbusters even though his wife won't let him listen to a lot of the stuff playing on the radio.[1]

When it's time to get serious, Gore does not fall back on stock patriotism, but instead sticks with delivering multi-layered messages aimed at the diverse constituencies that could form a new Democratic coalition in the suburban hinterlands of LA.

"Abraham Lincoln described the United States of America as 'the last, best hope of humanity,'" the vice-president begins. "That's still true today; in fact, it's more true today than it ever was before. Look at Bosnia and Rwanda . . . and all the problems all over the world, and how people in every nation on every continent, from every background, look to the United States of America as their hope for the future. We attract many of the best and the brightest from all over the world, and we feel we have a destiny as a nation to help chart a course towards a bright future for humankind."

Beyond the value of this speech as an obvious restatement of that classical conception of America as the beckoning light that shines from the Statue of Liberty, attracting the world's downtrodden with its promise of freedom, Gore's remarks are a skilful attempt to appeal to two separate constituencies that, in Orange County, have historically been at cross-purposes. By referring to Lincoln, a leading icon of the Republican party, Gore has issued an invitation to disaffected conservatives to join, as Roger and Janice Johnson did, a Democratic party that is considerably less liberal than it has been in the past. In addition, with the flattering description of immigrants as "the best and brightest," as people who come to the United States to share its values, the vice-president reiterates for that growing number of non-white newcomers in the California suburbs that it is the Democrats who can provide an alternative to the politics of xenophobia.

But beyond being an advertisement for his party, this riff on America as the "last, best hope of humanity" provides a way for the vice-president to segue into a lecture on what ails the American political system and what can fix it. For while the world still looks to the US with faith and confidence, he says, the same is not true of Americans themselves. An annual public opinion poll, taken for the past forty years, has asked Americans, "Do you trust the federal government to do the right thing most of the time?" While 77 percent of respondents answered affirmatively in 1962, the number fell to 17 percent by 1992, "and if you look carefully at the way the numbers went down," says Gore, "you can see the Vietnam War, you can see Watergate, you can see the 21 percent interest rates in the '70s, you can see a lot of shocks to the body politic that caused a plummeting self-confidence in our system of government." This leads, naturally enough for a politician, to Gore's self-congratulatory remark about how positive responses to that poll question have headed back upward for the first time ever under the Clinton administration, reaching 35 percent in 1998. The vice-president attributes this trajectory to his administration's commitment to providing better value from government by making agencies more flexible and cutting overhead and waste. So he crows about the milestones that have been reached: "200 outdated government programs" and "more than 60,000 pages of unnecessary regulations" have been cut, while the federal government workforce has become the smallest in absolute terms since 1962, and the smallest as a percentage of the country's total workforce since before FDR's New Deal. Overall result: the US government has become lighter by 350,000 employees and $137 billion, and the budget is balanced for the first time in recent memory.

Of course, many others will discount the idea that the federal government has slimmed down merely by embracing efficiency. During a morning panel before Gore's arrival, UCI Urban and Regional Planning professor Helen Ingram, who holds the university's chair in Social Ecology of Peace and International Cooperation, hinted that the crisis California's counties face in trying to pay for social programs is at least partly an outgrowth of federal belt-tightening. "Decentralization and devolving programs that were run out of Washington have real consequences," she said. "And streamlining and cutting and making the federal government more efficient has really meant that a lot of the things that used to be done at the federal level have now been passed down to lower levels of government." (This accusation will be familiar to Canadians who have seen federal transfer payment cuts linked to worsening conditions of homelessness and hunger in Canadian cities.)

But whatever you choose to call it — increasing government efficiency or simply shirking the responsibility for funding social welfare programs — it's clear that this exercise in "reinventing government" has been undertaken largely to still the rage of middle-class conservatives. Their belief that government has become remote, arrogant, and profligate, has undermined the sense of social legitimacy that allows governments to function. The challenge, as Gore sees it, is to "redeem the promise of representative democracy by renewing our self-confidence."

By this he means it's necessary to renovate the image of the public service so as to counter the entrenched hostility towards "professional politicians," "bureaucrats," and civic institutions. For decades populist revolutionaries from Goldwater to Reagan to Newt Gingrich — as well as legions of local politicians like those I encountered at the Westin South Coast Plaza — have been using the word "government" as a synonym for evil; many have even suggested that the only reason one should run for office is to be able to subvert the great behemoth, to be able to put sugar in the gas tank of that infernal machine that destroys everything in its path. Now, says Gore, it's time to invest some key phrases with new meaning. In much the same way the tag "made in Japan" was transformed from a signifier of shoddy workmanship to a mark of excellence in the 1970s, the words "good enough for government work," says the VP, can recapture their original meaning, acquired during World War II when the federal government spearheaded the war effort, as a phrase intended to inspire confidence and trust.

All of this, apparently, is much more than a matter of semantics; there are serious practical implications in the way the public views government and in the way government's functions are described. In a morning panel that foreshadowed the Gore speech, a collection of embattled civil servants and politicians complained of how this entrenched cynicism and the related momentum towards government-by-referendum — now a defining feature of California politics — have made it virtually impossible for public managers to manage, especially when managing means exercising some discretion over how funds are allocated.

It used to be that voters trusted politicians to make decisions on their behalf, drawing on the expertise in the bureaucracy and the dossiers of information that individual citizens might not have the time, inclination, or possibly the ability to digest — all with the under-standing the public could vote those representatives out of office at the end of their term if they didn't like the job they'd done. But that trust, apparently, has vanished. Now the California electorate want to dictate down to the letter, via the ballot-box initiative, exactly how politicians are going to run government and how they are going to spend their money.

What this means, in effect, is that those historic political innova-tions born in California of suburban angst and dislocation — such as the Reagan campaign's abandonment of traditional politicking in favour of TV appearances and high-tech marketing, and the triumph of Proposition 13 in pitting public outrage against a power elite — have perhaps not so much effected a reform of the existing system as led to the creation of something entirely new.

"You take what we've been guaranteed in our constitution: a republican form of government or representative form of govern-ment," explained Ron Bates, mayor of the City of Los Alamitos and president of the League of California Cities, "and then look at the direction that people are tending to go now, where they want to vote on everything, and you'll see we're being transformed into a kind of town-hall democratic process. To me that's a huge challenge for us as leaders trying to accomplish things. Because, in this technological age, we need more and more information to make appropriate decisions.

And you're asking voters to look at a thirty-second sound bite to vote on a major issue. It just can't be done."

In other words, citizens are telling politicians to adopt specific policies without sufficient knowledge of the mechanics of government or an understanding of what the spinoff implications of those policies will be. For Bates, the saga of the Orange County bankruptcy of 1994 illustrates the dangers of government-by-referendum. To begin with, many observers believe that county treasurer Bob Citron's decision to invest $7.6 billion of county money in a series of complex and highly risky derivatives-investment schemes was motivated at least partly by a desire to ford the gap between, on the one hand, voter expectations that the county government would deliver a high level of services and, on the other hand, the severe spending restrictions imposed by Prop 13. (A succession of annual polls conducted by UCI political scientist Mark Baldassare indicate that Orange County residents have a desire to see public services increased rather than cut, while holding the apparently contradictory belief that taxes and public spending are too high. When pressed, they most often explain the contradiction by pointing to unspecified government "waste" as the problem.)

And even after the county recovered from the bankruptcy, said Bates, plebiscite politics prevented long-term financial safeguards being erected to bar a repeat performance. One of the problems leading up to OC's financial meltdown was the lack of expertise by the elected officials who ostensibly oversaw the treasurer's activities to assess the risk involved with Citron's "creative solution" to bridging the services/spending gap. Bates said that Orange County did have an option in the wake of the disaster to change the system. It could have had "more appointed officials at the top reporting through a system that, from a management point of view, made some sense." But that adjustment had to be approved by referendum, and it did not pass. Voters chose instead to keep financial oversight in the hands of elected treasurers and county assessors, whose *political* credentials may prove to be more important in getting them into office than their *technical* ones. The decision may be rooted once again in the public's deep suspicions about government; the overriding concern was the "account-ability" issue, with an elected official being widely thought to be more subject to scrutiny and possible recall than an appointed official.

Yet for the most part, governments' challenges in trying to live within the dictates of multitudinous plebiscite decisions are far less spectacular than dealing with bankruptcy. On a daily basis, they have to decide which pressing social need or decaying piece of infra-structure will get some money thrown at it and which will not. This task has become all the more difficult since the passage in 1996 of Proposition 218, which was apparently aimed at closing up the "loopholes" local governments had been using to get around Prop 13's tight clamp on spending; these loopholes usually involved user fees and area-specific taxation targeted to improvements in particular neighbourhoods. The new legislation takes aim at these by requiring that any new fee, tax, or assessment, beyond the regular property tax dealt with by Proposition 13, must be approved by referendum.[2] "Under Prop 218," Bates told the UCI forum, "for anything we do now, to raise any kind of revenue for public programs, we need to go to the electorate."

And given the outcomes of previous tax-raising ballot initiatives, this does not bode well for governments scrambling to keep up with public expectations. Part of the problem, according to Stanley Oftelie, president and CEO of the Orange County Business Council (perhaps an unlikely proponent of higher taxes), is that citizens will invariably vote to reject tax hikes because it's the one economic sphere in which they have some real power. "People can vote to reduce their taxes. They can't vote to reduce the cost of gasoline and they can't vote to reduce the price of bread. We've set up a system where government is not playing on a level playing field," he said. The rules also appear skewed in the way that, to pass, all tax-raising initiatives require the endorsement of a "supermajority," or 66 percent of voters. Such a parameter gives an effective veto over important fiscal decisions to a small minority of voters.

Several members of that UCI panel believe, however, that in the long run local governments could come out winners in these contests if they could better communicate to the public how government spends its money. To that end, panellists had a host of suggestions, from beefing up school civics courses to distributing information packages to homes, but most ideas related to that great nemesis of any dedicated-but-not-so-sound-bite-savvy bureaucrat: the news media. County of Orange CEO Jan Mittermeier related that county officials have conducted intensive information sessions for the area's major newspapers to explain to reporters how to read financial-planning documents. Such documents are enormously complex, all the more so because of referendum-initiated budget restrictions and the questions of jurisdictional authority that make a tangled mess of the California political system. But beyond the imperative for reporters to have in-depth knowledge on financial issues is the matter of what is defined as glamorous enough to warrant coverage. Mittermeier noted, for instance, that in the election preceding the OC bankruptcy, one candidate for treasurer alleged that there was something seriously amiss with Citron's investment pool, yet the newspapers were either unable or unwilling to delve into the dry mechanics of the pool's management and so did not investigate the charges.

And that is the Achilles' heel of a system originally intended to give citizens the power to make sure politicians acted in the public interest, rather than in the interest of powerful lobbies: citizens can use that power effectively only if they have the necessary information, and they're unlikely to get it from the six o'clock news.

In fact, the referendum system was brought to California long before the age of television. Provision for ballot initiatives, referendums, and recall of elected officials were written into the California constitution in 1911, during the tenure of Governor Hiram Walker's Progressive party, which sought to release the state from the oppressive, monopolistic grip of the Southern Pacific Railroad Company. As Peter Schrag recounts in *Paradise Lost*, SP controlled the transport of goods to market and owned vast tracts of land, giving it control over prices in the market and the resources to buy the obedience of politicians in the legislature in Sacramento. The ballot initiative — originally a Swiss innovation that had been adopted in several other states such as South Dakota, Oregon, Utah, and Colorado before coming to California — was hailed as a means of returning government to the service of the public by pitting the will of "the great moral masses" against "the corrupt but powerful few." The premise was simple: voters would tell the politicians what they wanted done, and the politicians would be legally bound to follow their instructions.

Even as early as 1911, however, grim prophecies arose that the intent of the ballot initiative could be subverted by well-financed and well-organized groups who knew how to use confusion, distortion, or misinformation to their advantage. The *New York Times* editorialized that a flood of ballot initiatives would overwhelm voters' ability to critically judge each proposition, making it more likely that their votes would be based merely on the impression of what an initiative would do rather than on reality. "The new method is proposed as a check on the machines," the paper stated. "But the strength of the machines lies in the inattention and indifference of the voters, and the voters are sure in the long run to be more inattentive and indifferent in proportion to the number of questions forced upon them at one time. When the machine managers get familiar with the working of the new method, they will work it for their own ends far more readily than they work the present method."

Despite such dire warnings, the ballot initiative was adopted but remained a small footnote to California politics for most of this century. In 1914, at the height of the Progressive party's reformist crusade, six ballot initiatives were approved by voters; the next most productive year was 1934, when three initiatives were enacted. In total, between 1911 and 1978 (the year of Prop 13's passage), forty-two were initiatives approved by voters, most of them dealing with matters of minor importance. These unimpressive numbers are partly explained by the difficulty of getting a referendum question on the ballot; a statutory initiative requires the valid signatures of registered voters equal to 5 percent of voters in the previous election (the figure is 8 percent for a constitutional initiative), and gathering those signatures would have been a daunting task for most voluntary organizations.

But conditions changed by the late 1970s, when politicians and interest groups seeking political influence watched, awestruck, as Howard Jarvis's campaign for Proposition 13 scored a victory so huge it set California's fiscal agenda at least until the end of this century and humbled the wiliest of politicians. Within the new age of sophisticated demographic profiling and TV-based political campaigning, finding enough signatures to qualify a ballot measure no longer required momentous effort. True, it might be expensive, but the Jarvis victory showed that a successful referendum campaign was likely more than worth the cost. Also, a feeling prevailed that the ballot initiative had once again become right for the times, coming as it did in an age of political gridlock, when the diversity of California's electorate made it all the more difficult to achieve consensus or to build coalitions around major issues — a phenomenon that gave rise, in turn, to a public perception that politicians needed direct instructions to get things done. The late '70s and early '80s also saw several high-profile influence-peddling scandals, reviving the idea that the public needed some means of reining in the shifty politicians in Sacramento, of breaking the spell that gift-bearing lobbyists had cast over them.

And thus was born what Schrag refers to as "the initiative industrial complex." Not surprisingly the great pioneer of this new industry was the advertising firm Butcher-Forde, which had propelled Jarvis's Prop 13 campaign to victory with its precisely targeted, well-crafted direct mail campaigns and its powerhouse TV ads. Having been given ownership of Jarvis's mailing list for ten years, the firm was by the mid-1980s earning $12 million a year through their own use of the list and additional sums by renting it out to other firms. Butcher-Forde was joined by a host of other initiative manufacturers attracted by the huge revenue potential, and these consulting firms assumed a central role in a revived referendum process that saw a ballooning of the number of initiatives on the ballot. In the early 1980s, Butcher-Forde and its new competitors showed that commercial motivations, rather than ideological fervour or popular political discontent, could be the most potent mover of the process, when they began to test-market their own ideas for ballot measures and then hawk them to potential sponsors. This foreshadowed the shape of the industry today. Often the consulting firms themselves devise the issue and the campaign, pinpoint a demographic group likely to generate the required signatures, and then sell the sponsorship of the initiative to an industry group or business that might benefit, or to a politician who wants to be associated with a popular cause. In some cases, proposition sponsorships have been auctioned off to the highest bidder.

Today, it must be said, the whole process is animated not by volunteer labour but by vast rivers of money. The consulting firm generally subcontracts to companies that hire canvassers to collect signatures door-to-door or at tables set up in shopping malls. An alternative is to petition voters using direct mail. While the normal cost range for collecting signatures is typically between 85 cents and $1.50 a name, there have been some notable high-end exceptions. One insurance-industry-sponsored initiative involved the expenditure of $5 million to collect 400,000 valid signatures, an outlay that breaks down to more than $12 a name.

Critics scream that the one function not provided for within this assembly-line process is public education. Schrag quotes one consulting-firm executive as saying that canvassers are instructed not to conduct in-depth discussions with potential signers, since the more time spent in conversation the less cost-effective the signature-gathering process is. The other avenues through which citizens may learn more about the meaning and potential ramifications of these ballot initiatives are the companion fifteen- or thirty-second TV and radio commercials. Also through the direct mailings that contain the hundred-word-maximum official summary of the initiative (which has to be approved by the attorney-general's office to ensure that it presents a legally accurate portrait of the actual contents of the measure).

Most times, however, the complexity of the issues demands that citizens have far more knowledge than a TV or radio spot or a hundred-word précis can provide. There have been times when even experts have had difficulty understanding the full legal and long-term political implications of a ballot initiative. Schrag cites the 1988 drive to reform California's auto insurance system, wherein competing interests managed to qualify five different ballot initiatives on the matter, some of which contained much the same policy substance and differed only in the details. The full text of those initiatives together accounted for some one hundred pages of legalese, which would have made it practically impossible for the average citizen to grasp their relative merits. Schrag says the real danger is that, in presenting only selective reforms representing the interests of their sponsors, these initiatives would have prevented legislators from looking at the totality of options and crafting a complete package that would best address the shortcomings of the insurance system. However, despite an $80 million expenditure by insurance companies and trial lawyers (more than George Bush spent in his presidential campaign that year), was the special-interest measures were defeated; only one of the five ballot measures was approved: Ralph Nader's Proposition 103, which ostensibly introduced some new mechanisms to protect consumers. Yet the subterfuge that followed proves how far powerful business lobbies are prepared to go to control the eventual outcome of those populist-inspired processes. Although Prop 103 created a new commissioner's office to oversee the insurance industry, the commissioner's post fell into disrepute after the second commissioner, a Republican named George Quackenbush, was elected to the job partly on the strength of a $2.4 million contribution from the insurance industry over which he was supposed to be watchdog. The state's auditor-general soon reprimanded Quackenbush for failing to protect consumers against insurance-industry practices — a state of affairs that perhaps would not have surprised that *New York Times* editorial writer who cast such harsh judgment on the ballot initiative back in 1911.

Examples such as these provide some support for Al Gore's lament about the erosion of responsible government. The mechanisms of "direct democracy," intended originally to protect citizens against big business, have actually opened up a new and seemingly legitimate channel for well-heeled interests to promote legislation that favours them, all the while reducing elected representatives' ability to assess the "big picture" and to act in the long-term interests of their constituents. A major problem with ballot initiatives, it has been said, is that citizens can vote on abstract principles without having to acknowledge the multitude of potential consequences of the policies. While a harried voter might be inclined to take the "just do it" approach, a conscientious legislator is more likely to be concerned with questions of how, with the prospects that major trade-offs will have to be made to accommodate those shifts in policy.

In the case of fiscally oriented initiatives — Proposition 13 and its successors — there is an immense catalogue of subsidiary consequences few voters would likely have envisioned, most of which have to do with the erosion of services. Public education, for which California had been one of the top ten spenders in the US in the 1960s, has become so underfunded as a result of Prop 13–mandated spending caps that by 1996, 71 percent of California schools, by the reckoning of the General Accounting Office, were in need of major plumbing, electrical, or roof work; 54 percent of teachers, according to the National Education Association, didn't have enough textbooks to send home with students; and by 1994 this high-tech oasis had fewer computers per pupil in its schools than any other state. As California slipped to forty-first place in school funding per pupil by 1995-96, spending roughly $1,000 less per child than the national median, a range of indicators showed a predictable plunge in academic performance.[4] Declines have become evident in a range of other public services, including the judiciary, where underpaid appellate-court justices are more likely than not to retire early so as to enter the private, so-called "rent-a-judge" system, which offers well-heeled individuals charged with a crime the opportunity of having their case heard expeditiously if they shell out a hefty fee for a private judge to hear the case.[5]

A more general, less perceptible, but possibly more disturbing outgrowth of the "initiative industrial complex" is the hastened erosion of the sense of citizenship and shared responsibility that once underlined California's public programs. A series of ballot initiatives dictating how government is to spend its money have offered voters the option of picking and choosing, à la carte, which expenditures they support and which they do not. Because it is a natural inclination perhaps for voters to endorse spending that's of direct benefit to them, while rejecting that which isn't, this approach works against a long-held principle within representative democracies: government has a responsibility to protect the health of society as a whole, rather than merely meet the desires of an affluent, organized few.

But that old concept of citizenship — with its implicit acknowledgment of the comfortable's responsibility to ease the burdens of the poor, if only for the practical purpose of ensuring social harmony — seems to have fallen out of favour in recent years. This is reflected in the language often used to describe how governments should function. It was not surprising when, during UCI's morning panel on reinventing government, a seemingly innocent statement by Larry Higby, chairman and CEO of the private Health Management Organization (HMO) Apria Healthcare, became the flashpoint of an emotional exchange. Higby remarked that what "consumers" want out of government is the same as they want from private business: an organization "that delivers service without a hassle and delivers what it's supposed to deliver." For Higby, government's role and its responsibilities are no different from those of any company. "If you ask people to keep score on things," he said, "they don't know if Cox is providing cable television, or the federal government is providing cable television . . . Same thing in any number of services that can be provided."

This prompted Orange County CEO Jan Mittermeier to respond that "most of the people that use government services are not buying a service like cable TV. They are abused children. They are people who are in prisons or for whatever reasons do not have other options." In fact, these people are not the "consumers" of government services in the traditional sense of being people who lay down their money and expect to place their order. Rather, they are more like third parties to a process over which they have virtually no control — at the mercy both of the people who foot the bill and those who are contracted to provide the services. In a referendum-driven system, the disenfranchised — those abused children or prisoners — will have little say about whether or how taxpayers' money will be spent to their benefit. But how those people are treated will have an enormous impact on society as a whole. In reality, what governments sell, panel chair Helen Ingram suggested, may not be goods or services but more abstract commodities like "fairness and equity," social harmony, and ultimately a sense among disparate communities that the whole is worth belonging to.

California society has been moving in precisely the opposite direction, with taxpayers defending their right to dictate that their tax money be spent to advance their own, sectoral interests. An urban landscape increasingly divided between well-serviced, gated enclaves of privilege and the neglected neighbourhoods of the poor clearly depicts this. Some pundits believe that if the notion of a common good, of the sense that people pay taxes to create and maintain a society they feel comfortable living in, continues to erode, California will become even more Balkanized than it is today, to the point where individual social groups may opt out of the larger social contract and, in one extreme scenario, reformulate themselves under the umbrellas of armed gangs like the militias of Beirut. This is what a civic think tank known as the Los Angeles 2000 Committee refers to as "the Blade Runner scenario."[6]

The idea of disenfranchised communities seceding, through force of arms, from the society around them is of course a rather unlikely worst-case scenario. Still, this vision has some resonance in the public imagination because it is an extension of a situation that already exists to a degree in Southern California. Conditions of deprivation, poverty, and a militarization of the streets in many locales have already made it impossible for many middle-class Californians to feel safe venturing outside their own neighbourhoods. And so, mindful of this, Webster Guillory, chair of the National Organization of Black County Officials and Orange County's managing deputy assessor, told UCI's morning panel that the public should consider the "selfish" reason for supporting spending on social services and enlightened government programs. "We can define our obligations to the unfortunate in society as an obligation to ourselves and to our families," he explained. "Because, I don't care where you are today, where you live, you cannot avoid all the issues that impact upon our society." Some suggest that acknowledging this is the first step towards warding off waking up one morning and finding yourself a bit player in Blade Runner.

– – –

Is this what a generation or more of right-wing populist revolt has led to? Poor urban areas ruled by hopelessness and suburbs ruled by fear? Social divisions that are so profound that the body politic could shatter into tiny fragments with the next economic downturn? Liberals might say yes to all of the above, arguing that the birthplace of the Reagan revolution has become dangerously polarized and that something must be done to mend the social contract. Judging from the words of Al Gore and the policies of his party, it's clear how the Democratic leadership intends to tackle that task: by accepting criticisms that "big government" has been intrusive, inefficient, and profligate, and then by taking actions that will mute these criticisms and recapture the hearts of millions of Californians in the political centre. The Democrats are hopeful that by embracing fiscal conservatism and some of that powerful Republican rhetoric about the need to keep governments in check, they can lure disgruntled suburban

GOP voters into a new multi-hued coalition, breathing new life into representative government and giving legislators a new mandate to address the problems of an increasingly fractured society.

But out on the margins, there's a different view of how liberalism can halt the march towards Armageddon in Southern California. Larry Agran believes that Democrats who want to steal Republicans' main platform planks are on the wrong track. For years he's been trying to break down the isolationism — the exclusionary ethic — that's almost built in to the notion of suburbia. Unlike Gore, he thinks suburbanites need to be told about the case for stronger governments that spend more on projects undertaken outside the confines of their own neighbourhoods. Also unlike many Democrats, he believes that plebiscites and other tools of "direct democracy" are more a part of the solution than a problem.

These are ideas that Agran has brought to a mystifyingly successful Orange County political career. For six years he was the mayor of Irvine and on city council twice that long, and in 1992 he ran a dark-horse campaign against Bill Clinton for the leadership of the Democratic party, as the so-called "cities candidate." Today he is a registered independent, a fact that could be considered a protest against a party Agran believes has abdicated its responsibility to challenge the Republican policies he feels have created only turmoil and division in California. A strong case could be made in suburbia, he says, for spending substantial public funds to boost education, reduce poverty, and rebuild the economic engines of urban areas, which would pay high dividends to middle-class taxpayers who are tired of constantly peering over their shoulders for an approaching social cataclysm. While many might consider it naive to assume the affluent middle class would buy that message, Agran's own political history lends some credibility to the view. In a city where Republicans have a 2:1 lead in support over Democrats and independents, Agran several times has captured the mayoralty with an overtly liberal platform, at times leading a council dominated by progressives. Under his leadership, Irvine's council has successfully pushed for more subsidized housing, subsidized child care, and the maintenance of well-funded public schools across the city. All this in a community that was designed as a bedroom enclave for white-collar professionals, a place one might assume would be a prime breeding ground for suburban separatism.

But Agran insists that upper-income suburban voters, even those whose life experience is limited mostly to the workplace, the mall, and the tennis club, are generally responsive to the idea that social problems that aren't dealt with will grow and spread, to the point where there will be no refuge from other people's nightmares. "What I say to people is that, if they thought they were escaping problems in Los Angeles or Santa Ana by coming to Irvine, probably what they are buying is only five, or ten, or fifteen years before those same problems that go unaddressed in other communities are visited upon us," says the former politician, who has since returned to his law practice but was considering another run at the mayor's job at the time of our conversation. "Crime, drive-by shootings, drug problems, deteriorating schools — those problems just can't be contained; eventually they'll reach the suburban cities. It may take a while, but they'll get there. This has a very sobering effect on those people who are beginning to experience these things in the suburbs. People may have a very reactionary response at first, and I think this explains the lurch to the right which may be characteristic of new arrivals in Southern California. But then a more intelligent, sober way of thinking starts to prevail: 'These problems do exist and we're going to have to deal with them here, in Santa Ana, in Los Angeles, in Long Beach.' That's what I was hoping for, to be a voice for people in cities and metropolitan areas who in the main are desirous of taking care of these problems, not just fleeing from them."

Agran's tone, as he talks about stepping back from the brink, is measured and calm. This fits in with his general demeanour. A man just on the netherside of middle age with a few brushstrokes of grey around the temples and a squarish pair of wire-rimmed glasses planted on his nose, he projects a casual friendliness. The setting for our interview is the Agran family home, a 1960s-vintage detached dwelling that Larry and his wife bought in 1975, two years after her acceptance to UCI medical school prompted the move to Irvine from Sacramento, where Larry had been legal counsel to the state senate's health and welfare committee. (Today, Larry's spouse is a full professor at UCI, conducting research related to child safety in automobiles.) Their house is modest by the standard of today's real estate market, but warm. A skylight cut into the roof illuminates a wooden staircase that leads upward from the centre of the ground floor. The living room has two worn leather sofas and around the fireplace are plaques, plants, and a baseball trophy, on the piano a gallery of family photos. Here and there are African artifacts and over by the wall a large collection of CDs. A well-worn hardcover copy of the E.L. Doctorow novel *Ragtime* sits on the coffee table between the sofas.

Yet the most noticeable quality here, something that surely would have attracted many urban exiles when this neighbourhood was built in the 1960s, is the tranquillity. This house is situated on a quiet street of houses all surrounded by well-trimmed shrubbery and a car or two out front. The street, in turn, is a part of one of the several distinct "villages" that make up the city of Irvine, separated from the other villages around it by ribbons of green space and broad boulevards. Overall, there a feeling of seclusion, of isolation, making the wider world of traffic jams, crime, and social decay seem as distant as a bad dream.

But Agran says that the troubled outer world is actually very close at hand. The bedrock political reality for cities such as Irvine, he believes, is that they now function as interlocking parts of vast "metropolitan regions," social and political ecosystems that link the destinies of people who may appear to inhabit totally separate worlds. Thinking about metropolitan areas gives a clearer picture of the challenges facing communities than thinking about suburbs and cities does, he says, since communities that begin as suburbs soon face development pressures that transform them into cities in their own right. The separation of one city from another can also, on this landscape, be a pretty meaningless exercise, since cities bleed into one another across political boundaries, with the movement of people, money, goods, and problems continuing irrespective of where one jurisdiction starts and another ends. Irvine is the 188th-largest city in the US, says Agran, but the statistic is virtually meaningless. Far from being the kind of self-contained entity that New York or Philadelphia might have been in an earlier era, Irvine is recognized by everyone as just one component of the sprawling behemoth that is Southern California.

And what is the one major issue that should preoccupy the residents of this and probably every other metropolitan region in the US? Agran believes it is without a doubt the widening chasm between rich and poor. The span that exists between the "undreamed-of wealth" of the top households in the US and the grinding poverty of those at the bottom is without precedent in the United States, says the ex-mayor. "This is uncharted territory. We have between 35 and 40 million people officially living in poverty and about 15 million poor children. And this has just horrendous implications for the quality of life in cities." While municipal governments can work around the margins to soften the impact and to create the conditions where disparate social factions are more likely to get along, the one-time Democratic leadership candidate says life in America's great metropolises will only deteriorate if the federal leadership continues to ignore this most pressing concern.

"We are talking here about a six- or seven-trillion-dollar-a-year economy that could easily reduce child poverty to negligible rates," he says. "But it would take a ten-year commitment of the kind that the president and the vice-president — a vice-president who wants to be president — will not consider. These guys are just unwilling to summon the nation. I would like there to be a great national goal, and it could be a bipartisan goal, to cut the rate of child poverty by two-thirds in the next five to ten years. It might cost 50 to 100 million a year, but it's clearly doable in the interest of the nation. It should be through a mix of government programs, private organizations, volunteerism — whatever works — but in the end it's going to cost real money. The problem is we have all these gutless politicians who won't even talk about the possibility."

Although Agran is clearly disillusioned with the party he once campaigned to lead, he saves his harshest words for the "extremist" Republican leadership that has dominated politics in most of Orange County. After all, the Democrats' abandonment of their old social-welfare policies is merely a recent conversion to an outlook that Republicans have been pushing for decades. Agran insists, however, that although Republicans have been consistently rewarded at the polls in Orange County for espousing the rollback of socially inter-ventionist government, the average citizen is not in sync with GOP candidates who have made crusades out of issues like cutting off health and education benefits to illegal immigrants.

"It just drives me nuts," he says, "when you encounter people who are very wealthy who are so worried about whether some kid of Mexican extraction whose parents are here illegally, or who himself may be here illegally, whether he gets an education. Well, that's absurd. You think education is expensive, try ignorance — see what that costs. On top of that, it's been observed by a lot of people that these same well-off people who espouse these policies usually have got rich on the backs of other people. Almost all of them went to public schools or public universities at one time or another, had wonderful educations at the expense of others. They employ people as gardeners, nannies, cleaning their homes, their clothes, preparing their food . . . it's done by people who are typically in the low-income categories; often they are illegal, undocumented. Sometimes the hypocrisy of this drives me crazy. The racism and selfishness drive me nuts. But it's not most people of the county. Most people are much more reasonable, much more sensible, far less selfish."

I'm inclined to accept Agran's assessment of Orange County voters, to not dismiss his charitable words as sentimental wishful thinking, since he has made a career out of appealing to his constituents' good sense and compassion and has, against the odds, come out a winner. One possible explanation for his consistent success on terrain where other liberals have gone down in flames, is that, running as an independent in local races, he has been able to choose his slate of issues based on the community's lived realities, rather than having to toe a party line.

An albatross around the necks of candidates running under the Democratic banner — especially in Orange County, where many residents have fled from the sense of impending danger on LA streets — is the perception that the Democrats are "soft on crime." Crime is the chief hot-button issue in these parts, and Agran is convinced that liberals should not let their criticisms of the unfairness of the justice system undermine their resolve to keep streets safe. In fact, the one area where Agran supports Bill Clinton's adoption of Republican-touted policies is in his decision to increase funding to hire more street-level cops. "As a liberal," he says, "I would yield to no one in my determination to preserve that feeling of freedom and safety that people ought to expect in any community. Every community ought to be a safe community, where kids can walk outside and people can experience the entire environment."

Having said that, Agran does distance himself from the three-strikes-and-you're-out brand of justice that's established prison-building as a major growth industry in California.

Agran seems to have found a middle ground between the hang-'em-high prescription of right-wingers and the turn-a-blind-eye approach of some liberals. While advocating substantial funding for policing, he has simultaneously pushed for "positive investments in schools and programs of social support," which promise a long-term solution to the threat of crime. The most optimistic scenario here is that having a strong police presence as a deterrent to crime would actually boost public support for social spending. Since Irvine is recognized as one of the safest communities in Southern California, liberals might be better able to make a credible argument that the crime-rate decreases in communities that provide, as Irvine does, decent housing for its lower-income citizens, proper school funding, daycare, recreational opportunities, and a pleasant environment in which to live.

In fact, Larry Agran could be on to something that liberal mayoral hopefuls elsewhere may want to examine. Across the United States, the failure to assure the electorate that crime is under control has led to the collapse of the great liberal Democratic coalitions that once ruled major American cities such as New York, Los Angeles, Philadelphia, and Boston, says *L.A. Weekly* editor Harold Meyerson. Writing in the policy journal the *American Prospect*, Meyerson laments that "in the late 1990s, there are simply no remaining strongholds of municipal liberalism." Meyerson examined the voting patterns of traditional supporters of liberal mayors and found they have been drifting overwhelmingly into the camps of conservative Republican candidates such as Rudy Giuliani of New York and Richard Riordan of Los Angeles. The reason? That's easy. People simply want to feel they can walk the streets without fear.

Not that Meyerson advocates that liberals adopt the typical Republican hard line that sees the beginning and end of the solution to the crime epidemic in building more prisons and increasing the length of sentences. Like Agran, he warns against overly aggressive and socially insensitive police crackdowns. In cities where police blitzes against minor crimes amount to a "cloak for racially discriminatory law enforcement" and even "the [criminalization] of non-white young men as such," the results will not be safer streets but merely more injustice and a "rage and greater disorder" as police actions create a backlash. Nowhere has this been more evident than in Giuliani's New York, where high-profile travesties created a crisis for the mayor in 1999. In two horrifying cases, unarmed and innocent members of visible minorities had been either gunned down or savagely beaten by police — who had apparently been given free rein under Giuliani's anti-crime crackdown.

What progressives should support instead, says Meyerson, is community-based policing and the deployment of police forces that are representative of the racial mix of their communities. By doing this, they would be acting in support of one of the sacred ideals of municipal liberals over the years: the creation and defence of "public space." He elaborates: "Historically, the creation of public space was an achievement of progressives, and one defended by left urbanists against the encroachments of corporate sprawl or privatized enclaves. The parks and libraries in a city like New York are a remarkable universal entitlement, no less a triumph of progressivism than the free city colleges and the public hospital system were in their heyday." So the pledge by Riordin, Giuliani, and others to keep public spaces open and safe is actually a celebration by Republican partisans of long-held progressive, Democratic ideals. Indeed, Meyerson says that on balance, in the abstract at least, these popular law-and-order mayors bear much more resemblance to old-style liberals than to the crowd of Gingrich-ite conservatives in Congress. Giuliani's success at lowering New York's crime rate, for instance, repudiates the ultra-right's refrain about the uselessness of government bureaucracy by indicating that the public sector can be both effective and accountable. Meanwhile, none of the flag-bearers of the new municipal conservatism — Giuliani and Riordin — have shown much enthusiasm for the extreme right's wider agenda of busting unions, dismantling government, and privatizing services.

Ultimately Meyerson believes that an anti-crime stance can be a natural complement to a liberal, socially interventionist program that works to undo the conditions of poverty, despair, and injustice that have created mayhem on the streets. He cites the British Labour party's winning commitment to be "tough on crime, and tough on the causes of crime" — a rallying cry that seems to mirror the approach Agran has taken in Irvine.

Although striking a tough-on-crime pose can be morally and practically perilous, Meyerson is convinced it's a necessary first step towards reviving liberal urban coalitions. If they can get past this one issue, he feels, the chances of forming new alliances are good. He cites the growing number of Latino voters in many American cities who are conservative on issues such as welfare reform and "family values" questions, but overwhelmingly liberal when it comes to issues like labour rights and economic justice. This raises the possibility that left-leaning mayors could strike out into territory where the Giulianis and Riordins have refused to go, spearheading campaigns to improve working conditions and pay scales in industries like the garment trade and ensuring that lower-end workers who deliver public services — who in many cities have been union-busted and privatized into poverty — receive fair treatment and decent compensation.[7]

Meanwhile, in the more affluent suburbs like Irvine, Agran says, environmental issues provide the most solid ground for establishing progressive-led coalitions — which is not surprising, since the promise of a clean environment is one of the key aspects of the suburban dream that lured people out here in the first place. "Even conservatives will want agricultural lands and open spaces preserved. It's a very popular issue," Agran declares. "And it's allowed me to work with these conservatives and enjoy their support, while negotiating with the Irvine Company and other major developers about open-space preservation and other matters." At the same time, he says, such environmental-protection initiatives increased public confidence and provided a springboard for Agran to "convey to people that the local government can play a constructive role in other respects too — in curbside recycling, and affordable child care, affordable housing, strengthening our public schools, doing things that can dramatically improve the quality of life and the sense of community."

In this there seems to be a lesson applicable to almost any suburban community. If there is a soft underbelly to the neo-con platform of tax-cutting, privatizing, and gutting public services — appealing as those policies may be to stressed-out, over-mortgaged suburbanites who would just as soon contribute as little of their earnings as possible to the public coffers — it is its lack of attention to environmental protection. Suburbanites care a lot about trees, parks, and rivers, probably more so than people in remote areas where unspoiled land is abundant but the means to generate an income is not. Suburban-dwellers will feel betrayed when continual development threatens to take away those precious open spaces that looked so appealing in the developers' drawings. Seeing their suburbs start to look more like cities is one of the greatest hazards of a right-wing agenda that calls for government to get out of business's way and so offers little resistance to the forces that would pave over these bucolic suburban hinterlands.

Yet while environmental issues seem to provide a natural opening for liberal politicians seeking power in the burbs, the complicated political lie of the land in Southern California has made it difficult for most of them to play that card. A standard left/right view of politics would raise the expectation that Democrats would be the pro-environmental party in California and Republicans the reverse. But according to Mike Davis, author of *City of Quartz*, the two parties are far from straightforward on their stance on ecology. The Democratic party is as beholden to the powerful land-development lobby (or perhaps more so) as the Republican party. Republicans, despite a strong reliance on developers' money, owe much of their grassroots support to the homeowners' associations that support slow-growth policies intended to preserve suburban communities in their current form. Davis cites the case of LA's liberal Democratic ex-mayor Tom Bradley, a black politician with strong minority support who was deeply indebted to both the building-trades unions and the developers' lobbies that helped bankroll his campaign. In fact, when developers have campaigned against slow-growth legislation and ballot initiatives, they have portrayed themselves in their ads as champions of the poor and downtrodden. The builders like to claim that their support for higher densities and their opposition to land-use restrictions are motivated by the altruistic desire to create more affordable housing and to deflate real estate prices by increasing the housing supply. Davis writes that the intended targets of this propaganda have been able to overlook the fact that developers have done little for the poor in the past. The upshot, he says, has been a series of unlikely and contradictory alliances in which "minority groups, distrustful of white-supremacist homeowners, have jumped from the frying pan into the fire to support developers responsible for the creation of monochromatic suburban fringes in northern Los Angeles and southern Orange counties. [Likewise] powerful building-trades bosses for the most part continue to lock local labor federations . . . into supine coalitions with big developers, even when the latter are major backers of union-busting."[8]

Meanwhile, California's Republican party is enmeshed in an equally tricky and ideologically inconsistent set of relationships arising from the party's dependence on the powerful upper-middle-class home owners' associations, which provide it with grassroots muscle at election time. These groups are the primary force pushing slow-growth policies in the face of vast pressure to redevelop existing subdivisions and to build on undeveloped land. Resisting those market forces through slow-growth policies advances the interests of homeowners' associations in two major ways: by contributing to the "land inflation" that increases property values (by limiting supply in a time of high demand), and by discouraging the migration of lower-income minority groups into the suburbs, which many homeowners' groups want to preserve as the domain of the white and the wealthy. More importantly, however, slow growth ensures that the sprawling ranch house, with its big front yard and swimming pool out back, will remain the centrepiece of the Southern California lifestyle; that this quintessentially SoCal statement of abundance will not be driven into extinction by a new onslaught of apartment development. The single-family dwelling is a powerful symbol in this landscape. The established middle classes want it to survive.

These policies, however, have drawn Republicans into alliances as paradoxical as the ones Democrats have entered into, laying down some shaky common ground between conservative, affluent, multi-car-driving suburbanites and the environmental activists who might ordinarily find their core of support on university campuses or in the Bohemian enclaves of San Francisco. Davis insists, however, that the relationship is profoundly uneasy. The patrician concern with

But that doesn't mean they lack the means to defend their policies, especially when dealing with issues like land conservation that enjoy sizable public support. Agran says that local governments in California hold a key lever over business; it's what he calls "the power of no — the power to delay a project, to deny a project. You can bring that to the bargaining table. You can say, 'We'll say yes. But the price of us saying yes is [for you] to donate parklands, to help underwrite child care, to write affordable housing into your plans.' This is the kind of policy architecture we developed with the Irvine Company."

The city used this strategy for prying cash and concessions out of developers to establish its subsidized housing program. A standard demand was that 15 percent of new housing units be offered to lower-income families at reduced rents. The subsidized rent on an apartment that would normally go for $1,200 would be $700, $600, possibly even $500. The difference "then becomes absorbed by a mix of private and public subsidies," Agran elaborates, "allowing people to live side by side in the same community, but paying different rents." The former mayor says these policies have allowed Irvine to become much more diverse: while Irvine was close to 100 percent upper-income and white when it was founded, today it accommodates people with varying income levels and is 25 percent non-white. Although blacks are still drastically under-represented in the population — an indication, perhaps, that the racist history of American suburbanization still casts a daunting shadow over Orange County — there is now a strong presence in Irvine of Latinos and Asians, some of them recent immigrants working in low-paying service jobs.

Beyond negotiating contributions from developers, Irvine has also been able to use its own money to fund social programs such as child care, because municipalities in California are allowed to keep a portion of the sales taxes collected within their boundaries. By a quirk of fate Irvine is home to numerous high-tech firms that produce goods such as software, medical supplies, and sophisticated instruments, rather than services, meaning that the city reaps a sales-tax windfall when those items are sold.

Meanwhile, when what's required is the will to pass legislation, rather than the money to pay for programs, Agran says he and his allies have found the ballot initiative a useful tool. One initiative, to give the city's open-space policies the power of law, was supported by 87 percent of voters. "What was wonderful about that," Agran recalls, "is that the nature of the ballot initiative is to lock it in for all time," meaning that the struggle to save open lands from development doesn't have to be refought every couple of years. Irvine will also benefit from a rail-bond initiative, which was passed by voters and allots funds for the development of a light-rail system linking the city with adjacent communities. In fact, next to fiscal-control-related measures such as Prop 13, the ballot initiative has been used with greatest success in supporting environmental or health-related causes such as land conservation, pollution control, reining in the tobacco companies, or banning toxic chemicals.

But just because such measures seem to be in support of an overall public good rather than the pecuniary interests of a particular class doesn't make these initiatives any less controversial. Critics remain wary of a political process that diminishes the capacity of elected legislatures to act. Peter Schrag notes, for instance, that progressive consulting firms have had some success in overturning the thrust of Prop 13 by floating successful initiatives mandating new spending for zoos, orchestras, or land conservation. But he still complains that "each turn of what is now widely known as ballot box budgeting eats up an ever greater chunk of the public purse and makes it still harder for government to establish priorities and respond to new needs."[11] The ultimate effect of even the most progressive initiative, Schrag maintains, is that the disadvantaged are less likely to have their specific needs funded, especially if need arises out of an emergency, since

the plebiscitary dynamic — call it the ethics of the initiative — has precious little room for spending that immediately benefits someone other than those who must vote on it. It is not prone to generosity and is rarely respectful of minority rights, much less of minority needs. And while it's true that elected legislators often fail to do what their constituents wish . . . sometimes they also do a little better for those who are under-represented in the electoral process, something that the initiative process almost never does.[12]

Agran accepts these arguments to a point, but in the final analysis he stands with the populist politicians of that other stripe who say that legislative politics is dysfunctional enough to make such tools of "direct democracy" a necessity. "If we had a tradition of more flexible, more responsive national or state governments, people wouldn't feel they need the initiative instrument," he says. "I can tell you the initiative at the local level does a lot of good. It's responsible for all kinds of wonderful, innovative things getting done. A handful of people can organize the initiative, gather signatures and so forth. It's a more wide-open democracy."

All of this political talk is, by its very nature, abstract and some-times vague; which is probably why Agran suggests that we get into his grey Volvo and check out how some of these concepts have been cast into concrete. Crawling down the wide boulevards of Irvine — with the ex-mayor slowing nearly to a stop on many of the numerous times he wants to point out a particular landmark — it's obvious that he loves the nuts-and-bolts aspects of municipal government. A glimpse of a tree will prompt a discussion on the relative merits of planting eucalyptus versus pine trees in Southern California; the emergence of a condominium complex around a corner will trigger a proud recollection of how Irvine was one of the first communities to encourage row housing at a time when most people still felt that God had ordained SoCal as a preserve of single-family detached dwellings.

Mostly, however, the conversation is not about architecture or trees, but about how the physical structure of the community affects *people*. Much of our journey is through Irvine's residential quadrants — the self-contained "villages" with names like Woodbridge, University Park, and Turtle Rock, which are further subdivided into neighbourhoods, each having a rec centre, a pool, or a school at its centre. The idea was to create a focus for community life, to encourage people to get to know one another by spending time in public, and Agran believes it has worked. "I've noticed that people do have a strong identification with their village," he says. "You ask them where they live and they'll say, 'I live in Woodbridge,' rather than, 'I live in Irvine.'"

We pass by some exclusive neighbourhoods where the hillside homes sell for well over $1 million, and drive through some other ones where houses are expensive in a merely average sort of way. These are modest bungalows that were worth $20,000 when they were built in the mid-1960s but now trade for $300,000 or more. Unremarkable as these homes may seem, they are the everyday monuments to the "land inflation" that brought a political revolution to this state and dug a gaping chasm between the expectations of two different generations of middle-class Californians.

As we drive, Agran pays tribute to the "creativity" of the Irvine Company's original planners, although he says the firm has since devolved into a "cookie cutter" developer like most of its rivals. He believes the company's vision was responsible for people here being able to lead an abnormally relaxed and integrated life, where shopping, community facilities, and recreational paths are always within walking distance of home. These are particularly beneficial if you are poor, Agran says; securing subsidized housing in Irvine means you'll have an easier time of it than in Los Angeles or Long Beach. You'll be able to bike or take a bus to work, if you're employed locally, and won't need a car to get groceries from the local markets. And because lower-income housing is integrated seamlessly into the community, Irvine's poor have the use of facilities normally exclusive to "good" neighbourhoods, and none of the disadvantages that come with living in a low-income "ghetto."

"We do have some people on welfare who live here, but let's say you're a working family and your total household income is $23,000 or $24,000 a year,"[13] the ex-mayor postulates. "I think you could lead a relatively nice life here. The schools are excellent. Of course, the kids will have all the pressures to buy thank-yous, this and that, and expensive clothes. But that's no different from any other community."

Except, perhaps, that those pressures are probably stronger in Irvine, glittering high-tech boomtown that it is. A child of a low-income family, for example, must find it a deeply uncomfortable experience when his or her middle-class friends head out for an expensive few hours of diversion at the entertainment complex known as the Irvine Spectrum. Located smack-dab in the centre of Irvine's high-tech business area, at the intersection of two major highways, the Spectrum is testament to the fact that California's developers have elevated the creation of shopping malls to a fine art. Like the holo-deck on *Star Trek*, the purpose of its grand architecture is to transport patrons to a distant world. Modelled after a thirteenth-century Moroccan village, its outdoor terraces feature meandering pathways, while its restaurants and coffee shops are housed in cavernous rooms with domed ceilings inlaid with ceramic tile. There are even fountains spewing *hot* water, causing steam to rise like dry ice at a rock concert when the heated H_2O hits the ornate stones at ground level. This whole complex is dedicated to entertainment and leisure. There are twenty cinema screens, a Barnes and Noble superstore, a Blockbuster video emporium, and a vast Sega Genesis amusement centre. And it all costs money, lots of money. A person who toils at minimum wage would have to work close to an hour to cover the cost of a cappuccino at the mock-palace that functions as a coffee shop at the Irvine Spectrum.

Still, amidst all this delirium, this circus of consumerism, some people in this community have, remarkably, been able to break the spell of all these mesmerizing diversions and to think a little bit about the world outside. About how people who don't have big equity in their property or a large credit limit on their charge cards might be able to meet their own needs and aspirations.

That's one way Irvine seems profoundly different from elsewhere in Orange County. The other is in the peculiar way it has managed to reconcile that relentless urge to build with a respect for the natural environment. Driving by Quail Hill, the subject of that monumental clash between conservationists and developers, the panorama tells me this is the closest I will ever come to seeing what Southern California looked like before human society began to ooze out over its surfaces. Although the hills everywhere else are sure to have at least a house or two on their caps, you can look into the distance beyond Quail Hill and the only sign of human interference you'll see is a vague line marking the presence of a stray toll road in the distance (that was one that the environmentalists lost).

Agran marvels at the sight. "It happens to be a hazy day, but when it's bright it looks like Scotland out there. The green is so intense and the beauty so remarkable, you wouldn't expect it here." We motor on and see some equally unusual sites: horses and cows grazing on land abutting housing surveys; crops being harvested in a field close to the high-tech sector. These lands will continue to be agricultural perhaps centuries from now, having been protected in perpetuity from the developers' bulldozers by a conservationist ballot initiative.

Agran believes that the co-existence achieved in Irvine — between different economic classes, between human structures and the natural landscape — is the product of political vision and careful planning. The sprawl and social strife engulfing nearby communities comes thanks to a laissez-faire approach to building a society. Looking to the future, he sees challenges that market forces by themselves cannot meet. That's why, today, he's promoting several public-sector-dependent plans that he feels will ensure that this segment of Orange County remains livable. One is the light-rail system, the other a controversial design to transform the former El Toro marine air base into a complex of cultural and recreational facilities.

But this belief that achieving some public good is dependent upon a vital public sector, rather than being the accumulated product of individual self-interest, is more alien to many parts of Orange County than grazing cattle and untouched hillsides. With continued rapid population growth in the suburban fringes of LA and the threat of escalating social problems, the clash between these two worldviews seems sure to intensify. On one side are the traditionalists who still see the West as the land of freedom and the home of the rugged individualist, on the other the worried adherents of the Blade Runner scenario, who believe that only by embracing a new kind of politics will this paradise escape being spoiled forever.

I think back to that Reform Party campaign office a few miles from Toronto and to the offices of Opposition leader Preston Manning on Parliament Hill. It was in these places that I heard passionate calls for a new system of "direct democracy" in Canada, based on mechanisms similar to the ones that have transformed California. That suburban-ites are apt to embrace these types of devices — plebiscites, recall votes — is directly linked to the landscape's impact on politics. Campaigning is rarely done in person in these sprawling, centreless amalgams, but through television; the privatized, compartmentalized style of life, meanwhile, not only has shut off many suburbanites from their neighbours but also has left them alienated from their govern-ments. Even observers like Larry Agran, who believe that a system of referendums is better than the status quo of electing politicians and letting them rule from afar, give evidence that politicians gener-ally have done a poor job of making people feel involved in their political system.

Yet people in other parts of the world who advocate a similar system of government-through-referendum should take a hard look at the California experience. To some, that experience clearly shows that direct democracy has accomplished precisely the opposite of what was intended. Instead of reining in greedy corporate interests by subject-ing their avaricious intentions to public scrutiny at the ballot box, the referendum process seems only to have given the corporations another tool to bamboozle the people. Some say the use of referendums has not led to more democracy but to mob rule; to a situation where decisions are made without thought; where politicians no longer have the discretion to do the right thing; where self-interest carries the day.

But there is no real sense of inevitability about this or any other aspect of suburban politicking. Canadians may look south and see how the overwhelmingly suburban metropolises of California and elsewhere have voted consistently for anti-spending measures and for politicians who promise tax cuts. They might draw the fatalistic conclusion that there is something about suburbia that makes taxation such an all-consuming issue, diminishing any sense of a broader public good that needs protecting and nurturing. Yet the experience of Irvine, deep in the heart of ultra-conservative Orange County, puts the lie to that notion. Irvine's recent history shows that plenty of other issues stir the hearts of suburbanites; these might be considered "quality of life" issues, and chief among them is environmental protection. Irvine's experience illustrates, as well, that conservative suburbanites will even get on-side with such typically liberal projects as subsidized housing and child care. They need only a rational debate about how those projects can enhance life in the community as a whole, promoting security and a more general sense of community well-being.

9 | It Comes Down to Neighbourhoods

On a balmy spring night back in upscale Tierrasanta — San Diego's "Island in the Hills" — the community rec centre's several acres of parking lot are jammed with minivans and SUVs. But make no mistake; this crush was not caused by a sudden collective urge to shoot hoops. Rather, the unusually large crowd has come for a meeting of the Tierrasanta Community Council. The fourteen members have gathered in a stuffy, crowded conference room, flanked by Old Glory and the bear-emblazoned flag of the "California Republic." The high turnout is a boon for local office-holders seeking re-election. In advance of a wide range of midterm contests, several incumbents have sent their representatives to invite residents to upcoming "coffees," where they can chat with the candidates. The candidates use the opportunity to expound briefly on a pet issue that might strike some chord of interest with voters. An assistant from a state assemblyman's office notes, for instance, the need to "do something about our schools" following the defeat of a bond measure that would have raised funds to repair battered educational facilities. Another calls for a federal inquiry into alleged price-fixing by oil companies, who have been charging San Diegans consistently more at their gas pumps than their relatively downscale counterparts around Los Angeles.

But these are mere sideshows. As nice as it would be to think that tonight's buzz is about ballot-box democracy, this throng has little interest in election pitches. Nor have these people come to witness the council's presentation of a $500 cheque to the lacrosse team of Junipero Sera High School, or to receive an update on construction at the adjacent Miramar military base. Most people are here for a discussion of the local covenants, codes, and restrictions, commonly referred to as CC&Rs, an acronym that generally requires no explanation in these parts. CC&Rs are a set of rules that specify what homeowners can and can't do with their property. Most suburban neighbourhoods in California have their own customized slate of CC&Rs, which are usually written by the developers at the time of construction and attached to the deeds of individual properties. So when someone buys a home in practically any suburb in this state, there will be clauses in their land deed telling them they are legally bound to paint their shutters only certain colours, to retile their roofs in a hue that matches their neighbours, to refrain from making certain types of renovations, to store their trash cans in a particular location.

Tonight, outgoing council president Mike Smiley and maintenance-committee chair Fred Zuckerman will try to convince Tierrasantans that they should make a greater effort to have their own local CC&Rs enforced, that the long-term health of the community depends on it. The genial though clearly fuss-budgety Zuckerman, a tall, grey-haired man wearing an open-collared white dress shirt and tennis shoes, will do most of the talking. It's a task he undertakes with the quiet determination of a social crusader and the methodical, plodding stance of, say, a scholar of religious law. In fact, Zuckerman is something of a CC&R scholar; his persuasive brief on the subject — "The Broken Window Theory: Keeping Tierrasanta Healthy" — was recently published on the front page of the local *Tierra Times*. In case you are unfamiliar with the broken window theory, which has served as the intellectual reference point for many petty-crime crackdowns in urban centres across the US, its basic point is that if you don't sweat the small stuff, you'll soon be on the slippery slope to hell. Or as Zuckerman summed up for the *Tierra Times*, "Many case studies have been conducted where a random building has had a window broken and left unrepaired. It never takes long for additional windows to get broken. More vandalism appears, graffiti follows, then litter . . . However, if a broken window is promptly repaired, the process is halted. Over and over again it has been shown that neglect and indifference beget more neglect and indifference."

Not that there are any broken windows on display in Tierrasanta. Far from it. But by applying this theory of escalating criminal behaviour, it's easy to see how smashed windows might be an obvious next step if people are allowed to violate the norms of good taste. And that is happening today, says Zuckerman, who tells the overflow crowd at the rec centre that the three most common offences are: (1) people putting antennas on their roofs, (2) people not storing their trash containers in a shed, and (3) people having boats or motor homes parked visibly on their property. In fact, Zuckerman has recently and successfully taken to court one of his neighbours who had parked a boat in plain view in this residential district. Although he did not collect the cash settlement — "That was not my purpose," Zuckerman explains to the crowd — "The point is that he did move the boat."

Later in the unfolding of this narrative I start to feel disoriented, wondering if all this talk about forcing people to tear down TV antennas and store their trash cans in such a precise manner could really be happening in Southern California. This after all, is the cradle of libertarian revolt, the place where Goldwater and Reagan's musings about the threats (from big government) to Americans' personal liberty first took root. This feeling contains a certain undercurrent of paranoia. If the courts can condemn renegade boat-parkers, I think, can they force me, a scruffy outsider — or to use the Americanism, "alien" — in their midst, to get a haircut and change my mismatched socks?

Reassuringly, other members of this assembly are experiencing a similar unease. For instance, the youngish woman with long brown hair and dressed in elegant earth tones who recalls how the community association at her previous home had tried to bar her developmentally handicapped teenage son from using the swimming pool alone. They had sent her a letter arguing that the boy's actual age did not reflect his mental age, and therefore he should be regarded as a child and not be allowed to use the pool without supervision. The association backed off when she threatened to sue, but she is obviously wary of intrusive, nosy-parker neighbours. "The last thing I want as a homeowner is for my committee to tell me what to do," she says. "I want them to be on my side."

A stocky, goateed man in his early thirties, wearing a red T-shirt emblazoned with a floor-design company's logo on the back, displays similar indignation. Turns out the man is also a boat owner, and yes, that boat is parked on his lawn. "Doesn't anybody here like to see anyone else having fun?" he complains. "I fail to see how the boat in my front yard can cause damage to anyone. It's a $20,000 boat; if anything, it should raise the property values."

That last remark elicits titters of disbelief from the crowd. Property values are the primary concern of most people here tonight and all seem to agree with the real estate agents' credo that uniformity, rather than creative embellishment, is the way to signal to potential buyers and to the market in general that this is a solid middle-class community, sound of mind and morals, uninfected by drugs, gangs, or tight cash flow. In a landscape where the distinction between haves and have-nots is so clear — and where the route from the former to the latter can be one misguided step over a precipice — the most trivial signs of decay stir a panic.

Thus the sense of urgency in the voice of a woman in her mid-fifties, a redhead who's going grey, who warns, "If we don't enforce the CC&Rs, soon you'll start to see people fixing their cars in their driveways. I've been here for twenty years and there are some things going on that really impact my property values. Some of them really look like ghetto homes, with clotheslines and the fences and the whole works. I invested in this community because of what this community has to offer. I think the value of the properties is determined by the people around me."

This is the sentiment that carries the evening with residents and their council representatives, who unanimously pass a motion renewing their support for the principle of CC&Rs. But when the practicalities arise, things get complicated. Fred Zuckerman explains that there have recently been changes in the law allowing charges of non-compliance with CC&Rs to be heard in small-claims court. The problem is that the case has to be brought to court by an affected resident; the community association, which is strictly an advisory council, has no legal power to enforce the CC&Rs. The most it can do is write to a resident requesting compliance; if the resident doesn't respond, the council has no further recourse. But Zuckerman thinks he's got a solution. He proposes a pilot program in which the Tierrasanta Community Council would underwrite the legal costs of residents who want to take their neighbours to court. This move presumably would encourage residents to litigate against their neighbours by taking them off the hook for the $50 court costs.

At this point, solidarity among council members begins to break down. One woman says she feels uncomfortable with the idea of a non-profit community organization getting into the business of suing its members. She fears that the decision would "come back to haunt us." Still, the motion passes — twelve to one, with two abstentions — an outcome that Mike Smiley believes might be the first step towards establishing an appropriate sense of vigilance in the community. "Perhaps this is the little push that gets things moving," the outgoing council president muses, "to the point where the violators say,

'There's a mood in this community. They're mad as hell and they're not going to take it anymore.'"

It's impossible not to see this scene as representative, at some level, of a stereotypical, small-minded suburban mindset immortalized in such classic 1960s pop ballads as "Harper Valley PTA" and the Monkees' "Pleasant Valley Sunday." There's a certain comic weirdness about a parochial political organization whose reaction to a concern about some trivial local issue is an earnest, determined, and sometimes brutal sense of *realpolitik*.

On further reflection, I've got to take that back. The work of community associations like the one in action here is not that comic and, actually, far from trivial. The real point of all this wrangling over parked boats and unconcealed trash cans, it later strikes me, has to do with the deadly serious business of establishing borders in a borderless world. Seen in this light, adhering to those silly rules governing the exterior appearance of one's property has a similar function, for the suburbanite, as parading the gang colours if you're a Blood or a Crip in south-central LA. It's something that establishes identity, cordoning off a little piece of psychological and physical territory for a group of the like-minded, reclaiming a little space in a world where most of the traditional social walls have been razed by high-speed modems and cable TV.

If any group of people realizes how fluid today's world is — with disparate, distant cultures constantly colliding, with one reality endlessly on the verge of morphing into another — it should be the residents of upscale, suburban San Diego. Close to the geographic nucleus of what has been called the "futuropolis" — a high-tech enclave spanning San Diego County and the southern half of OC — many people who work and reside here are computer professionals who live by the Microsoft slogan "Where do you want to go today?" They talk with relish of an open, global economy and culture made possible by the miracle of modern computing technology. Openness. Expansion. Interaction. These are the frequently lauded values of the computer age. But in daily life they are as frightening as they are inspiring, prompting a threatened North American middle class to seek separation and seclusion, to erect barriers around their communities that, while allowing them out to trawl for experiences in the wider world, will not allow outsiders in.

One very large form of barrier, of course, is the border between the United States and Mexico. A crossing point can be found just half an hour away from Tierrasanta, where the traffic crawls from south to north, but moves much faster in the opposite direction. The purpose of this border has always been to separate two very different realities, but now there is a special sense of urgency about that task, since those realities now function, from an economic point of view, as two aspects of a single entity. People on both sides of the border have been drawn together in the service of a unified, continental economic machine — one-half providing managerial and technical direction, the other half the low-cost labour to produce and assemble the products marketed by multinational corporations. Yet, despite the economic connection, their worlds could not be more different. The workers who earn their daily bread in suburban Tijuana's neat, boxlike, windowless pastel factories — branch plants of major US and Asian firms — live in shacks made of rough-hewn wooden boards and sheets of tin, which are draped over the nearby hillsides like a ragged quilt. They obviously do not share the burning concerns of their counterparts in US suburbs like Tierrasanta, who fret over the correct placement of rubbish bins. To many residents of neat American suburbs, the apparent chaos that rings Tijuana is a fearful sight, and one that, in the era of free trade, is especially difficult to put out of mind, since they are now directly connected to it economically. In this respect, in today's global village, borders are fortified, not demolished.

In most cases, however, the barriers that go up around communities are not physical but psychological. The 1950s notion of the suburb as a place of order and social certainty is continually being attacked and reviled in today's culture. Ozzie and Harriet may live on each night in reruns on Nickelodeon, but with one twitch of the finger on the remote control, those comforting images can be supplanted by taunting rap singers on MTV or some seamy spectacle on Jerry Springer. In short, this is a battle for hearts and minds, rather than just territory. And so it is here, in the cultural arena, where the broken window theory holds greatest sway, imploring middle-class Americans desirous of upward mobility to help police their peers, to insist on certain cultural and social standards, lest they wake up one morning surrounded by "trailer trash" who leave broken beer bottles on their doorsteps. Seen in this light, those silly rules about storing your trash cans properly and painting your shutters the right colour seem highly significant: they are psychological cues, the equivalent of a password or secret handshake denoting membership in a club that has committed itself to making sure your neighbourhood doesn't slide into the dreaded abyss of downward mobility that swallowed a major chunk of the contented middle class during the '80s and '90s.

Of course, there's also a practical side to all this. It overlaps with the more abstract questions about how the middle class can preserve its sense of unity and fellowship, but can still be isolated as a freestanding issue. The fact is that conformity — though it may grate at some level — is good for one's personal finances. Neighbourhood compliance with design restrictions figures prominently in the calculation of property values, and in these parts, property values are an obsession, almost a matter of life and death. As Mike Davis puts it, Southern Californians "love their children, but they love their property values more." And so they are willing to make great sacrifices to keep those property values high, even when those sacrifices involve their personal liberty.

Moving slightly north, back to Orange County, we encounter evidence that it's this factor — the impact of CC&Rs on property values — that allows homeowners to stifle their normally overwhelming concern with individual freedom. UCI political scientist Mark Baldassare, who for twenty years has kept tabs on the *Zeitgeist* of OC through his Orange County Annual Survey, reports that the locals have a high degree of awareness of what they are giving up — and what they are gaining — when they throw in their lot with this new level of government, the homeowners' association.

"When we do surveys on that topic," recounts Baldassare in a wide-ranging interview, "people always have internal conflicts about the trade-offs they have made. The thing that attracts them [to the associations] is the feeling that they and their neighbours can control their environment in what otherwise is viewed as a dangerous and sometimes hostile larger world, and that this will protect their economic interests such as property values. They don't make the trade-off without some complaint, I might add. They say, 'What about my freedom?' but they also say, 'What about my property values? What about my biggest investment in life?'"

Practical considerations, it seems, have a way of overriding abstract ideals.

"As long as these associations can provide people with decent pools and stable or rising property values," Baldassare continues, "middle-class people seem willing to make the trade-off. Upper-middle-class people are going to be much more negative, but they can afford to live in neighbourhoods that aren't going to change for the worse. You know how it works: the very best neighbourhoods will remain the very best neighbourhoods, but it's the middle-class neighbourhoods that can be at risk, through aging or immigration or economic down-turn. The rules and regulations that a homeowner association imposes are often seen as a buffer against that."

If the average middle-class citizen faces inner conflict over the sur-render of freedom for economic security, a professional Republican warrior must feel that doubly. That's why I was eager to talk to Don Gilchrist, a staffer for the state senator, John Lewis. Initially he suggested we conduct our interview at the ball park a couple of blocks away, during the course of a match between the California Angels and the visiting Toronto Blue Jays. Since we both had doubts about the practicalities of that, we wind up in his office, in a long, low-rise wooden office block in the City of Orange, facing a courtyard festooned with tropical plants. We sit chatting across a Cadillac-size desk piled high with papers and reports. The walls are lined with photos that capture the smiling visage of Gilchrist's boss as he shook hands with presidents Ronald Reagan and George Bush, along with a gallery of political cartoons. A white-haired grandfatherly man with a slight stoop — he turned seventy a few weeks earlier — the amicable Gilchrist is a veteran of California's suburban revolutionary wars, having moved from his native Los Angeles to a community in the San Fernando Valley when he took on a managerial job with an aerospace company in the 1950s. Soon after the move, he joined the whirlwind of Republican activism that was sweeping through these new suburbs, and today he is an elder statesman of this area's party machine — a member of the OC Republicans' Central Committee and a staffer for one of the original tax-bashing candidates ushered into office during the Prop 13 revolt.

His political pedigree aside, Gilchrist is also well acquainted with homeowners' associations. He was a board member of California's Community Associations Institute, an umbrella group that advises homeowners' organizations on how to run their business. He also helped draft a new section of the state's civil code defining exactly what policies homeowners' associations have the legal right to impose. To have undertaken this task shows that Gilchrist is not just a blustering ideologue — a conclusion also suggested by his deliberate, almost ponderous manner of speech — but more of a details guy, someone who's happy to examine the fine points. Indeed, there are a lot of those fine points in this new body of law; the section of the legal code Gilchrist sent me runs to forty-three pages of small print, expounding on issues ranging from the homeowner's right to challenge the "reasonableness" of the CC&Rs — a complete ban on satellite dishes, for instance, was found to be unreasonable — to allocation of responsibility for repairing damage by termites, to the norms for administering community association funds. The reason for such exhaustive elucidation, explains Gilchrist, is that homeowners' association issues, because they straddle the public and private arenas and are full of ambiguities and uncertainties, have recently given rise to a huge range of legal challenges, unleashing a feeding frenzy amongst litigation lawyers eager to capitalize on residents' differences.

"We have more lawyers per square mile than any other place on the planet, probably — Orange County specifically and California in general," says Gilchrist with a resigned smirk. He says that when he was on the board of the institute "the lawyers were hovering around as they saw the beginning of this stream of litigation on all kinds of issues . . . The other thing is that the attorneys draft all these rules and regulations — the CC&Rs and the board bylaws — so they have a certain amount of paperwork fees that they can build in for themselves from the outset. They also help craft the laws so that they will foster more litigation. It's a fascinating piece of business."

Gilchrist does acknowledge the ironies that flow from the overlapping allegiances of conservative Californians to both Republican ideals and their local homeowners' associations: the paradox of remaining ever vigilant against Big Brother government while submitting willingly to a tyrannical Little Brother who's in your face daily; of decrying government red tape and bureaucracy while becoming entangled in the legal red tape that has been strewn about by avaricious lawyers. But, like Baldassare, Gilchrist believes that the practicalities help vociferously independent spirits to short-circuit any feelings of unease they may have about submitting to the iron hand of the homeowners' association.

"In some cases," he explains, "people have made a conscious choice [to belong to a homeowners' association], and often it's a choice between evils. You live in a community where you don't have to worry about who cleans the streets and who takes care of the landscaping, so you get out from under a certain amount of nitty-gritty manual labour. The exteriors of the buildings are all maintained and so are the roofs. Some people relish that opportunity to retire to the suburbs and live in an association and not have to mow the grass."

— — —

So, to recap, the libertarian ethic running through Southern California's recent history is not fixed and absolute. People are prepared to accept limits on their freedom as long as those limits produce some practical benefit, such as keeping property values high and taking care of lawn mowing.

But let's examine this phenomenon in a different context. How would these same people react to proposals put forth by liberals such as Larry Agran — that Southern Californians enter into a similar kind of contract with local government, whereby more power and money are ceded to the public sector to create assets such as a light-rail system? In this scenario the payoffs to the public — the equivalent of having someone cut your grass or fix your roof, except on a broader, social scale — would include cleaner air, less gridlock on the roads, shorter travelling time to and from work, and fewer deaths in traffic accidents.

I got a hint of what the Republican response to that suggestion might be during an earlier phone conversation with Gilchrist, when he referred to the transit planners who are pushing light-rail development as "social engineers." It was a throwaway line, so I wasn't sure if he had used that phrase in a neutral way or to convey some feeling of disdain.

"Oh, that's pejorative, absolutely," Gilchrist clarifies when we meet in person. "It would be one thing if they laid their strategies on the table and said, 'Okay, this is what we have to do . . . We have to (a) reduce the number of cars on a daily basis, and (b) plant these vertical residences along a transit line in an urban setting where people need to be for their jobs.' But they don't do that. They're saying, 'We're going to craft these light-rail lines, and we think if we put them there, people will come.' What they are modelling them after is the old eastern cities. We had the recent past mayor of Sacramento coming to town and regaling the locals here about how successful the light-rail system is in Sacramento, and how reminiscent it is of her childhood days in Philadelphia. And everyone says, 'Oh, this is what you want to have us look like — downtown Philadelphia, right?' And everyone says, 'Not here, not soon, and not downtown Irvine.'"

The fear, then, is that new transit corridors will be used as a lever to clandestinely alter the style of development in Orange County by moving from suburban- to urban-scale densities (a shift that history suggests is not an automatic outgrowth of the presence of mass transit, since the county was served by the Red Car light-rail line in the '30s and '40s, when densities remained even lower than they are today). If densities do increase around the transit corridors, however, it's a good bet that land values would rise in those areas out of proportion with land values farther from the transit lines. This brings us back into the familiar terrain of the conspiracy theory — ground well-known to populist SoCal Republicans who, paradoxically, while being fully committed to upholding corporate rule, are deeply suspicious of large corporations. And there is plenty to tweak their suspicions around this issue, since it's no secret that some powerful interests are backing the transit line. The Disney corporation, for instance, which is virtually doubling its original Disneyland theme park in Anaheim, is desperate to see some form of economical, efficient transit to transport its low-wage, mostly Latino labour force to work from their homes in Santa Ana and elsewhere. This low-paid workforce has become essential to the tourist industry, with its multitude of hotels and retail outlets; it is unrealistic to think that people working at or near the minimum wage can support two-car families. But beyond Disney's interest in getting its employees to work, Gilchrist suspects that powerful, Democrat-connected developers may be looking — à la the Jack Nicholson film *Chinatown* — for an inside track on where the transit line would be developed and what it would do to land values. "You have the prospect of all kinds of conspiracies," he declares.

But perhaps a larger objection — one that's likely more potent than the spectre of high-level manipulation by real estate interests and "social engineers" — is the threat that light rail poses to the primacy of the private automobile, that great icon of personal freedom, as beloved to the modern-day suburbanite as Trigger was to Roy Rogers. During our interview, Gilchrist spends considerable time telling me what seem like horror stories about lives spent commuting. In one, a husband and wife team he knows have to commute with their child a hundred miles one way from a mountain suburb east of San Bernardino to their workplace in Fullerton. They leave early in the morning, then at the end of the day the woman picks up the child from daycare and proceeds to bide the evening in town with the child before picking up her husband after his night law classes. After this, it's time for the long commute home. To me this seems like a diabolically stressful way to organize your family life, but Gilchrist views it differently. He insists that people around here relish the freedom to live where they please — and if they seek cheap housing, that could be a long way from work — and have learned to adjust to long drives. To bolster the point, he calls in legislative aide Lee Kersten. Besides working in Senator Lewis's office, she is completing a PhD in political science at a nearby university.

"This young lady, Lee," he tells me, "has chosen to live at the beach, not because she has to. She has chosen to live at the beach, period. She has plenty of demands on her time, and is commuting . . ." The veteran politico doesn't know quite how far, so he turns to the woman he has jokingly called a "professional student" and asks her how far it is from home to school.

"It's about forty miles," Lee responds. "It's seventeen miles here. And I guess it's another twenty-five miles to where I go to school. I used to live five miles from here."

Gilchrist asks if it bothers her to have to drive that far.

"No, I want to live at the beach," she says.

For my benefit, Gilchrist reiterates the results of this little Q&A: "She's made a conscious decision to [commute] and is willing to put up with all the wear and tear on her vehicle and all that stuff."

True enough, there are a lot of people in these parts who love their cars with a blind and powerful passion and are resolutely unwilling to entertain any arguments against automobile use, whether those arguments revolve around road congestion, pollution, or public safety. That seems to be the case for Howard Scott of Placentia, who penned the lead letter-to-the-editor in the *Orange County Register* of April

30, 1998. Under the headline "The media fall prey to government's attacks on freedom," Scott writes:

> My take on the April 22 article about the death ratios of trucks, vans and SUVs is as follows: The print media have totally surrendered to being a conduit for liberal government propaganda ("Big vans, pickups deadlier than SUVs," Business, April 22). Obviously, heavier vehicles cause greater damage to smaller vehicles in accidents. To gullibly infer that these vehicles should somehow be controlled, penalized or restricted is absurd.
>
> The free market choice to purchase these vehicles reveals loud and clear that the added safety provided, in spite of higher cost to purchase and operate, is what the buying public prefers. What is obvious, but not pointed out, is the fact that lighter, fuel-efficient cars required by government mandate cost lives.
>
> Let's be honest here. The government spinmasters who take every conceivable poll and statistic and twist it into yet another avenue for interference in and control of our lives need to be challenged. Has the dumbing down of our students by the public schools reached news reporters and prevented them from questioning the validity of such propaganda? The freedom of the road is one of the last refuges of The American Dream the government has not eliminated.

Despite Howard Scott's eloquent equation of automobile travel with the American way, others argue that any proposed programs to reduce the volume, size, and energy consumption of automobiles are not part of an ideological assault but practical responses to a looming catastrophe. Larry Agran says, for instance, that while future increases in automobile traffic may necessitate a new round of hugely expensive and environmentally destructive freeway construction, existing freeways would become 30 to 40 percent more efficient if only 10 percent of commuters could be persuaded to take light rail.

The need to do something to forestall new freeway construction and preserve air quality and open space seems all the more pressing if you accept the prediction, reported recently in the *Los Angeles Times*, that the population of Southern California is likely to increase by a staggering 43 percent between 1998 and 2020 — adding 22.35 million people, equal to roughly two Chicagos, to the area. Planners quoted in the *Times* story say that many parts of Orange County will be gridlocked by the new growth unless a variety of new transportation strategies are put in place.

Certainly the current state of the roads in Orange County — which are jammed in many parts during long rush hours — suggests the need to de-emphasize the car. Yet Gilchrist takes a contrarian approach, insisting that today's congestion merely reflects a temporary disequilibrium that will work itself out. He says it's all part of a natural cycle; although many people have recently moved far from their work in search of cheaper housing, causing them to spend a lot of time commuting, in a few years new jobs will migrate to the population centres, and the pressure will be off.

"I've seen several generations of housing cycles and job creation and job migration to housing areas," Gilchrist recalls. "There's not an easy answer to the question, 'Which came first, the housing or the jobs?' In the early '80s there was a place called the Marino Valley, and housing prices were maxed out there, so a lot of families were moving out to the suburbs fifty or sixty miles away, and they were driving on the freeway. That became a problem. Since then, jobs have developed out there, so the commuting has lightened and the freeway system has improved."

According to Mark Baldassare, the majority of Orange Countyans share neither Gilchrist's optimism about the self-correcting nature of traffic problems nor Scott's philosophical attachment to private transportation at any cost.

"Most of the public opinion polls that I've done or seen elsewhere suggest most residents believe that there is a place for light-rail transit in the transportation planning of Orange County," Baldassare says. "People understand that, just in terms of traffic congestion and good planning, there's a need for alternatives to the car. They want more choices and they want some other ways to reduce traffic congestion."

This suggests something greatly at odds with the image that Orange County projects to the world. If a majority of people are prepared to accept a public, communitarian solution to gridlock, then maybe this place isn't such a pillar of right-wing libertarianism after all; perhaps the public mood actually favours making decisions on practical, rather than ideological grounds, even if those decisions support the intervention of government in their insular, independent suburban lives. And it's not just public opinion on freeways and automobile traffic that points towards this more moderate image of the average Orange County resident. After decades of public polling, Baldassare believes that OC, despite the outcome of its electoral battles, is at its social core just as middle-of-the-road as anywhere else.

"There's a big gap between the views of people who are elected and the public at large in Orange County, within which I would include average Republicans, on issues as wide-ranging as environmental issues and abortion and gay rights," he says. "The county, including people registered as Republicans, is actually much more socially tolerant and environmentally aware than the Republican leadership feels comfortable with."

How does one explain this gap between the leaders and the led? Baldassare suggests it is an outgrowth of the fact that many citizens feel disconnected from electoral politics. The pollster says his surveys show that a big chunk of the citizenry are turned off by everything from the tone of political advertising, to the lack of content in political addresses, to the extremist stances of the candidates.

"There are a lot of people, both Democrats and Republicans, who just don't know what the point is to voting anymore," Baldassare reports. "It's not that they are disengaged from politics. They are very engaged. They know exactly what is going on, but they have become so cynical and alienated by the process that they just don't know what the point is."

In the hands of skilful political fixers, however, this sense of alienation is not a neutral entity but a tangible, active force that can be cultivated and successfully deployed as a campaigning tool. Such is the case in OC, claims Baldassare, where a hard-line Republican leadership has realized that "the higher the turnout, the more people who come out to register to vote, the more tenuous their hold on power," and so they have consistently rebuffed non-partisan efforts to increase voter turnout to the levels of urban areas like Los Angeles and San Francisco.

Not that the politics of resignation is entirely the creation of Republican strategists. This is a two-party system, and both parties have to accept blame for too many people in Orange County staying home on election night (for example, two major referendum votes in the wake of the OC bankruptcy — in June 1995 and March 1996 — had turnouts of 34.5 and 43.3 percent respectively). The problem, says Baldassare, is that while many OC voters perceive Republican candidates as extremists, a lot of them don't believe the Democrats present a credible alternative. In his estimation, the Orange County Democratic machine has been "dysfunctional" for years. Having "failed to do the basic organizing activities that parties need to do," Democrats have watched their vote stagnate during a time of rapid population growth. The one bright spot for the party is the organizing that has taken place in the Latino community, resulting, for instance, in the election, and then re-election in the 1998 midterm, of Loretta Sanchez. But Baldassare believes the Latino vote has been a gift rather than an earned reward for the Democratic leadership. He notes that Latinos are no more liberal in their values than average Californians; generally they have been pushed into the Democratic camp by the Republicans' anti-immigration policies rather than having been actively wooed by Democrats.[2] And despite this boost from a vital Latino membership, the Democrats still suffer from incoherence on key policy issues, notably environmental protection.

"I'll never forget being at a meeting," recalls Baldassare, "where there was both Larry Agran and Richard O'Neill, who is a millionaire developer, probably the most prominent Democrat in the county.[3] They were at each other constantly. You wouldn't see that amount of animosity between a Republican and a Democrat on environmental and growth issues. And the whole Democratic party in Orange County has this kind of tension running through it."

The inability of Democrats to repair their internal rifts has meant that most of OC has remained "a one-party county," which may explain many residents' decision not to participate in electoral politics. (Many, however, came back to the polls in the '92 and '96 federal elections, during which time Orange County gave independent Ross Perot one of his strongest bases of support, possibly in protest of the lack of choice that the established parties have offered it.)[4]

But putting aside the peculiarities of the local scene, there may be some broader lessons to be taken from this portrait of Orange County as a place of political paralysis. Perhaps one such lesson is that the natural outlook of suburban cities is not one of reflexive conservatism, as some have extrapolated from poll and election results, but rather a pervasive sense of alienation and apathy.

Baldassare argues that an insular mindset, a tendency to retreat from public life, is to some extent an inevitable product of the organizational and design principles that have been built into suburban metropolises like Orange County. Communities with privatized recreational facilities and with enormous political powers devolved to the micro-level of the homeowners' association "have isolated people from the region they live in . . . and reinforced people's isolation from the world of political debate and regional policy issues," he says. This became strikingly evident during the time of the Orange County bankruptcy. Then, citizens reacted with an eerie aloofness to what at first appeared to be a financial meltdown in their region, when vital services across Orange County were about to end because the money had simply disappeared with the collapse of the county's investment pool.

"The ship had hit the iceberg," recalls Baldassare, "and how did people react to it? It was like, 'So let it sink.' Here was a real community crisis, and people couldn't care less. They all looked at it in terms of their own city — was their own city okay? Not was the county okay. If they felt they were getting the services they needed in their area, they weren't going to get worked up about it. They didn't feel there was a larger whole that needed to be saved."

In *Postsuburban California*, authors Kling, Olin, and Poster describe Orange County as an "anticipatory region" or a "window on the future" — an area that, throughout the post–World War II period, has provided the model of how most of the rest of us would wind up living. This was, after all, the birthplace of typical post-war suburbs. And as those suburbs grew and bled into one another, Southern California gave the world its first glimpse of a new urban form — the "Edge City" in Joel Garreau's terms, or the "Postsuburbia" that Kling, Olin, and Poster speak of. This mixture of the multiplicitous functions of a typical urban area with the low-density, privatized architectural attributes of suburbia is now the norm in many metropolitan regions of the United States and Canada. Southern California also showed the world that suburbia could produce its own brand of politics. The original Reagan revolution and the Proposition 13 tax revolt were believed at first to be merely self-contained, wacky, West Coast phenomena. A few years later, however, they would be seen as the blueprints for similar neo-conservative coups taking place across the United States, and as far afield as Canada, Britain, and New Zealand.

Not that what originates here must inevitably travel, unmodified, across the globe. In Ontario's 905 land, for instance, an intensified process of privatization may, indeed, lead to the formation of California-style homeowners' associations to take on the functions that governments abandon. There are already a scattering of US-style gated communities in the area, so why not these homeowners' groups? Such an outcome, however, is not a certainty: Canada's cultural preference for "peace, order, and good government" above the ideal of protecting one's private property suggests some reluctance to give up the town hall in favour of a private quasi-government. And being latecomers to the process of constructing a suburban-centred politics, we have the luxury of being able to reject earlier models.

Overall, though, if events in California have foreshadowed larger, sometimes global trends, what does the current state of chaos and confusion in Southern California's sprawling suburban metropolises say about the future of other regions that have embarked on similar journeys? Perhaps the one conclusion that can be drawn from five decades of frantic suburban expansion in Southern California, as elsewhere, is that the suburban dream is indeed finite, that any story that has a beginning and a middle must also have an end, that perhaps the suburban era is now bumping up against its own limitations. The darker side of this sun-soaked narrative is that, although you can run from urban problems, eventually they will catch up with you. Sooner or later there will be no place left to run, probably not enough asphalt to accommodate the cars, and eventually not enough land left to cut into neat parcels and cover with Kentucky bluegrass. Which brings us back to the sad realization that this is no longer the 1950s, and the dream of the good life has grown considerably dimmer.

This sorry tale of despair and disappointment should, however, provide some encouragement for those who believe that human beings can use human institutions and a certain collective foresight to solve the problems that face us. The mythology of the New Right — that individuals freed from the yoke of government will build brilliant new communities on the suburban frontier, and that self-interest and market forces will ensure that these are better places to live than communities whose shape is influenced by government planners — has dominated for most of the post–World War II period. But the shortcomings of that approach have by now become evident. It means lives spent commuting on clogged highways, the loss of natural spaces to suburban sprawl, a growing gap between affluent enclaves and the foresaken pockets of poverty, and disjointed communities where it's necessary to drive to buy a carton of milk and where neighbours never speak. Today there are no shortage of ideas on how to remedy these problems. Most of them require, however, shucking the old ideas of the post-war period — that resources are infinite, that individual, private solutions are invariably what people want — and realizing that we're into a new era where the good life is perhaps still attainable in burbs, but not in the ways we've previously imagined.

part 3 | # Where Does It Go From Here?

10 | Encore: Back In the 905

It is late May 1999, just about two years to the day since I last ventured onto the smooth asphalt surfaces of York Region in Ontario. A provincial election — the "referendum on the Mike Harris revolution," as the papers have taken to calling it — is set to occur in eight days. I'm feeling a bit like Rip Van Winkle, waking up one morning in the air-conditioned chill of the Dodge Suites Hotel in Vaughan to discover a landscape that in some ways has become unrecognizable in a mere twenty-four months.

The locals say this is the fastest-growing clump of communities in Canada, and the scenery bears that out. The major landmarks are the same ones from two years ago — when I came to watch the federal candidates duke it out — but as the flow of concrete, cash, and consumer goods has intensified, this place has continued its metamorphosis into something new and weirdly out of proportion.

Vestiges of a rural past — holdout agricultural parcels, the occasional barn — have been disappearing, replaced by giant cinema complexes, warehouse-scale café-bookstores, and ever more housing subdivisions. Banners and sandwich-board signs advertising new accommodation have blossomed like dandelions up and down Yonge Street, providing a graphic indicator of the pace of growth on the northward trek from Steeles Avenue to Newmarket. Building permits issued in the 905 belt are now apparently returning to dollar values last seen during the great building bonanza of the late '80s.[1] This revival corresponds, depending on what political point you wish to make, either to Harris's tax-slashing first term in office or to the ongoing surge of Canadian exports, propelled by the federal government's exchange-rate policies and a steady demand from our trading partner south of the forty-ninth.

Whatever the reason, the past few years have been good to York Region. It feels, in fact, as though the 1980s never ended here. Although the big cities have been afflicted with the *fin de siècle* scourges of homelessness, beggars, and the moral angst they produce, here in the post-industrial suburban heartland recession was fleeting and has left few obvious traces and even fewer second thoughts. Granted, the tone of today's boom is a little different from that cocaine- and hot-money-fuelled Monopoly game played out during the late '80s. Down on the southern perimeter of the Yonge corridor, for instance, close to where York Region and the City of Toronto meet, you can find new developments that speak of restraint and even some ecological concern. For example, a townhouse complex where tall units have been bound together, Old World style, into one dense and stately block of stone and concrete, like a New York brownstone or a little piece of Amsterdam. It makes the consoling statement that some people around here don't mind living close to their neighbours, that there is some room in their worldview for the concept of community.

For the most part, though, people continue to be drawn to York Region — "Ontario's Rising Star," as the billboards on arterial roads now proclaim — for the same reasons as before: the promise of space, the sheen of luxury, the benefits of exclusivity. A few miles farther north, a more typical pitch leaps out from a billboard across from a strip mall parking lot. It advertises, "executive living in Newmarket. Traditional Estate Homes on Forested 1/2 to 1 acre lots priced from $399,900." Note the word "from." Note also that neither concerns about the ecological impact of sprawl nor the deepening, wrenching crisis of poverty unfolding in established urban areas has done anything to diminish the appetite for "traditional" real estate values (expensive houses on large lots) up in these aristocratic 'burbs. And finally, note that there are political implications to these things, as everyone is about to rediscover eight days from now as Ontarians line up at the polls.

— — —

It is May 25 — a big day. Most of the recent polls show Mike Harris widening his lead over Dalton McGuinty's challenging Liberals, reversing a trend that, towards the beginning of the campaign, showed voters — even in the 905 — so spooked about cuts to health care and education that they were considering tossing the Tories out. The premier will be addressing a joint chambers of commerce luncheon today at a Vaughan banquet hall called the Hollywood Princess.

This event is significant not because Harris has made himself scarce around these parts; on the contrary, the 905 vote is so crucial to the Tories that they have been spending a great deal of time up here. In fact, Harris launched the PC campaign less than a month earlier from the backyard of a supporter's home up in Newmarket. No, what makes this particular event noteworthy is that it comes at a point in the campaign when Harris has clearly caught his stride. Ever since McGuinty's disastrous performance in the televised leaders' debate the previous week, the Liberals — the only serious challengers in this race — have been playing catch-up, allowing Harris the luxury of spinning the issues his own way, without wasting too much time responding to his opponents' attacks. So today Harris, unencumbered by the need to perform damage control, will have the chance to tell suburbanites what he thinks they want to hear. I'm anticipating that this will afford a clear view of exactly what it is in the Tories' revolutionary pitch that appeals to these techno-burb voters.

I am also awaiting with some eagerness — and a little dread — the opportunity to witness a spectacle that by now has become emblematic of the polarization of life and politics in Ontario under Harris. At each Tory campaign stop it's been the same: The premier, eyes fixed forward, is whisked into a building to address his well-heeled supporters, while a coterie of protestors — during this campaign they've been arriving in school buses and ambulances to symbolize Harris's cuts to hospitals and education — are kept at bay by a wall of cops.

When I pull into the parking lot of the Hollywood Princess late in the morning of May 25, the police are out in force, although the protestors haven't arrived yet. There's a mobile command unit, and clusters of cops have taken up their posts at every entrance to the lot. A York Region policeman approaches our valiant little Honda Civic, vintage 1990 (which performed admirably on the trip from Ottawa, thanks to a replacement radiator and new front brake pads), and asks for my reservation confirmation for the luncheon. Nobody gets near this building without the proper documentation; it's a bit like one of those Cold War spy flicks where some guy in uniform is standing by a checkpoint demanding, "Papers, please."

Despite passing this first test, I actually feel a bit nervous — a shadow, perhaps, of what it must be like to be a Mexican going through the immigration checkpoint on the freeway to LA — given the clear set of sociological indicators that separate those who are attending this event from those who are likely to disrupt it. The Civic, for one, with its flecks of rust sprouting around the wheel rims, is clearly set apart from the sea of late-model luxury cars that fill the parking lot. Mercedes-Benzes, I observe, though not yet as common as in Southern California, have clearly been gaining in popularity amongst this crowd.

Once past the parking lot patrol, I'm met with another wall of police at the entrance to the building, and beyond them, an additional platoon of enforcers who look like bar-room bouncers squeezed into business suits. These guys, the PCs' own private security squad, carefully scrutinize the crowd for interlopers and party-crashers. They have apparently learned their jobs well. This afternoon, for instance, some hawk-eyed security agent will recognize Joel Hardin, an official with the Canadian Federation of Students (making him a junior "union boss," in Harris-speak), apprehend him, and charge him with trespassing — even though he has bought a ticket to the event and caused no disturbance. A mark of the Tory bouncers' professionalism is that they will chuck this unwelcome observer discreetly, without a fuss, leaving me and the rest of the folks at my table unaware of the ejection. (The incident, however, will be reported on the TV news.)

Beyond the curtain of muscle that separates the protest and the pro-business camps, it's time to schmooze. The obtrusive security in itself is an obvious topic of conversation, and on this matter a small sampling of guests seem to harbour mixed feelings. For Carl, an exporter from Scarborough (his company sources Canadian-made goods requested by clients in Asia and Latin America), the remaking of the Hollywood Princess into a fortress is confirmation of his view that Harris has been maliciously targeted by an unruly rabble seeking to drown out his message. "That, to my mind, is not the right way to do things — it's dirty pool," Carl tells me after our conversation moves away from the ice-breaking topics of the Stanley Cup playoffs and the unusually cool May weather. Quizzed about whether the heated protests that follow Harris may be part of a more general breakdown of social order — signs of rot similar to the proliferation of squeegee kids or the increase in panhandling, both of which Harris has promised to crack down on — Carl professes to have some special insight into these particular issues.

Having at one time been an importer, as well as an exporter, a job that required some travel to Asia, Carl had his fair share of dealings with beggars and unlicensed vendors. On one of his trips to the Far East, for instance, he was riding in a friend's car — "He had quite a nice car," the merchant recalls — when a couple of ragged street vendors approached them after they had stopped in heavy traffic.

When his friend waved them off, the vendors expressed their displeasure by snapping off the car's windshield wipers and running away.

"We used to chuckle about them [beggars and street vendors]," Carl recalls. "We'd talk about how this kind of thing could never happen in Canada." Time, of course, has proved him wrong. Today there are squeegee kids on many Toronto street corners, and in some Canadian cities young children beg on the streets.

For many people outside this hall, Carl's story would likely contain a chilling message about the descent of an egalitarian society into a Third World–style polarization between rich and poor. In other words, what happens when government gears its policies towards rewarding entrepreneurial moxie and forgets about those on the fringes? Just the day before this meeting, for instance, Campaign 2000 — the national coalition dedicated to eradicating child poverty in Canada — released a study showing that while child poverty across most of the country has fallen, there has been a steep rise in Ontario since Harris took office, slashing the welfare rates by 22 percent and allowing rent controls to be waived as soon as the tenants change.[2]

But Tory policy-makers are betting that their core constituents in suburbia will see squeegee kids and beggars not as a sign of systemic political failure but as a problem that needs to be dealt with in the same way as those protestors who dog Harris: with a big police presence and more trespassing convictions. Carl seems to buy that solution, when he gets around to giving it some thought. He agrees that police need more power to get people off the streets, although "crackdown may be too harsh a word" for what he has in mind.

Others here are more agitated by the militarization of Ontario politics. Standing beside a window that reveals that the protest buses have now arrived, I exchange a few words with a Québécois journalist who seems ill at ease with the massive police presence. Having travelled with both Harris and McGuinty during this campaign, he concludes that the security at Harris's stops is well beyond the norm; on the Liberal tour the mood was relaxed and access to the leader was open, he says.

Soon after the correspondent makes this comparison, we have confirmation that we are truly privileged to be ensconced within this fortress. Breezing past us, smiling, uttering a few words of greeting in French to the Québécois journalist, and projecting a strange in-person resemblance to Rodney Dangerfield, is the most intensely loved and intensely hated Ontario premier in living memory, Mike Harris. With him comes the realization that one has indeed crossed over some magic threshold and entered "the bubble," as it's known by government critics — that meticulously controlled environment designed to protect the premier from the chance of a misstep, the whiff of dissent, the threat of spontaneity.

This bubble, so some commentators maintain, has very little to do with sheltering Harris from noisy protestors who would hijack the democratic process, as Carl and many others believe. Instead, it fuctions as part of a recently imported political machine designed to turn the conventions of campaigning upside down. It replaces old-style electioneering, in which a political campaign was seen as a *public* process, where voters could grill politicians on their records — some of you may remember when a politician's worth was measured partly by his ability to match wits with hecklers on those cross-country whistle-stop tours — with a spectacle that's ready-made for television, something cordoned off and remote from casual scrutiny, a tightly scripted and choreographed piece of theatre in which unauthorized audience participation is not welcomed.

According to *Globe and Mail* reporter Richard Mackie, television images of Harris mingling with the common folk have been, consistently throughout this campaign, the product of "detailed planning and careful logistics designed to ensure that the only people who get close to the Premier are those whom party strategists want in the pictures." Case in point: Harris and his wife visit a library in Smiths Falls, meeting with parents and promising that the province will force school boards to accept input from school councils, a move that presumably would allow parents to do things like replace the tattered children's books in the Smiths Falls library. But it's not a message delivered to a non-partisan throng. The locals who form the cheering section on this campaign stop have been carefully selected from the ranks of pro-PC parents.

The main benefit of controlling campaign optics in this way, writes Mackie, is that it allows the Tories to skirt the issues that opponents want them to respond to. Therefore subjects like homelessness, hospital closings, and a new school curriculum that won't be ready for the next school year are ignored, so public attention can be focused on the "hot-button issues" that research shows will elicit the desired Pavlovian response from voters. Each day the Tories try to narrowcast those messages to the desired audiences with as little interference as possible from outside commentators. Their promise of an additional 20 percent income tax cut, for instance, may not have had broad appeal during this election, but it is crucial to shoring up support amongst men earning less than $30,000 a year. This is the group that responded most positively to the workfare proposal in the 1995 campaign, since low income earners are likely to be highly resentful of people who pick up a government cheque without having to punch a clock each morning.[3]

By operating this way Harris's party had been able to extricate itself from much of the rough-and-tumble of public debate, enabling it to beam well-crafted messages directly into the psyches of targeted voters. One day the issue is mandatory teacher training (a plank that scored well with parents, promising that they might forget about the past four years of chaos in the schools); another day it's new laws to clamp down on squeegee kids (used with moderate success to woo otherwise liberal women voters in the downtown areas who have become frightened by the rapid decay of urban life during Harris's first term).[4]

Of course, it doesn't take a rocket scientist to figure out that politicians want to avoid being on the defensive, being so caught up in responding to criticism that they can't make their own case. But some of the stories of this campaign, showing how far Harris's party is willing to go to replace real life with brazenly manufactured images, seem almost surreal.

Witness a Mike Harris campaign spectacle played out at the Air Canada Centre, the massive sports complex that recently replaced Maple Leaf Gardens as the home of Toronto's NHL hockey team. The occasion: Team Harris celebrating Ontarians who had moved off welfare and into gainful employment. Big event in a big venue. Big crowd, right? Well, not quite. Covering the event for *eye* magazine, Tom Lyons writes that the Tories rented this monster facility to stage a spectacle that in reality was "nothing more than a press conference in an empty arena. Harris looks directly into the TV cameras and says he is 'here to congratulate' former welfare recipients, leaving viewers at home to assume that there must be *something* going on, perhaps a group of reformed crackheads shuffling up to receive honorary Leaf jerseys after the speeches. But there are only empty seats and the giant scoreboards flashing triumphant slogans about how many people have disappeared from the welfare rolls. Twelve people every hour! Three hundred and eighty thousand altogether! Enough to fill the Air Canada Centre twenty times over! (Where they have all gone remains a point of bitter debate.)"

In Lyons's estimation this episode shows that the Tories are running a campaign that "exists only on TV . . . its boundaries guarded by police." And faced with this D.W. Griffiths version of political campaigning, the government's detractors are left with little choice in their quest to be heard but to crash the party as noisily as possible. "Anyone who wants to approach the Premier with a question must get past the police to break into TVland," concludes Lyons. "The reward for breaking through is a brief turn as a TV star, followed by a stint in jail."

And indeed, that is exactly what happened that day. The question about where people dropped from the welfare rolls have gone continues to be raucously debated out in the real world — on the street outside the Air Canada Centre, as it happens, where anti-poverty activists have gathered to promote their version of reality. Even here, however, the professional spin-meisters may have gotten the upper hand. After the "congratulations, you're now off welfare" show at the ACC came a defining moment of the 1999 Ontario election: A crowd of angry demonstrators surged towards a departing Harris and his seven-year-old son Jeffrey, causing police to go after the protestors with cattle prods, and Tory representatives on TV political panels to condemn agitators who would sink so low as to implicitly threaten the premier's son.

Lyons quotes a longtime news photographer who says the clash seemed like a set-up concocted by Harris's handlers. The premier and his family, who rarely accompanied Harris on these trips, could easily have avoided the protestors by taking the exit used by hockey players.[5] Which raises the spectre that this pushing-and-shoving scene was actually *designed* to elicit sympathy for the premier and to neutralize the protesters who dogged Harris at every campaign stop, identifying them in the public mind as violent rabble who terrorize little kids. It's a bit like that scene in the movie *Bob Roberts*, where the title character, a right-wing populist demagogue played by Tim Robbins, stages his own shooting in order to boost his popularity.

— — —

Whether or not life was imitating art to quite this extent, it seems clear that Harris and his technicians have learned the key lessons set forth more than thirty years ago by another actor — Ronald Reagan. You may recall that Reagan's 1966 campaign to become California governor was a pioneering work in the sinister science of electoral stagecraft. It recognized that reaching a suburban electorate is all about making it work on TV, that election campaigns can no longer be ad lib affairs but, rather, tightly scripted and meticulously blocked theatrical productions. Reagan showed that the point of a political campaign in the age of TV and suburban living is to forget about the live audience — they're just props on a set — and to speak directly to the targeted viewer, trying to hit those nerve endings that the research has revealed.

The 1999 Tory campaign followed to the letter the commandments brought down from on high by Reagan and solemnly adhered to by campaigning politicians in the US ever since. Harris's handlers stressed the importance of having a relaxed, reassuring, and well-rehearsed candidate, sheltered from the stress and the potential for miscues that come with Main Street strolls and impromptu barbecue flips. They armed their candidate with a polished script that had been tested and refined by polling gurus and other "hidden persuaders." And they saturated the airwaves with partisan advertising for up to a year before the election was actually announced, softening up their targets in preparation for the final assault.

It's not surprising, really, that Harris and his party should adopt this approach, given that a key core element of the constituency live out here on this endless post-suburban plain. On the short drive from the Dodge Suites to the Hollywood Princess, for instance, I can't get it out of my head how much this place has come to resemble suburban California. In a mere five-minute jaunt through Vaughan I've passed three of those mega–movie complexes — the Famous Players Colossus, an IMAX wide-screen theatre, and a thirty-screen AMC entertainment palace — the Buck Rogers–style architecture of which has been a long-standing feature of the SoCal landscape, but which has only started to rise above the desolate spectre of retired southern Ontario farmland in the past couple of years. Then there are the highways, the central defining feature of the landscape. Visible a few hundred metres to the south on the drive down is Highway 407, the newly privatized toll road. My route, meanwhile, is along Highway 7 (Vaughan's equivalent of Main Street), which runs past Tory candidate Al Palladini's Lincoln-Mercury dealership, in front of the Hollywood Princess, and on eastward to link up with a daunting corridor of hydro-electric transmission towers. Adding to the feeling this landscape produces that I've suddenly been transported across three time zones — is the sign that sits in front of a square brick building across from the Hollywood Princess: "We sell guns — Y2K food, guns." It is as if some wacky survivalist cult had migrated from the Western US along with the amusement-park architecture and Mike Harris's neo-Reaganite revolution.

— — —

The similarities between the 1999 Ontario election and earlier rounds of US political pugilism aren't limited to the stage management and the suburban scenery. On matters of substance as well, this election has the feel of an American slugfest, with the two leading parties (Harris's Tories and McGuinty's Liberals) staking out policy ground very similar to that normally occupied by Republicans and Democrats during state races in the US.

The Tories have extended the motif they introduced in 1995 with a Republican-style platform combining deeper tax cuts, crime-fighting, and exhortations in favour of personal responsibility and against the "cycle of dependency" allegedly promoted by welfare. The Liberals, caught in a predicament similar to that of the Democrats south of the border, have been shoved to the right by the unexpected appeal of 1995's Common Sense Revolution and had no option in 1999 but to accept the earlier income tax reductions as a fait accompli. They have, however, held firm in their view that additional tax reductions will have to wait until new funds are pumped into health care and education, and until the deficit is eliminated; all the while pursuing a small-*l* liberal moral high ground by pushing for a cleaner environment and some government intervention to remedy the worst of the crisis of homelessness, child poverty, and the widening income gaps that have gripped the province since the Tories were first elected.

Both of the leading parties' platform documents (the Tories' *Blueprint* and the Liberals' *20/20 Plan*)[6] contain examples of agenda-stealing, with each party trying to cover an exposed and vulnerable flank. The Liberals, despite the preamble that "police tell us incidence of violent crime is actually declining," still attempt to deal with the "soft on crime" tag. They pledge harsher penalties for "those who would exploit our youth" — at one point the party announces it will introduce mandatory two-year sentences for criminals who deal drugs or bring weapons near schools — and they promise to confiscate the property of narcotics peddlers and to boost police funding to fight child pornography. The Tories, meanwhile, try to short-circuit criticisms that they have gutted environmental protection — laying off most of the Environment Ministry's inspectors, turning Ontario into a haven for toxic-waste dumpers — with promises to increase penalties against polluters and to hold corporate executives accountable for their companies' environmental performance.

But these attempts to cover their weaknesses — or to usurp the most appealing aspects of their opponents' platforms — do nothing to fudge the clear and massive distinctions between the two parties. Just a glance at the competing campaign documents make it obvious that Ontarians may never before have had such a clear philosophical choice at the ballot box. At the root of this divergence, it strikes me, are two fundamentally different interpretations of the dominant mentality in those ever-expanding suburban communities — that middle ground between city and country that now forms the middle-class mainstream of Ontario society, and which any party must woo if it is to have any realistic hope of seizing power.

Reading the PCs' *Blueprint*, with its overwhelming emphasis on crime, punishment, and the correction of the morally impure — themes largely absent, with the exception of those juvenile boot camps, from the original Common Sense Revolution of 1995 — you must assume that the targeted suburban voter is motivated largely by paranoia and resentment. These people have either been battered by unpleasant interpersonal dealings in daily life or terrified by violence on TV, and are now eager to see criminals, deviants, malcontents, and non-conformists of all sorts either locked up or somehow brought down a few notches.

Next to economic development and taxation issues, which give the Tories the opportunity to crow, the big hot button in the Harris re-election bid is crime. Criminal-justice issues take up five pages of densely packed print in the party's fifty-two-page brochure, yielding a cornucopia of policies — crackdowns on squeegee kids and panhandlers, making parents pay for property damage done by their kids, having convicted criminals pay for their own stay in jail, and so on. A visit to the Conservative web site at the height of the campaign reveals an even greater emphasis on law-and-order issues; two of five recent press releases filed under "news" hammer away at this topic. "Harris to Parolees: Doing Crack? You're Going Back!" shouts the headline above a press release, written in the style of a tabloid crime story, which reiterates the premier's belief that paroled offenders caught by random drug testing should be ushered straight back to jail. Another missive restates the Harris commitment to "take back our cities from aggressive panhandlers, squeegee kids, and drug dealers." This item provided a magical moment of nostalgia for me. Reading that "Harris' Blueprint to crack down on street crime is based on the 'broken window' strategy of crime control," I was suddenly transported back to the Tierrasanta Community Center in San Diego, where this ubiquitous "broken window" provided the symbolic justification for campaigns against unsanctioned trash containers and boats parked in driveways.

Indeed, the paradox that underlies life in suburban California — where conservatives will espouse radical libertarianism in the economic sphere but submit to all manner of intrusive regulations and restrictions in other aspects of life — appears to be sprouting in Ontario, if Harris's election platform is any indication. His talk of freeing business from the yoke of high taxation and government red tape is matched by endless prescriptions for a more intrusive and authoritarian government presence in social affairs. It's not just that Harris wants the province to be a more effective jailer. In many other areas of social endeavour, the Tories are saying that things will get better if the authorities just get tough. Want your kids to learn better at school? Then put them in school uniforms and set up "strict discipline programs" for students who won't co-operate. While they're at it, the Tories also think it's a good idea to legally obligate kids to sing the national anthem each morning.

So what gives? Why has this brand of moralistic social conservatism suddenly become a major plank of a party that, in the last election, had such success appealing to voters on the basis of pocketbook issues alone? In the US, it's clear that similar pitches to restore the declining moral character of society have been propelled onto the agenda by a strong fundamentalist Christian lobby. But Canada seems a different case; we've always thought of ourselves as being much more socially tolerant.

Part of the answer may be practical; perhaps by focusing on perceived flaws within the human character, it becomes easier to justify the growing gap between rich and poor. Forced drug testing for welfare recipients, for instance — "those who refuse treatment or who won't take tests on request will lose their benefits," *Blueprint* states — has an air of Victorian paternalism. It contains the implication that people wind up on welfare because of some personal failing like a weakness for alcohol or drugs. This notion has some utility, especially in a society increasingly divided between those with Mercedes-Benzes and those with worn-out shoes. Focusing almost exclusively on alchoholism, drug abuse, and mental illness as contributing factors to poverty makes it easier to ignore the fact that the minimum wage is too low and rents too high, that welfare rates aren't adequate in most urban areas to rent a place to live. Similarly, concentrating on more intangible attitudinal elements affecting, say, education — kids aren't learning because teachers can't discipline them and they don't sing the national anthem in the morning — provides a convenient distraction from the proposition that, just maybe, cutting a couple of billion dollars from the school system might have negative consequences on the quality of education.

A competing explanation for this retro-conservative social agenda is that Tory strategists have figured out that when people move to the suburbs to raise kids and drive minivans, they embark on a one-way journey back to the '50s, seeking to recapture the comforting moral certitudes of *Father Knows Best*. Feeling that the world is a threatening and unpredictable place full of temptations for their kids, they set aside the mushy liberalism of those parenting books and opt to re-create a world where good kids will prosper and all others will feel the wrath of punitive cops and school principals. The scariest thing about this proposition is that it may well be true.

One final clue about the raison d'être for this expanded anti-crime, pro-authority platform may be found in the presence of all those spirited Reform Party partisans who labour under the Ontario PC banner; perhaps the "strict discipline" promises are a sop to them. The Reform crowd has embraced the Harris mission with unabashed delight. Having suffered through the 1997 federal contest in which the party failed both to win a single seat east of the Manitoba border and to shuck its image as a posse of dangerous rednecks, York Region's Reformers have been, throughout this provincial contest, close to ecstatic with the realization that a party espousing most of Reform's policies — low taxes, more law-and-order, a return to traditional values — stand on the brink of a stunning second electoral triumph.

"I could see during the last federal election that [Reform] had a chance to make major inroads in Ontario, but they didn't," complains Doug Clark, whom I first met two years ago amidst the plush-carpeted splendour of the Aurora Golf and Country Club. Today he is traversing another broadloomed expanse, this time in the lobby of the Hollywood Princess.

"I talked to the head guys in Ottawa who were running the campaign," he continues, "and they refused to listen. I said, 'You're going to get massacred in Ontario if you keep this up — you have a chance on certain issues,' and I even explained it, and they said, 'No, we disagree with you; we think you're wrong and we think we're right.'"

But the provincial Tories are different; they really understand Ontario. Take the crime issue. It's been stirring something of a panic up here, says Clark, who relates that his car has been broken into twice — "The police figure it's an organized ring from Toronto that comes up and does its thing" — while a friend of his "was basically accosted with a loaded gun while he got out of his car" in an underground parking lot.

So when the Harris Tories talk about getting tough with criminals, it really resonates with suburbanites who believe there's a wave of criminal activity moving north from the big city. In the last federal election Clark, who is now Reform's riding president for Vaughan-King-Aurora, as well as a door-knocking foot soldier for Al Paladini's provincial re-election campaign, urged Reform strategists to put greater emphasis on criminal justice, which is much more relevant to Ontarians than a triple-e Senate or the supposed "special privileges" for Quebec. But they didn't bite.

Yet there's more to a good campaign than just one issue. Clark believes that the Tory platform hits enough bases to give it a general foothold across the province. Then there's the leader himself. Clark speaks repeatedly and reverentially about "Mr. Harris" having "broad appeal" for a major chunk of the electorate, an appeal that has been enhanced by Harris's success at keeping his credibility quotient high.

"What it will come down to," Clark tells me, "is that the basic core supporters will say, 'He said he was going to do it, and he did it.' Right or wrong, he has followed through on what he said he was going to do."

And so, in this contest, the mood of Ontario Reformers is very different from that in 1995. All that energy and enthusiasm, that fire and brimstone, seem to be leading someplace. This has given Reformers hope for a brighter future on all fronts. The *Globe and Mail* reports, for instance, that a large contingent of Reformers in the new riding of Oak Ridges have been integrated so seamlessly into PC MPP Frank Klees's campaign for re-election that it is now touted as a model for the "Unite the Right" campaign urging the linking of PCs and Reformers nationally.[7]

One of the Reform foot soldiers working the phones on Klees's behalf is Bill King, who gave me his business card before leaving the campaign office of federal candidate Maralyn Hazelgrove back in 1995. So I phoned up to ask if Bill might be able to pull some strings, to have me tag along with some Klees campaign workers as they went door to door. His response was basically "No dice — everyone's too busy getting the vote out to talk with a reporter."

Still, our conversation was illuminating, shedding some light on how Harris's campaign pitch has been playing with its most zealous supporters. It also confirmed that King still holds to his unconventional beliefs about widespread and interlocking conspiracies in the halls of power: one of his first items of business today, for instance, is to try to peddle me a copy of a book entitled *Fraud, Deceit and Manipulation*, written by a friend in Richmond Hill. It is an exposé, King explained, of "how the feds are acting illegally on income tax" — too hot for most bookstores, except a few independents run by political renegades — and is based partly on documents Bill alleges have since mysteriously disappeared from the National Archives.

When talk turned to the current provincial election, King predicted, correctly, that Harris would easily walk back into office. This prompted King to move away from his commentary about skulduggery and misdeeds in high places to express a rare sentiment of contentment. The imminent re-election of Harris, he said, will mark the first time in recent memory that Ontario voters elect a premier not just to repudiate the previous leadership (for example, Harris being elected in 1995 to get rid of Bob Rae; Rae being voted in previously to get rid of David Peterson; Peterson to get rid of Frank Miller, etc.) but to express endorsement of a sitting premier's policies.[8]

As for what it is in the Harris platform that has captivated his own attention, King hinted that the socially conservative drift of the Tories' policy book ranks high alongside the Harris commitment to more and deeper tax cuts. He explained that he was looking forward to the Oak Ridges all-candidates' meeting — which, in a blow to the democratic process, was ultimately cancelled — so he can confront Liberal candidate Vito Spatafora with a statement made by his leader.

"Dalton McGuinty believes that homosexual couples should be able to adopt children," King complained, segueing seamlessly into another conspiracy theory. "This is another example of the heinous way in which the morals of our country are being purposefully destroyed." (On the issue of gay rights Harris himself has been coy. Responding to a Supreme Court decision supporting same-sex spousal benefits, the premier stated that while same-sex unions are "not my idea of a family," Ontario is committed to upholding the law.[9] In this way Harris skilfully avoided looking bigoted, while at the same time sending a signal to rank-and-file supporters — who may have no such qualms — that he personally shares their beliefs.)

Indeed, this ability to deliver calculatedly ambiguous messages on sensitive issues is surely one of the secrets of Harris's "broad appeal," which leaves Reformers like Doug Clark awestruck. In much the same way that Ronald Reagan, running for California governor in the 1960s, was able to take a radical right-wing policy platform — the appeal of which had hitherto been limited mostly to conspiracy-minded members of the John Birch society — and make it sound reasonable, even compassionate, so too has Mike Harris been able to neutralize the more caustic qualities of his party's actual program.

It's a reasonable assumption, for instance, that most people dwelling in the comfort of a spacious 905 bungalow would likely choose not to support the tax-cutting, budget-slashing programs of the Harris Revolution if they felt they were directly linked to the rise in the number of families sleeping in hostels, or people freezing to death in the winter streets. Indeed, one of Harris's toughest jobs during this campaign has been to persuade voters that no such causal relationship exists — and it was a task he performed with consummate skill.

Take the televised provincial leaders' debate — a turning point that halted the Tories' decline in voter approval and jumpstarted their final-stretch surge back into power. Confronted with a question about the ballooning number of people whose home is now a stretch of sidewalk, Harris thanked his inquisitor for the question, adopted a solemn look of paternal concern, and proceeded to reframe the question in a way that would clear the conscience of many voters whose moral qualms might otherwise dissuade them from voting Tory.

"There is no question," began Harris, adopting the tone of some-one who's willing to concede a point to his critics, "that even with a booming economy and even with 540,000 more people working and 380,000 now off welfare, because Toronto is booming in the last four years, we are a magnet for a lot of people. They're coming here, they are seeking jobs, they come from areas where there are not jobs, and we are getting more and more people showing up in Toronto and looking for help. And we have to respond to this."

Harris went on to say, as he had at other points in the debate, that his government is following through on the recommendations of Anne Golden's report on homelessness, commissioned by the City of Toronto. And it's the feds, he added, who need to "come to the party" so that all levels of government can address homelessness "in a meaningful way, in a way that not only is affordable but in a way that will truly put the needs of the homeless first, and help give them a job."

It was an audacious response, but one you might expect from the leader of a party whose manufacture of campaign images for TV has bordered on fictionalization. In one fell swoop, Harris attempted to reverse a deeply held perception of the issue, recasting the epi-demics of homelessness and deepening poverty not as failures of his government but as unintended consequences of its success. The home-less are not Ontarians who have been cast to the wolves; they are job seekers from elsewhere who have come to share our prosperity. The revolutionaries at Queen's Park are not the ogres their critics portray; in fact, they are more concerned about the homeless than anyone else and are more committed to finding a solution.

Problem is, this doesn't square with the most credible interpreta-tions of the problem. While the premier obviously based part of his narrative on data contained in the Golden report, he also clearly distorted that document's central messages, particularly with respect to the province's role in creating and helping to solve the homelessness crisis. True enough, Golden's findings do back some of the statements Harris made. Her report clearly chastises the federal government for policies such as cuts to Employment Insurance. And Golden's assertion that 47 percent of people using Toronto's shelters come from out of town lends limited credibility to the premier's claim about homelessness being an imported problem.

But that's only a small aspect of the crisis, and Harris clearly referred to it out of context. For the report makes clear that the underlying problem — for hostel users of local origin and from far away, for homeless people who don't go to hostels, and for the thousands more in danger of losing their homes — is simply one of deepening poverty, and on this score much of the blame accrues to Harris's own administration. Golden reveals that incomes for the 40 percent of Toronto families on the lowest end of the scale dropped by more than 20 percent between 1991 and 1996. At the same time, low-rent accommodation has been disappearing, thanks partly to Harris's gutting of rent controls. These factors have led to the current squeeze in which more than 106,000 Toronto families are spending more than 50 percent of their incomes on rent, a situation that could lead to many more people losing their accommodation if incomes drop further or rents continue to rise.

Golden repeatedly states that this crisis is partly a product of Harris's policies: the cut in welfare payments, "in particular, the shelter component of welfare payments, which is too low to cover typical rental payments in Toronto," the report reads; the scrapping of rent controls; and the province's downloading of responsibility for social housing, more of which could help ease the shortage of low-cost accommodation, to the municipalities. Golden is equally straightforward in her assertion that the homeless crisis could be alleviated by reversing those policies, some of which are cornerstones of the Common Sense Revolution. "By launching housing programs to create low-cost housing and by passing legislation to protect and increase the number of affordable units, we can begin to address the affordability crisis," the Golden report states.[10]

And yet, despite Golden's high-profile assertion that the Harris government has played a key role in worsening the problem of homelessness — "homelessness is largely caused by poverty and it is the province that is responsible for income maintenance programs," her report concludes — the campaigning premier persisted in spinning the issue in the opposite direction. He held fast to the notion that his administration has given lower-income Ontarians a new, shining sense of hope where before had been only despair.

That is one of his main messages, in fact, when he takes to the podium at the Hollywood Princess. He devotes much of his speech, naturally, to his government's overall economic record, telling this business crowd all about how the Common Sense Revolutionaries have cut red tape, cut taxes, and laid down the foundations for the province's ongoing economic boom — and pledging more of the same in their second term. Yet what's surprising is that in this pep talk Harris consistently returns to the theme of how these economic policies have benefitted the poor. It's as if he and his handlers are aware that, even out here in this isolated enclave of affluence, there are plenty of uneasy consciences that need soothing.

So here is Harris once again trumpeting those magic numbers: 540,000 new jobs and 380,000 people off the welfare rolls. Harris keeps these figures front and centre with the help of two visual aids, mock population signs reading, "Growth Ontario Pop: 540,000" and "Opportunity Ontario Pop: 380,000."

Cynics, of course, may question whether those 380,000 people no longer receiving welfare have indeed been transported into this bright new world of Opportunity. The reality of the downtown streets suggests that many of those people, rather than assuming a new place as wage-earners in today's booming economy, have merely been made ineligible for welfare (if you lose your accommodation and have no address, for instance, the government will no longer send you a cheque). There's also no proof that among those who did find work, incomes are adequate to provide some security of tenure or to keep them away from the province's increasingly overburdened food banks.

For Harris, however, the shrinking of the welfare rolls is unequivocally a good news story, an epic and uplifting tale of success. "Opportunity Ontario has a population of 380,000 people," he tells the crowd. "That's more people than live in the entire city of Ottawa, the capital of Canada. That's the number of women and men and children who have escaped the welfare trap in less than four years." And then he gets personal. "People like the young man who came running out of the doughnut store that I walked by recently. And he came up to me and he gave me a box of doughnuts. And I said, 'Thank you.' And he said, 'No.' He said, 'Mike' — and he called me Mike, you know, my mother calls me Mike if I'm being good, Michael if I'm being bad — he said, 'No, Mike, I thank you.' He had been on welfare and now he had the dignity of a job, and he wanted to thank me personally for turning welfare into workfare into a job and into opportunity."

To me that doughnut-shop bit seems apocryphal, an unlikely occurrence related in the context of the even more unlikely scenario that Harris has suddenly become a hero to Ontario's poor. How everyone else in this room has taken it is another matter. Whether or not a particular story has the ring of truth is likely to depend on the listener's own life experiences and what he or she needs to believe in order to uphold their existing attitudes and values.

— — —

Lunch is being served; it's time for an impromptu little focus group. The folks here at table 33 in the main hall of the Hollywood Princess seem pretty representative of York Region's upper-middle-class mainstream. To my left sit Woodbridge lawyer Joseph Paradiso and his wife, Letitia. To my right is Avi Barkin, chief financial officer with the firm Crown Cork and Seal, who's come to this event with two of his co-workers. None of this group are party activists or even members; instead, they fit the mould of the typical suburban "swing voter," who holds to a clear set of political beliefs but is unwilling to make an automatic commitment to a party, choosing to weigh the options carefully before each trip to the ballot box. Joseph, for instance, says that although he hasn't joined the PCs, "at this stage of my life [he looks to be in his early sixties] I'm tending towards the Conservative party." Avi, who happens to be a friend of the Liberal candidate in Thornhill,

Dan Ronen, is even less equivocal. He says there's a good chance he's going to cast his ballot for Harris, but he won't make a firm decision until he's read the Liberals' 20/20 plan.

What has caused these voters to lean this far into the Tory tent? Well, it certainly isn't crime or Harris's related crusades against disruptive kids or profane T-shirts in class. "I don't think crime has been a big issue in this campaign at all," says Avi when I raise the topic. "The police have not made a big noise about funding, and everything you hear about crime statistics is that they are down."

When the discussion inevitably moves towards squeegee kids — a hot button the Tories have pushed often during the campaign — the tone is light and dismissive. Joseph says squeegee kids "are more of a nuisance than anything else. They're making a living. If a person wants to give them a buck, they give them a buck." Letitia explains the phenomenon with a similar nonchalance, refusing to see squeegee kids as emblematic either of the breakdown of law and order or the failure of society to provide a future for its young. "They are showing they are against the status quo," she says. "'I do my own thing.' It's their way of showing they are independent. It's not begging, but on the other hand it's not like having a responsible job."

So these are clearly not right-wing extremists, people with axes to grind or crusades to launch. They seem almost to have been immunized against the hot-button approach. Even when expounding on issues in which they have a personal stake — a matter of special interest to Joseph, for example, is the possibility that private schools might someday get public funds — they are open to considering the complexities of the issue.

"My concern," Joseph explains, "and I haven't really worked it out in my own mind, is that there has to be something for people to make a choice. I understand why the public school system is there and why it should be strong and why it should be supported. I am a product of it . . . My wife and I sent our four boys to a private school. We made this choice and we could afford to do it. But on the other hand, why should I pay twice when most people just pay once?"

Overwhelmingly, though, the issue that has propelled this group into the Tories' orbit is economic performance. But on this score as well, their endorsements are not unquestioning. Avi Barkin, the company CFO, says he still has qualms about the government borrowing more to pay for tax cuts, a move that will defer the elimination of the deficit. He also believes that much of Ontario's recent boom comes courtesy of American policy-makers, although he gives Harris credit for giving the economy a further shove with his income tax cuts. How much of the boom came from south of the border, and how much from Queen's Park? "I don't really think about it that much," Avi replies. "I'm just grateful for the way the economy's going and I hope it continues to do well."

Indeed, most members of the highly leveraged suburban middle class, with their hefty mortgages, car payments, and demanding kids, are also grateful for good economic times and fearful of the reverse. Which explains why a central theme of the Tories' TV advertising blitz was that a vote for the Liberals, the party that wants to re-open urban hospitals and introduce an income support program to cut the rate of child poverty — buys you a ticket to economic slowdown and more unemployment. An inseparable strand of criticism woven into this message is that firm leadership is an essential precondition for economic success. So the Tories have played up the image of Harris as the guy you know, the politician you can trust to do what he promises (whether you like his promises or not), while hammering away at McGuinty's previous changes of heart and cost calculations which, in the estimation of both the Tories and the NDP, don't seem to add up.

This is a script that plays well for Joseph Paradiso, who at one time might have been expected, by virtue of his Italian heritage, to automatically cast his vote for the Liberals. Contemplating what it is exactly that makes him feel comfortable with the PCs, the lawyer concludes that "you can't pinpoint a specific policy. It is just a general outlook. The fact that he did what he said gives you some confidence.

We're used to politicians saying one thing before the election and doing the opposite afterwards."

At this point the spectre of a politician who has long since left the stage emerges. "I'm always reminded of Trudeau," Joseph continues, "when he was going against Stanfield, and there was [discussion of] the wage and price controls. Before the election Trudeau said, 'No way,' and Stanfield battled it out in a campaign across the country: 'We need it, we need it.' The day after the election, Trudeau just — bang! — brought in the controls. Well, I don't think that is fair. And Chrétien said we are going to do away with the GST, and now it's here to stay."

But while Harris is lauded by supporters as someone who keeps his word — a trustworthy, rock-solid leader — he is also reviled by his critics as a cruel demagogue who has victimized the poor and power-less and divided the province more sharply between haves and have-nots. When talk turns to this less flattering portrait, the guests at table 33 indicate a general willingness to accept Harris's version of things: that the tide of affluence has lifted many people out of poverty, that the government has actually done well by the poor. And none of them wants to see the province get back into the construction of social housing or the imposition of rent controls. Such measures are seen around this table as the marks of a return to the dreaded "big government" and a violation of business's right to a free marketplace.

"Maybe it's just my age, my time of life," says Joseph, "but I'm leaning towards the idea of less government. But what do you do, though? I think a government that tries to govern less doesn't necessarily have to forget compassion. As Christ said, there will always be the poor amongst us. Whether it is the individuals' fault or whether they are sick or whatever it is, there will always be the poor amongst us.

"But it is better to have a government which proceeds with less governing, allowing people to do the best they can, allowing me to decide even to whom I give my charity . . . Part of the problem will be taken care of by the economic activity created by the lesser tax. There was a time when I would have said, 'Tax the rich.' At this point I say, create the atmosphere in which there are jobs."

And then there is the suspicion, encouraged by Harris's talk about mandatory drug testing and snitch lines, that people on social assistance are likely either con artists or drug abusers, rather than victims of circumstance. Here the conversation turns suddenly brittle, as words like "dependency" and "fraud" get thrown around the table.

"I think that humans, by nature, are very greedy," says Letitia. "If they can get something for nothing, they will. I'm not saying that there are not legitimate cases where the need is there, but there are many more cases where people want to get something for nothing."

And thus, at our table, we have collected many abstract statements of principle: that people are greedy and will rip off society when they can; that the public sector has no place competing with business in the private marketplace (in areas such as housing); that less government and lower taxes are good because they stimulate initiative and growth.

But how do these abstractions measure up against the solid, practical realities of everyday life? It's almost unassailable that speculation and heavy demand have pushed rents — in hot markets like Toronto — into the stratosphere. Meanwhile, earnings at the bottom end of the income scale have either plateaued or dipped to the point that they can't begin to cover the costs of living. This has led observers like Anne Golden to the conclusion that calamity can be averted only through new government assistance, such as shelter allowances and the building of new subsidized housing.

Such conditions are part of many people's daily reality. Residents of exclusive suburbs may never have to face them, but perhaps they should. So I ask the people around the table, as the dessert and espresso coffee are starting to arrive, how it would be possible to survive in this expensive real estate market making minimum wage.

Joseph pauses for a quick calculation and then concludes, "It's impossible . . . You are right. The person who works for minimum wage — what is it, $6.85 or something now — even at $7 an hour, forty hours a week, is less than $300. After you pay some taxes, what kind of a family can you keep?"

Avi sees the math leading to the same conclusion. "I don't think minimum wage was meant to support families," he says. "I agree."

So everyone starts contributing ideas for how low-wage earners can be brought up to some reasonable standard of living: maybe through a "negative income tax," in which the government pays money back to people who earn less than a minimum figure; maybe through a rental subsidy where government pays landlords if their tenants can't afford the rent; maybe by topping up paycheques in cases where employers can't afford to pay a real living wage. The irony is, however, that none of these suggestions is contained in the policy document of the party everyone here will be voting for.

But out here it's easy to concentrate on the moral certitudes, the grand pronouncements of conservative ideologues — and not be distracted by the particulars, by practical questions such as how it is, exactly, that one is supposed to make ends meet on minimum wage or a monthly social assistance cheque. After all, these new burbs were designed as sealed, self-contained vessels of middle-class consumer culture where hardship is easily hidden.[11] (Perhaps as an antidote to this condition of isolation, the well-off in York Region should read Pat Capponi's book *Dispatches from the Poverty Line*, in which the author delves into the details of living life on welfare — the ways of rationing toilet paper, for example, and how an adult can live for a week on stale bagels and coffee.)

And now, increasing numbers of people are biding their lives entirely within the orbit of 905. The folks at my table, for example, all live in one part of York Region and work in another, making a daily east-west trek within suburbia instead of the north-south one downtown. Indeed, as Letitia Paradiso remarks, the whole point of living in the suburbs is to shelter yourself and your kids from the grittier realities of life, from the unhappy circumstances that are more prominently displayed in an older city.